Into His Presence

Spiritual Disciplines for
the Inner Life

Ian Bunting
General Editor

THOMAS NELSON PUBLISHERS
NASHVILLE

3368

American version published in Nashville, Tennessee, by Thomas Nelson, Inc. UK version published by Scripture Union as *Closer to God*.

The rights of Ian Bunting, Michael Vasey, Colin Matthews, Graham Pigott, Roger Pooley, Philip Seddon, Russ Parker, Amiel Osmaston, Deborah Seddon, Michael Botting, Alison White, John Pearce and Jane Keiller (the Grove Spirituality Group) to be identified as authors of this work have been asserted by them in accordance with the Copyright, Designs and Patents Act 1988.

Unless otherwise indicated, Scripture quotations are from the New King James Version of the Bible, © 1979, 1980, 1982, Thomas Nelson, Inc., Publishers.

Other Scripture versions quoted include:

AMPL   THE AMPLIFIED NEW TESTAMENT, © 1958 by the Lockman Foundation and used by permission.

CEV   CONTEMPORARY ENGLISH VERSION, © 1991 by the American Bible Society and used by permission.

NIV   The Holy Bible: NEW INTERNATIONAL VERSION, © 1978 by the New York International Bible Society. Used by permission of Zondervan Bible Publishers.

PHILLIPS J. B. Phillips: THE NEW TESTAMENT IN MODERN ENGLISH, Revised Edition, © 1958, 1960, 1972 by J. B. Phillips. Used by permission of Macmillan Publishing Co., Inc.

Library of Congress Cataloging-in-Publication Data

Into his presence : spiritual disciplines for the inner life / Ian
  Bunting, general editor.
      p.   cm.
    British ed. has title: Closer to God.
    ISBN 0-8407-3315-1
    1. Spiritual life.   2. Devotional exercises.   I. Bunting, Ian.
  BV4501.2.I548   1993
  248—dc20   93-5819
                                                         CIP

Printed in the United States of America

1 2 3 4 5 6 7 8 — 00 99 98 97 96 95 94 93

Contents

1. Getting Started   1
2. The Daily Mirror   33
3. Keeping Company with God   59
4. Praying Together   86
5. Devotion in the Dark   116
6. Imagination and Spirituality   151
7. Physical Spirituality   178
8. Deeper into Scripture   208
9. Wisdom for Living   235
10. Spirituality and Politics   269
11. Practical Spirituality   295
12. Corporate Spirituality   319
13. To Be a Pilgrim   358

— 1 —

Getting Started

———— ◆ ————

We come to God because we believe God is. God made us. God loves us and we can know God. When we take up a book like this, it is a sign of hope. We want to get to know God better, and he has given us signposts and markers to make this possible. We find them in the world about us: "The heavens declare the glory of God; and the firmament shows His handiwork" (Psalm 19:1). We discover them in our soul-searching, as the psalmist David discovered them:

> For You formed my inward parts;
> You covered me in my mother's womb.
> I will praise You, for I am fearfully and
>   wonderfully made;
> Marvelous are Your works,
> And that my soul knows very well.
> My frame was not hidden from You,
> When I was made in secret,
> And skillfully wrought in the lowest parts of
>   the earth.
> Your eyes saw my substance, being yet
>   unformed.
> And in Your book they all were written,

The days fashioned for me,
When as yet there were none of them.
                    —Psalm 139:13–16

Above all, the Bible shows us the way to know God. "Your word is a lamp to my feet and a light to my path" (Psalm 119:105). And the central theme of the Bible is the story of Jesus Christ and how we know God increasingly through him. We can become part of that ongoing story as we travel in the power of God's Spirit.

We're All Different

Christians are all different. This may seem obvious, but we sometimes create problems for ourselves and others when we forget it. Often we feel that everyone must conform to the same pattern, and so be just like us. If they don't, then we feel something is wrong. Yet because we are all made differently, we think, act and respond differently. Nothing is wrong with this. It is how God made us, and it will affect *how* we get to know God.

For example, some of us are feelings oriented, some practically, some achievement, and some thought oriented. Now we all have characteristics of each, but we usually lean in one direction more than another. Some who read this book will set great store by their feelings. One could call them "Mary" Christians. Mary, for example, was deeply moved by feelings in her relationship with Jesus when she anointed his feet and wiped them with her hair (John 12:3). For readers who share her temperament, it will be important to *feel* God's love. To be a Christian is to enter into a love-relationship with Jesus Christ, much as two people share a love-relationship in friendship or marriage. As time goes by, the relationship may deepen to the point of passionate feelings, where neither words nor signs are needed to express the love-relationship. You just know and love Jesus, and he loves you, and this is all that matters.

Other readers will be much more matter-of-fact about believing in God and following Christ. If Christianity is to mean anything to these, it must be practical. It must work. Things must change. I must change, these believers say. We could call these disciples "Peter" Christians. The trouble with Peter, however, is that he usually failed while trying to change. He was always spoiling his discipleship. He tried to walk on water (Matthew 14:28). He tried to be faithful to Jesus and, if necessary, even to die with him (Matthew 26:35). But he kept on slipping up. Nevertheless, through knowing God, Peter was changed. The time came when he did miracles like Jesus (Acts 3:6) and was faithful when challenged (Acts 5:29). According to tradition, he died for his faith. Christians like Peter are probably looking for personal change. They know what is bad within themselves, and they want to see it replaced by what they know to be good—for example, the fruit of the Spirit: love, joy, peace, longsuffering, kindness, goodness, faithfulness, gentleness and self-control.

Other Christians will be achievement-oriented, go-getting sorts of Christians. They see targets and aim to reach them. They are "Paul" Christians. Paul knew what he wanted, and, having identified his goal as that of being united to Christ, he committed himself to achieving it:

> *"I press toward the goal for the prize of the upward call of God in Christ Jesus."*
> —Philippians 3:14

Such Christians have a clear sense of purpose. They concentrate perhaps on seeing relatives and friends converted, on raising a Christian family, on serving overseas, or on keeping the faith, like Paul, to their dying day.

Thinking disciples are "John" Christians. John looks for a faith that can be understood, for a faith that makes sense, that fits the facts. He wrote that his friends might know and be assured of their faith in Christ:

> *"These things have I written to you who believe in the name of the Son of God, that you may know that you have eternal life, and that you may continue to believe in the name of the Son of God."*
> —1 John 5:13

There is a sense, as we noted, in which we are all feeling, practical, achieving and thinking Christians. Even in the above list, many readers will have placed John in the "feeling" category, and perhaps Paul in "thinking." Fair enough. But they were strong in the characteristics described above too. The point is that we are likely to respond more readily to messages that challenge or stimulate us along the lines of our strongest personality traits. It is good to become aware of what those are. It is not that we want to be unresponsive to other kinds of messages, but to recognize the particular ways in which God speaks to us according to the strengths of the personalities with which God created us.

Discipleship

The first Christians got their name because they followed Jesus Christ (Acts 11:26). This holds true for all Christians. Even though we are all different, we are all travelling the same road of following Jesus. On this road we are always learners or apprentices. We never travel as far as the Master has gone before us. In fact, like the Israelites who crossed the Jordan, we have never been this way before. The road is new, each step is new. This is why experienced Christians remind us that it is a continuing walk and learning process day by day.

Lord Jesus Christ, we thank you for all the benefits you have won for us, for all the pains and insults you have borne for us. Most merciful redeemer, friend and brother may we know you more clearly, love you more dearly and follow you more nearly, day by day. Amen.

And yet, we often get stuck on the path. Maybe we get tired. Maybe following Jesus now seems to lack promise, the road becoming hard and rough. Maybe we still love the world too much. Maybe we think we have arrived; there's nothing more to be learned. Yet there is always more to love, more to grow, more to achieve, and more to know. This is why in the New Testament "discipleship" is often called a struggle. Of this, St. Augustine wrote, "In this life, there are two loves fighting each other in every temptation; love of God and love of the world, and whichever wins draws its lover in its train as by a weight." It is first a struggle with ourselves because we often find that we want to become, or to accomplish, more than is within our power. Paul experienced this problem, along with the profound disappointment that comes when we fail to keep our standards or God's.

But Christians also find themselves struggling with enemies outside themselves. This struggle may be with other people, or perhaps even with demonic powers. Such struggles can bring fear or hopelessness, and it is tempting to give up.

The Bible assures us that we are not alone. Jesus promises that God will come to his disciples and make a home with them. "If anyone loves Me," Jesus said, "he will keep My word; and My Father will love him, and We will come to him and make Our home with him" (John 14:23). When we grasp the way that God—the Father, Son and the Holy Spirit—accompanies us, the picture changes from one where we are travelling without hope and struggling in despair to one in which we have a traveling companion. We are soldiers with victory in sight and our commander alongside and even inside with us. Yet it is even more promising than that, because in Christ each of us is "a new creation; old things have passed away; behold, all things have become new" (2 Corinthians 5:17). Furthermore, with God making a home in us, our view of the world changes. We begin to see the path with God's perspective.

Which Way?

We have been describing a journey of discovery about God, ourselves and each other. Every traveler is grateful for maps and guides that tell what others have found. The Bible is like this. It is the guidebook, or handbook, for everyday living. It reflects its writers' joys, sorrows and temptations, and their discoveries along the way. It is not just a history book. It is a journey planner for Christians who want to move into unexplored territory. It could be that you want to get moving again after a period of standing still. Or, you may want to try a different path, a new way to pray, or other kinds of spiritual experiences in order to get nearer God, to get to know him better. John Newton said, "If you want to love

Him better now while you are here. . . . Trust Him. The more you trust Him, the better you will love Him. If you ask, How shall I trust Him? I answer, Try Him. The more you make trial of Him, the more your trust in Him will be strengthened."

Christianity is an *experimental* religion. It is for people who want to experience God. Being a Christian is a question of discovering truth through believing God and following Jesus' teaching. "My teaching is not my own," Jesus said, "It comes from him who sent me. If anyone chooses to do God's will, he will find out whether my teaching comes from God or whether I speak on my own" (John 7:16–17 NIV).

This book offers suggestions for those who want to experience more of God. And it is designed for all sorts of Christians. For instance, as a "Mary" Christian, one who depends on how you feel as an indicator of where you stand in relation to God, there will be many ideas to help you along the lines of your God-given personality. You may find it stimulating to experiment with the use of your senses in prayer, or to use bodily movements in praise, penitence, or worship as you approach God. For the feeling-oriented Christian who is further along the road, a creative entry into silence may open a new vista to the depths of God's love.

The practical "Peter" Christian may find it helpful to join a prayer group in which there is honest sharing. It may be helpful to start a spiritual journal as a way to take a periodic spiritual check-up on your growth as a disciple. Further on? A spiritual director could serve as an inspiring personal consultant.

The achieving, "Paul" Christian may benefit from a new, perhaps unfamiliar, spiritual challenge. It could be to tithe your income for the first time, or to fast and pray for a particular miracle you believe God wants to perform. It might involve taking a fresh look at one or two areas of your life with a determination to set some goals for change and begin working towards them.

The reflective "John" Christian may love to read new Christian books. But have you discovered the treasures to be found in older writings? The lessons of believers who come from another age and a different culture are rich and, in some cases, a strange (to us) way of getting to know God better! Yet their experiences can spur us along our paths of discovery today.

We all can learn from spiritual practices and insights that at first may seem unappealing or even threatening. In the same way that jogging is rough on the unfit, a spiritual discipline that threatens us could be just what we need. In fact, just as the people of the Western world are too comfortable in terms of wealth, possessions and leisure—at least in relation to the Third World— so Christians easily fall prey to a comfortable Christianity that demands little and fails to lead one to spiritual maturity. This book will challenge you to greater spiritual discipline and suggest how you may go about it.

Great Christians from the past have an important part to play in deepening our discipleship. It is easy to forget the debt of gratitude we owe the saints in heaven, who have left us their example and teaching. This book is illustrated with some of the pithy sayings, poetry, practices, prayers and examples of Christians who are now in glory, but who have left us a gold mine of encouragement for the Way.

For some of us, appreciating these saints of the past may be like learning to appreciate the skills of yesterday's artisans, who made pre-twentieth-century watches or pianos. We get so used to today's digital watches and electronic keyboards that we take for granted the achievement of those inventors and craftsmen. Thankfully, in the late twentieth century, many are grateful for the "real thing," the thing of quality unsurpassed, whether in watches, pianos or, far more importantly, in getting to know God.

A few readers will feel anxious about some of the suggestions in this book; for example, the use of icons, making retreats, or fasting. Icons do not automatically involve one in superstition. Retreats, though they may seem a terrible waste of time to an activist Christian, can be vital for being refilled with the Holy Spirit. And fasting can be a spiritual discipline to concentrate one's mind and sharpen spiritual perception.

Though the authors, therefore, all relate easily

and naturally to the traditional disciplines of evangelical spirituality, we have also learned to appreciate the ways in which believers from other Christian traditions have discovered how to experience and live closer to God. Catholic, Orthodox, African, and Asian Christians have all contributed to our understanding. We have been willing to enhance our spiritual life through insights from other traditions that are in accord with the Bible's teaching, and we encourage other Christians to do the same. For example, in prayerfully walking through the Stations of the Cross in a Catholic church, we may receive a much deeper perception of the event that lies at the heart of our faith: the death and resurrection of our Lord Jesus Christ. A biblical parallel of this is seen in the institution of the Passover, which is a visual reminder detailing the Jews' practical experience of God's salvation. If some of the ancient ways or insights from outside the evangelical tradition strike you as strange or unappealing, you still may want to try one or two. And there will be many for you to use that are much more familiar.

BEGINNINGS

There is no "right" way to go through this handbook. If you want to go straight through this book from cover to cover without taking time to do any of the spiritual exercises in the "Take 7 Days" material, so be it. This book, however, was not written or intended to be used like that. The chief purpose is to provide people with 7 days' worth of opportunities for spiritual development. You may see one or two exercises in a particular "Take 7 Days" section that you want to respond to all week.

Another way to proceed is to take a week with each chapter and its "Take 7 Days" section. Another way is to peruse the chapters and their spiritual exercises and begin with the ones that catch your attention. Others may want to start with material that looks familiar; others, with the more unfamiliar.

The idea is not to feel pressured to participate in each spiritual exercise before you move to the next chapter. A tip: how about placing a check mark by the ones you have done, or any that you may want to return to do later? We grow as we travel and win more ground, as we face new experiences and adventures with God.

But before you begin your new journey, here are some questions you may want to think about. Try out the first set of questions as an exercise in self-awareness and the second set as an exercise in sensitivity to others. Work through the checklists thoughtfully, thinking especially about areas where repentance is needed. For that is a good beginning all of us can make.

Self-Awareness

1. What is your relationship with God now?
2. What changes, for better or worse, can you detect in your life during the last year?

3. What goals have you achieved or failed to achieve?

4. In what way has your knowledge of God has increased?

5. Where are you resisting God?

6. What inhibits you from going further?

7. Are there any spiritual enemies hindering or attacking you?

8. How well are you disciplined in the areas of food, sleep, fitness and leisure activity?

9. Do your reading habits broaden or narrow your horizons?

10. What will you pray for as you work through this book?

If we are disappointed about some of our answers, let us not hate ourselves, but remember that God still loves us. Our assurance of his love is that he has sent his son Jesus Christ to die for us. Nevertheless, our honest answers may have made us aware of our sin. Yet sin is not only our personal shortcomings that offend against God's love. It goes deeper. Sin speaks of a rebellious heart, mind, and will that is set against God. In short, sin is the offense of a fundamentally anti-God nature. And we do not sin against God alone but against others too. Here, then, is the second checklist.

Sensitivity to Others

1. How is your relationship with your spouse, or parents or close friends (if you are unmarried)?

2. In what ways are the relationships improving or worsening?
3. Has your relationship with your spouse or your friendships suffered as you have tried to achieve your personal goals?
4. How highly do you rate the suggestions of others to help you get to know God better?
5. What are your outstanding and unresolved conflicts with other people?
6. How well are you coping with your sexual desires at present?
7. Are your friendships with unbelievers healthy and rewarding?
8. How do you think using this handbook will help you improve your relationships?

Repentance

Wherever we are disappointed in answering these questions, genuine repentance is the key for redeeming the situation. In the words of Gordon MacDonald, "There are no words to describe the inner anguish of knowing that you have disappointed and offended God, that you have violated your own integrity, and that you have betrayed people you really love and care for." This begins the process of genuine repentance that puts right our relationships with God and others.

Some who read this may feel like they never have had a loving relationship with God. If so, you can begin right now in the quietness of your heart to ask God to forgive you and to help you discover him.

Sometimes, however, we feel paralysed by sin and unable to change. Sometimes we do not know how to respond to God. It may help, therefore, to see repentance—the process of having our sins dealt with—as a series of steps.

Recognize the Sin

First we need to identify our sins, to name them. This is different than recognizing the *effects* of our sins, as disastrous as they may be. The effects are not the causes. We cannot repent of the causes until they are identified. For example, consider a man who prays that God will help him improve his relationship with his wife. It is not very helpful for him to say, "Lord, I want to confess to you that my relationship with my wife is not very good." This man needs to name the precise things he is doing that contribute to the breakdown of the relationship. Maybe he needs to confess; "Lord, I do not pay attention when she talks, and I lie to her about my friends."

Repent of the Sin

To repent means to turn from sin to God. We will probably do this only when we feel that deep regret over sin which is the start of repentance. The husband whose situation we've been considering might need to say to God, "I thought these sins did not hurt my relationship with my wife, but now I see them as selfishness. I am sorry. I will turn away from this. I don't want to be like that in future."

Receive God's Forgiveness

Now we need to believe God has forgiven us, and we need to receive his forgiveness. God's word promises forgiveness for specific sins. "If we confess our sins, He is faithful and just to forgive us our sins" (1 John 1:9). You may find that a physical act such as unclenching your fist, to symbolize repenting of sin, and lifting your open hand to God, to symbolize receiving forgiveness, can help. Or breathing out, as a sign of giving sin to God, and breathing in, as a sign of receiving God's forgiveness, may help you know deep down that God has offered forgiveness and you have received it.

Look to the Future

Now we need to think about the future. If we are contrite over past sins and willing to change, we should determine to be different. "Next time my wife wants to tell me about her day after I get home from work, I will put down the newspaper and turn off the television so that I'm not distracted, and I will listen to what she has to say." That exercise of the will is what makes repentance a change of direction: we are going to stop going in the wrong direction and start living God's way.

Ask for Help

Finally, we should pray for the help of the Holy Spirit. We need the Spirit's help throughout the Christian life, but never more so than when we are struggling to leave sin behind and live God's way.

Now you're ready to "try out" the first seven day's exercises. They will help you think about what you are like, where you are and where you want to go. Enjoy your journey!

TAKE SEVEN DAYS . . .

DAY 1: *An Exercise in Feeling*

▶ *Scripture*

As the deer pants for the water brooks,
So pants my soul for You, O God.
My soul thirsts for God, for the living God.
When shall I come and appear before God?
My tears have been my food day and night,
While they continually say to me,
"Where is your God?"
When I remember these things,
I pour out my soul within me.
For I used to go with the multitude;
I went with them to the house of God,
With the voice of joy and praise,
With a multitude that kept a pilgrim feast.
Why are you cast down, O my soul?
And why are you disquieted within me?

Hope in God, for I shall yet praise Him
For the help of His countenance.
O my God, my soul is cast down within me;
Therefore I will remember You from the land of the
  Jordan,
And from the heights of Hermon,
From the Hill Mizar.
Deep calls unto deep at the noise of Your waterfalls;
All Your waves and billows have gone over me.
The LORD will command His lovingkindness in the
  daytime,
And in the night His song shall be with me—
A prayer to the God of my life.
I will say to God my Rock,
"Why have You forgotten me?
Why do I go mourning because of the oppression of
  the enemy?"
As with a breaking of my bones,
My enemies reproach me,
While they say to me all day long.
"Where is your God?"
Why are you cast down, O my soul?
And why are you disquieted within me?
Hope in God;
For I shall yet praise Him,
The help of my countenance and my God.

—Psalm 42

▶ *Exercise*

Find a quiet place where you can read through Psalm 42.
As you read, pause briefly at the words that stir emotions.
For example, *pants, thirsts, joy, disquiet, mourning.*

Now imagine yourself standing or sitting by a fast-flowing river. In the middle of it there is a huge rock, unmoved as the white water rushes past it. Think about that rock's unmovableness, its unshakeableness. In your imagination, place yourself on that rock, standing or seated.

Psalm 42:9, speaks of "God my Rock." Think of how rewarding it is to have God himself as your Rock amid all the emotional ups and downs of life.

Now close this exercise by re-reading the Psalm in this context and pausing to think about, or thank God for, any passages that are of special interest to you.

▶ *Hymn*

THE ROCK THAT IS HIGHER THAN I

O sometimes the shadows are deep,
And rough seems the path to the goal,
And sorrows, sometimes how they sweep
Like tempests down over the soul!

O then to the Rock let me fly,
To the Rock that is higher than I;
O then to the Rock let me fly,
To the Rock that is higher than I!

O sometimes how long seems the day,
And sometimes how weary my feet;
But toiling in life's dusty way,
The Rock's blessed shadow, how sweet!

O near to the Rock let me keep,
If blessings or sorrows prevail,
Or climbing the mountain way steep,
Or walking the shadowy vale.
                              —Erastus Johnson

DAY 2: *An Exercise in the Practical*

▶ *Scripture*

I say then: Walk in the Spirit, and you shall not fulfill the lust of the flesh. For the flesh lusts against the Spirit, and the Spirit against the flesh; and these are contrary to one another, so that you do not do the things that you wish.

But if you are led by the Spirit, you are not under the law.

Now the works of the flesh are evident, which are: adultery, fornication, uncleanness, lewdness, idolatry, sorcery, hatred, contentions, jealousies, outbursts of wrath, selfish ambitions, dissensions, heresies, envy, murders, drunkenness, revelries, and the like; of which I tell you beforehand, just as I also told you in time past, that those who practice such things will not inherit the kingdom of God.

But the fruit of the Spirit is love, joy, peace, longsuffering, kindness, goodness, faithfulness, gentleness, self-control. Against such there is no law. And those who are Christ's have crucified the flesh with its passions and desires.

If we live in the Spirit, let us also walk in the Spirit. Let us not become conceited, provoking one another, envying one another.

—Galatians 5:16–26

▶ *Exercise*

You may want to use a notepad or notebook for this in order to keep a kind of record of how you're doing. Call it your spiritual journal. As you read through Galatians 5:16–25, you will see the contrast between what the old sinful nature produces and the fruit of the Spirit. Verses 19 to 21 supply a veritable index of the sins we are capable of committing. Of course, you may not spot yourself in any of those. But, then, how deeply, how thoroughly, do you see yourself expressing the fruit described in verses 22 and 23?

In your journal, list the nine types of fruit of the Spirit. Now choose two or three areas where you know more maturing is needed. These can be either in your relationship to God or to others, or both.

After you have written down the areas in question, note in your journal what may prevent the changes you want to take place. Then decide what course of action you will take help reach your goal.

Close this exercise by reading verses 16, 18, and 25. They remind us that in the strength of God we change. Take comfort in this as you pray for God's help.

▶ *Hymn*

SPIRIT OF GOD, DESCEND

Spirit of God, descend upon my heart;
Wean it from earth, through all its pulses move;
Stoop to my weakness, mighty as Thou art,
And make me love Thee as I ought to love.

I ask no dream, no prophet ecstasies,
No sudden rending of the veil of clay,
No angel visitant, no opening skies;
But take the dimness of my soul away.

Hast Thou not bid us love Thee, God and King?
All, all Thine own, soul, heart, and strength, and mind;
I see Thy cross, there teach my heart to cling:
Oh, let me seek Thee, and oh, let me find.

Teach me to feel that Thou art always nigh;
Teach me the struggles of the soul to bear,
To check the rising doubt, the rebel sigh;
Teach me the patience of unanswered prayer.
                                        —George Croly

DAY 3: *An Exercise in Achieving*

▶ *Scripture*

But I want you to know, brethern, that the things which happened *to me have actually turned out for the furtherance of the gospel, so that it has become evident to the whole palace guard, and to all the rest, that my chains are in Christ; and most of the brethren in the Lord, having become confident by my chains, are much more bold to speak the word without fear.*

Some indeed preach Christ even from envy and strife, and some also from goodwill: The former preach Christ from selfish ambition, not sincerely, supposing to add affliction to my chains; but the latter out of love, knowing that I am appointed for the defense of the gospel.

What then? Only that in every way, whether in pretense or in truth, Christ is preached; and in this I rejoice, yes, and will rejoice.

For I know that this will turn out for my deliverance through your prayer and the supply of the Spirit of Jesus Christ, according to my earnest expectation and hope that in nothing I shall be ashamed, but with all boldness, as always, so now also Christ will be magnified in my body, whether by life or by death.

For to me, to live is Christ, and to die is gain.

But if I live on in the flesh, this will mean fruit from my labor; yet what I shall choose I cannot tell. For I am hard-pressed between the two, having a desire to depart and be with Christ, which is far better. Nevertheless to remain in the flesh is more needful for you.

And being confident of this, I know that I shall remain and continue with you all for your progress and joy of faith, that your rejoicing for me may be more abundant in Jesus Christ by my coming to you again.

I can do all things through Christ who strengthens me.

—Philippians 1:12–26; 4:13

▶ *Exercise*

As you read Philippians 1:12–26, you will see the apostle Paul's single-minded determination to preach the Gospel. And that determination was not watered down despite adverse circumstances. Take a few minutes to review the important things you have determined to do today, this week or this month. Is there anything you can think of that may dampen your ardor to achieve those goals? If so, take a few minutes to memorize Philippians 4:13. Then close this exercise by taking time in prayer to ask God to help you achieve your God-given goals with determination.

▶ *Hymn*

HIGHER GROUND

I'm pressing on the upward way,
New heights I'm gaining every day;
Still praying as I onward bound,
"Lord, plant my feet on higher ground."

Lord, lift me up and let me stand,
By faith, on heaven's tableland,
A higher plane than I have found;
Lord, plant my feet on higher ground.

My heart has no desire to stay
Where doubts arise and fears dismay;
Though some may dwell where these abound,
My prayer, my aim is higher ground.

I want to live above the world,
Though Satan's darts at me are hurled;
For faith has caught the joyful sound.
The song of saints on higher ground.

I want to scale the utmost height
And catch a gleam of glory bright;
But still I'll pray till heaven I've found,
"Lord, lead me on to higher ground."
                                    —Johnson Oatman, Jr.

DAY 4: *An Exercise in Knowing*

▶ *Scripture*

Who shall separate us from the love of Christ? Shall tribulation, or distress, or persecution, or famine, or nakedness, or peril, or sword?

As it is written:

"For Your sake we are killed all day long:
We are accounted as sheep for the slaughter."

Yet in all these things we are more than conquerors through Him who loved us.

For I am persuaded that neither death nor life, nor angels nor principalities nor powers, nor things present nor things to come,

nor height nor depth, nor any other created thing, shall be able to separate us from the love of God which is in Christ Jesus our Lord.

                                    —Romans 8:35–39

▶ *Exercise*

A large part of "knowing" involves persuasion. As you read Romans 8:35–39, notice the convictions held by the apostle Paul because he had been persuaded of them. Though you may not have reached such depth and height of knowing, you can.

On paper, list several biblical truths about which you are already persuaded. Maybe they are about the certainty of salvation, or God's promise to save a loved one, or the knowledge you have from a favorite verse. These mark significant periods in your life when you came to know, to be persuaded, of these things.

Now put verses 38 and 39 into your own words. For example, "I am persuaded that _____ and _____ are true, and that neither death nor life, etc., can change this." As you are reassured, close this exercise by asking God to persuade you of something wonderful! Maybe that will be something as vital as the love of God which Paul knew so thoroughly.

DAY **5**: *An Exercise in Traveling*

▶ *Scripture*

Now behold, two of them were traveling that same day to a village called Emmaus, which was seven miles from Jerusalem. And they talked together of all these things which had happened. So it was, while they conversed and reasoned, that Jesus Himself drew near and went with them. But their eyes were restrained, so that they did not know Him.

And He said to them, "What kind of conversation is this that you have with one another as you walk and are sad?"

Then the one whose name was Cleopas answered

and said to Him, "Are You the only stranger in Jerusalem, and have You not known the things which happened there in these days?"

And He said to them, "What things?" So they said to Him, "The things concerning Jesus of Nazareth, who was a Prophet mighty in deed and word before God and all the people, and how the chief priests and our rulers delivered Him to be condemned to death, and crucified Him.

"But we were hoping that it was He who was going to redeem Israel. Indeed, besides all this, today is the third day since these things happened. Yes, and certain women of our company, who arrived at the tomb early, astonished us.

"When they did not find His body, they came saying that they had also seen a vision of angels who said He was alive. And certain of those who were with us went to the tomb and found it just as the women had said; but Him they did not see."

Then He said to them, "O foolish ones, and slow of heart to believe in all that the prophets have spoken! Ought not the Christ to have suffered these things and to enter into His glory?" And beginning at Moses and all the Prophets, He expounded to them in all the Scriptures the things concerning Himself.

Then they drew near to the village where they were going, and He indicated that He would have gone farther. But they constrained Him, saying, "Abide with us, for it is toward evening, and the day is far spent." And He went in to stay with them.

Now it came to pass, as He sat at the table with them, that He took bread, blessed and broke it, and gave it to them. Then their eyes were opened and they knew Him; and He vanished from their sight. And they said to one another, "Did not our heart burn within us while He talked with us on the road, and while He opened the Scriptures to us?"

So they rose up that very hour and returned to Jerusalem, and found the eleven and those who were with them gathered together, saying, "The Lord is risen indeed, and has appeared to Simon!" And they told about the things that had happened on the road, and how He was known to them in the breaking of bread.

—Luke 24:13–35

▶ *Exercise*

Before you read Luke 24:13–35, recall that the Christian life is a journey filled with daily activities, some of which seem pretty mundane! What sort of a day was it for you yesterday or today? What kind of week have you had? Did anything significant change? Have you seen anything in a different light? Was it the same old routine?

Now read the passage. As you join the two disciples on the road to Emmaus, notice their concerns that day as they walked along (vv. 17–24). But more than this, take note that for a long time it did not make any difference to them that Jesus himself was with them during the day. In fact, they did not even know he was there with them (v. 16).

Close this exercise by trying to recognize the signs that Jesus was involved in your day or week. Then try to discern the signs of his presence that you missed. Ask God to help you be more alert to his presence in your daily activities.

▶ *Hymn*

SAVIOUR, TEACH ME DAY BY DAY

Saviour, teach me day by day
Love's sweet lesson to obey;
Sweeter lesson cannot be,
Loving Him who first loved me.

With a child's glad heart of love
At Thy bidding may I move,
Prompt to serve and follow Thee,
Loving Him who first loved me.

Teach me thus Thy steps to trace,
Strong to follow in Thy grace,
Learning how to love from Thee,
Loving Him who first loved me.

Thus may I rejoice to show
That I feel the love I owe;
Singing, till Thy face I see,
Of His love who first loved me.
—Jane E. Leeson

DAY 6: *An Exercise in Soldiering*

▶ *Scripture*

Finally, my brethren, be strong in the Lord and in the power of His might. Put on the whole armor of God, that you may be able to stand against the wiles of the devil. For we do not wrestle against flesh and blood, but against principalities, against powers, against the rulers of the darkness of this age, against spiritual hosts of wickedness in the heavenly places.

Therefore take up the whole armor of God, that you may be able to withstand in the evil day, and having done all, to stand.

Stand therefore, having girded your waist with truth, having put on the breastplate of righteousness, and having shod your feet with the preparation of the gospel of peace; above all, taking the shield of faith with which you will be able to quench all the fiery darts of the wicked one.

And take the helmet of salvation, and the sword of the Spirit, which is the word of God; praying always with all prayer and supplication in the Spirit, being watchful to this end with all perseverance and supplication for all the saints.

—Ephesians 6:10–18

▶ *Exercise*

No one enters a battle without some kind of protection, and some offensive weapons. This is no less true concerning the spiritual battles we enter. As you read Ephesians 6:10–18, note both the protective defenses and the offensive weapons. Note also that it takes all of it to be "the whole armor of God." And that is the point, it is the armor *of God*.

We cannot avoid engagement with the powers of darkness. Yet we will not battle them in our own strength. God himself is both our defense and offense.

Close this exercise by memorizing verse 13. Let it be a strength to you the next time you face a spiritual battle. And then, as a soldier of God, having done all to stand, stand.

▶ *Hymn*

O GOD, OUR HELP IN AGES PAST

O God, our help in ages past,
Our hope for years to come,
Our shelter from the stormy blast,
And our eternal home!

Under the shadow of Thy throne
Thy saints have dwelt secure;
Sufficient is Thine arm alone,
And our defense is sure.

Before the hills in order stood,
Or earth received her frame,
From everlasting Thou art God,
To endless years the same.

A thousand ages in Thy sight
Are like an evening gone;
Short as the watch that ends the night
Before the rising sun.

O God, our help in ages past,
Our hope for years to come,
Be thou our guard while life shall last,
And our eternal home.
—Isaac Watts

DAY 7: *An Exercise in Unity*

▶ *Scripture*

For as the body is one and has many members, but all the members of that one body, being many, are one body, so also is Christ. For by one Spirit we were all baptized into one body—whether Jews or Greeks, whether slaves or free—and have all been made to drink into one Spirit. For in fact the body is not one member but many. If the foot should say, "Because I am not a hand, I am not of the body," is it therefore not of the body? And if the ear should say, "Because I am not an eye, I am not of the body," is it therefore not of the body?

If the whole body were an eye, where would be the hearing? If the whole were hearing, where would be the smelling? But now God has set the members, each one of them, in the body just as He pleased. And if they were all one member, where would the body be?

But now indeed there are many members, yet one body. And the eye cannot say to the hand, "I have no need of you"; nor again the head to the feet, "I have no need of you." No, much rather, those members of the body which seem to be weaker are necessary. And those members of the body which we think to be less honorable, on these we bestow greater honor; and our unpresentable parts have greater modesty, but our presentable parts have no need.

But God composed the body, having given greater honor to that part which lacks it, that there should be no schism in the body, but that the members should have the same care for one another. And if one member suffers, all the members suffer with it; or if one member is honored, all the members rejoice with it.

Now you are the body of Christ, and members individually.

—1 Corinthians 12:12–27

▶ *Exercise*

Before you read 1 Corinthians 12:12–27, take several minutes to look over your body and actually see its various parts. Sound silly? Think about this. While you are highlighting to yourself various body parts, consider that "difference" is essential to a properly functioning body.

Now read the passage with that in mind and listen prayerfully to what the Holy Spirit is saying to you about this. You may feel that you have been guilty of looking down on a member of Christ's body. You may feel guilty that you have used "difference" to cause division. You may feel conviction from the Holy Spirit because you pride yourself in being one of the stronger members. You may feel angry about being a weaker member.

Such attitudes betray one's need for repentance because of a failure to appreciate the differences that God has set in the body of Christ (v. 18). Take some time in prayer to humbly acknowledge your faults. And the next time the situation arises, remember this prayer and your new appreciation of "difference." Resolve to work toward unity within the diversity that is Christ's church.

▶ *Hymn*

BLEST BE THE TIE

Blest be the tie that binds
Our hearts in Christian love;
The fellowship of kindred minds
Is like to that above.

Before our Father's throne
We pour our ardent prayers;
Our fears, our hopes, our aims are one,
Our comforts and our cares.

We share our mutual woes,
Our mutual burdens bear;
And often for each other flows
The sympathizing tear.

When we asunder part,
It gives us inward pain;
But we shall still be joined in heart,
And hope to meet again.
　　　　　　　　　　　—John Fawcett

— 2 —

The Daily Mirror

———— ◆ ————

Going to the Bible to find the truth may sound like a comfortable thing to do. But this is not often the case. A willingness to face biblical truth may take considerable courage and honesty if spiritual development and genuine growth are to occur. Without this challenging Voice from outside ourselves, explorations of spirituality may become mere exercises in self-indulgence or sentimentality. Jesus still says to us today, "You are in error [if] you do not know the Scriptures," (Matthew 22:29 NIV). And the apostle Paul wrote that "All Scripture is given by inspiration of God, and is profitable for doctrine, for reproof, for correction, for instruction in righteousness" (2 Timothy 3:16). Again, it may not be comfortable being faced with making personal adjustments according to Scripture.

Biblical Truth Faces Us with Reality

The truth of God comes to us as a mirror (James 1:23), or a light (Psalm 119:105), or a hammer (Jeremiah 23:29), or a sword (Hebrews 4:12). Sometimes its message is as sweet as honey (Ezekiel 3:3). At other times it will burn with intensity (Jeremiah 20:9). But however it comes, it is the truth that brings us face to face with God, with ourselves, and with others.

So what truth does the Bible present? First, it tells the truth about "beginnings." It tells how all things began, including human beings. And it tells who made these things. Second, it tells how things went wrong when the primary human family sinned. Third, it tells a true story; the story of God's love for his people, and it tells that story through the history of particular people, the Hebrews. It is therefore a story of characters, times, and places, even of peoples who live outside the central story.

The Bible also reveals the character of the one true God who is the Father of the Lord Jesus Christ, and it discloses what human nature is like. And the Bible presents us with values to choose between. Some choices are set out clearly. Others are slightly ambiguous, in the sense that we may need to dig for the biblical principles behind what is being said.

The above are but several examples of the truth the Bible presents. So it is not only a collection of statements or a true record of events. It is the truth about reality. We can choose to face this truth or to run from it. Our choices shape our lives.

As we choose, God responds. Sometimes the choice seems costly in its outworking. A senior executive and financial expert in a multinational company knew how to make money work. Although he had been a Christian for a number of years, the amount of money he gave away was tightly controlled and very limited. Then he was challenged to face seriously what the Bible said about money. He began to ask God's help about how to earn it, spend it, and give it away. This eventually led to his resignation from a corporate position on a matter of principle. It also produced a change whereby he made giving to God's work a priority. His account is that only then did he begin to develop as a person and as a Christian.

Sometimes when we face up to the truth of the Bible God really surprises us. A man in his twenties became a Christian and discovered as a consequence that Jesus was Lord of his sexuality. This meant the immorality with his girlfriend had to stop, even though they were fond of each other. He dreaded sharing his decision with her, and as he did his girlfriend began crying. She too was a Christian, but she had run away from God for several years and was struggling with great guilt. Her boyfriend's honesty and courage brought her back to the Lord, and they were able to seek God's future for their relationship.

Not every story of obedience, of course, leads to an immediate happy ending, but God's commands are gracious, whatever the results, and obedience to them is vital for spiritual development.

To know the Bible is to know the mind of Christ for our lives. Such truth is not neutral. It challenges us to make choices and in the power of the Holy Spirit to change. Both our wise and unwise decisions have consequences, and God responds to either. We choose to move into the light or to remain in the shadows.

Heavenly Father, I do not want to read your Word without doing what it says. In fact, your Word says that the person who hears but does not obey is like a man who looks at his face in a mirror and, after looking at himself, goes away and immediately forgets what he looks like. Help me become a person who looks into your perfect law that gives freedom, and, not forgetting what he has heard, does what it says, that I may be blessed in what I do. (Based on James 1:22–25)

GUIDELINES TO FOLLOW

For some people an encounter with the truth is exhilarating and liberating: "Come, see a Man who told me all things that I ever did. Could this be the Christ?" (John 4:29). For the rich young ruler, however, the encounter with reality was more than he could bear: "'Go your way, sell whatever you have and give to the poor, and you will have treasure in heaven; and come, take up the cross, and follow Me.' But he was sad at this word, and went away grieved" (Mark 10:21–22). Whatever it may be like for each of us, here are some practical guidelines to help us follow through when facing the truth of the Bible. We'll begin by looking at some danger areas.

We go to the Bible for comfort and reassurance. Life is difficult, and we need to be sure that God is still with us, that he is in control. Yet a penchant to find comfort may cause us to distort our use of the Bible. For example, we could be in danger of treating the Bible like a sort of divine chocolate box, constantly searching for a passage, phrase, verse or idea that will make us feel better. So we skim over pages of text until we find something that comforts us, even though God, perhaps, desired to bring some correction.

Another pitfall is to go to the Bible to find quick and easy answers. We want the Bible to work for us like a super-computer. Input a problem and a text with the answer will come up on the screen. This, however, may be merely an excuse so that we do not have to do our part in praying, listening, understanding, and testing.

Another temptation is to "read in" to the Bible only what we want to hear or discover. This is to *escape from* rather than to *face* reality, and the penchant for such fantasy is heard throughout Christianity: "The only reason Christians are ill is because they don't have enough faith." "God wants every Christian to be successful and wealthy." "The Lord has chosen our country and government to prosper in his world."

In response to these misuses of the Bible, here are several practical guidelines about how to use the Bible correctly.

1. Be Honest

Sometimes we prefer tact to honesty. Jesus was not always comfortable to be around because he was honest with everyone. And because he was honest, one of his chief enemies was hypocrisy. He will discover that in us too, even if we call it tact!

Jesus opposed hypocrisy because it is a denial of the truth. Of course, God in his mercy doesn't show us all the truth about ourselves at once. He knows how much we can bear. Our part is to respond obediently to what we are shown and so develop spiritually.

This will mean being honest about our desires, doubts, difficulties, and failures. It will mean honesty with God and others, as well as with biblical texts. This may cost us more than we have previously been willing. Yet it is another way in which God leads us to know more of himself.

2. Explore Unfamiliar Territory in the Bible

Our readings may be based solely on a wide selection of passages that are "familiar favorites." Although we may follow a theme, character, or biblical book, we still may not branch off into unfamiliar territory. If you have never read through the entire Bible, this is a good way to launch out into uncharted waters.

And when you go exploring, let the Bible speak to you in its own terms. Here is a quick look at three questions that will help you accomplish this:

- What is the natural meaning? (What do the English words mean, without any fancy interpretation? A dictionary is very useful here.)

- What is the original meaning? (This means trying to find out what the words meant to the people to whom they were first addressed. Here a good Bible dictionary, handbook, and commentary are well worth the investment.)

- What is the general meaning? (This is to compare the meaning of one passage with that of a similar or contrasting passage within the entire context of the Bible. Again, reference books are essential for this, but should be used only after you have studied the Bible itself.)

Obviously this can take a little time! And it may sound a little cold and clinical. Yet throughout this book you will find ideas about how to use the Bible for meditation, prayer and worship. If you take time for the occasional "cold and clinical" Bible study, it will greatly enrich whatever "Take 7 Days" exercises you do. The danger, you see, is to take into these exercises what was never in the Bible in the first place. And then we are back in fantasy land.

3. Look for Insights into God's Nature and Character

Sometimes a text will "come up and hit us," and at other times God guides us through clear principles. We do not need to keep asking "Is

it wrong to steal?" But God guides us also by
showing us more and more about his character
and personality. As we read about him in the
Bible and get to know him through the work of
the Holy Spirit, we get a deeper sense of what
he likes and dislikes. This is another reason for
reading widely in the Bible, for it opens to us
another dimension of spiritual development.

4. Ask Other Christians What They Have Learned

"Let the word of Christ dwell in you richly,
teaching and admonishing one another," (Colossians 3:16). Sometimes we forget to tap into the
knowledge that trusted Christian friends have
acquired from facing the reality of the Bible. But
this verse from Colossians shows that we can
test the truth of our guidance and choices with
God's people.

This practice is particularly helpful where
Christians are divided on an issue. Then it is
essential that we seek the truth *together*, sharing
our views in trust and humility and in a spirit
of honest inquiry. This joint search may not lead
to instant unanimity. But it displays a willingness to change where we may be wrong, which
is the only way to move forward into the truth
together. And as a way of checking our preju-
dices and blind spots, it is valuable to discover
the biblical knowledge of believers from other
nations, backgrounds, or Christian traditions.

5. Expect Insight from God

We do not need to make God speak. He has already promised to do so. We need to expect to hear from him. Expectancy produces an active kind of listening, and it involves much more than reading the text. Reading the text is merely a task to do. *Listening* engages us in a personal encounter with the author. We *read* a newspaper. We *listen to* a letter from a friend.

Listening to God as we read the Bible means that we come to him expecting to hear something new, living, and fresh, perhaps a word about our hopes, fears or concerns. A promise. A reproof.

What will we hear? Who knows? That is for the sovereign God to decide. That is the adventure. That is the excitement.

6. Be Wise in Understanding

Wisdom, according to the Bible, is about what you know *and do,* what you believe *and practice.* It is not just a "head trip." When James wrote that "faith by itself, if it does not have works, is dead," this is what he meant. Think about this before you move through the "Take 7 Days" material below. Time spent reading the Bible alone, listening to God, is useless, even harmful, if we do not follow through on what we hear.

TAKE SEVEN DAYS . . .

DAY 1: *Facing Just Ourselves*

▶ *Troubleshooting*

This is a simple exercise. It does not entail using the Bible, but you will write a letter at the end. You will use the Bible in the following exercises, but here the idea is to help you discover how you approach the Bible.

When we come to the Bible, we bring all of our inner baggage with us. Some of it is healthy, some not so healthy. In either case it affects *how* we use the Bible. Read through the following list of questions carefully, but without giving too much thought to them just yet. Then read the instructions at the end of the questions, which will help you finish the exercise.

▶ *Red Flag Questions*

- When I read the Bible, am I willing to let it make me uncomfortable?
- Am I willing to test my understanding of biblical passages with Christians *outside* my church or peer group?
- What do I think about my parents when they offer advice?
- Am I a member or a faithful attender of a particular church?
- If I went to my minister for counseling would I trust him to the point of following through on what he said?
- Have I been wounded by a Christian authority figure?

- Do I imagine God as sitting on his throne with lightning bolts ready to strike?

- Or do I imagine God as a kind of indulgent Father-Christmas figure?

- To what degree do I hold back from obeying the Bible because of what my friends think?

- Can I identify one area of my life during the past six months where I have changed a particular action because of being challenged by the Bible?

- If it could be shown to me today that an area of my life is clearly inconsistent with the Bible, am I willing to change no matter what the cost?

▶ *Application*

Now is the time to re-read as many of the questions that were of particular concern to you, and to think about their affect on how you listen to the Bible speak to you. Is there a clear readiness on your part, or some hesitancy in letting it really speak into your life?

Under the ministry of the Holy Spirit, letter writing can be therapeutic, in the sense of revealing, cleansing, and renewing. Pick out one or two areas above where you now realize that your inner baggage is hindering a readiness to let the Bible really speak to you. Write a letter that begins, "Dear God," and in it name what has occurred to make you hesitant. Cite specific circumstances and honestly express your feeling about why they influence you to shy away from biblical instruction at times. Close your letter by admitting your fault here and by asking God to heal and change your responses to his Word. Thank God in faith, believing he will answer your letter. Sign it with your full name and place it in your Bible. You'll be reminded to pray through it again, and perhaps again, until you feel a break-through.

DAY **2**: *Facing the Bible as a Mirror*

▶ *Troubleshooting*

The truth of the Bible comes to us a mirror.

> *Don't, I beg you, merely hear the message, but put it into practice. The man who simply hears and does nothing about it is like a man catching the reflection of his own face in a mirror. He sees himself, it is true, but he goes on with whatever he was doing without the slightest recollection of what sort of person he saw in the mirror.*
>
> —James 1:22–24 PHILLIPS

This passage is set within the context of regeneration, and when the grace of God so transforms us it carries with it an obligation to obey. In this context James admonishes us that when the Word of God shows a Christian to himself as he is, he may just give it a glance and hurry off. Now this person, in glancing, has heard the Bible speak to him, but he does not act on it.

This mirror reflects self, that entity we are called to deny daily by picking up the cross. Self has many aspects, and the mirror of the Word of God reflects them all to us.

Pause here, and take several minutes to recall one or two aspects of your self-nature that you have given only fleeting attention from the Word of God.

A promise. James sees another man. This man does not give a fleeting glance. He looks with an intense gaze, and when he does, he sees what the other man would have seen had he taken time for reflection. The second man sees an amazing thing, that the Word of God liberates when obeyed. He sees this when he lets himself become steeped in the Word whenever it challenges him. The first man goes away deceived (v. 22 NKJV), the other person after taking some time goes away blessed (v. 25 NKJV).

> *But the man who looks [gazes intently] into the perfect mirror of God's Law, the Law of Liberty, and makes a habit of so doing, is not the man who sees and forgets. He puts the Law into practice and he wins true happiness.*
>
> —James 1:25 PHILLIPS

Think about it.

▶ *Hymn*

I SURRENDER ALL

All to Jesus I surrender,
All to Him I freely give;
I will ever love and trust Him,
In His presence daily live.

I surrender all,
I surrender all;
All to Thee, my blessed Saviour,
I surrender all.

All to Jesus I surrender,
Make me, Saviour, wholly Thine;
Let me feel the Holy Spirit
Truly know that Thou art mine.

All to Jesus I surrender,
Lord, I give myself to Thee;
Fill me with Thy love and power,
Let Thy blessing fall on me.
                                    —Judson W. Van DeVenter

DAY 3: *Facing the Bible as a Light*

▶ *Troubleshooting*

The truth of the Bible comes to us as light.

Your word is a lamp to my feet and a light to my path.
—Psalm 119:105

A little verse, but so much spiritual clout. A light can illuminate an entire room so that all of its contents can be seen, or it can be a shaft of light shining upon one area at a time. The light of Psalm 119 shines at our feet, perhaps to keep us from stumbling or to reveal a new direction on the path that God wants us to go. Here we are shown practical applications of the Word.

Christian applications of the Word of God are many and varied. We'll just consider one here: the practical use of time.

Setting aside the question of the amount of time that goes for work, sleep, church attendance, and inescapable activities like preparing meals, shopping and caring for the children, how sensible is our use of time? Let's narrow it even further to media consumption. Take a minute to add up the hours a week you spend in front of the television or video, reading magazines and newspapers, listening to CDs.

How many hours did you come up with for the seven-day period? Ten? Twenty? Thirty? More? Less? Whatever number you arrived at, this is the number of hours per week you spend on the path listening to the media. Do you think the amount is a practical use of time? Compare that amount to the hours per week you spend tuned to God's voice through the Bible.

▶ *Application*

Some Christians receive much more instruction and direction from the media than from the Bible. But how different are their visions of what the truly good life is!

Take several minutes now to let the Word light the path of your use of time. One minister discovered he needed to break his habit of monitoring all the radio and TV news programs he could. A Christian couple decided they would not have a television in their home. A family strictly enforces one hour of television viewing per evening.

The Word of God is radical, not lukewarmly reasonable about stewardship of time.

> *Blessed is the man*
> *Who walks not in the counsel of the ungodly,*
> *Nor stands in the path of sinners,*
> *Nor sits in the seat of the scornful;*
> *But his delight is in the law of the* LORD,
> *And in His law he meditates day and night.*
> *—Psalm 1:1–2*

> *Rejoice always, pray without ceasing.*
> *—1 Thessalonians 5:16–17*

> *And whatever you do in word or deed, do all in the name of the Lord Jesus.*
> *—Colossians 3:17*

Think about it.

▶ *Hymn*

GIVE OF YOUR BEST TO THE MASTER

> *Give of your best to the Master,*
> *Give of the strength of your youth;*
> *Throw your soul's fresh, glowing ardor*
> *Into the battle for truth:*

Jesus has set the example,
Dauntless was He, young and brave;
Give Him your loyal devotion,
Give Him the best that you have.

Give of your best to the Master,
Give Him first place in your heart;
Give Him first place in your service,
Consecrate every part:
Give, and to you shall be given,
God His beloved Son gave;
Gratefully seeking to serve Him,
Give Him the best that you have.

Give of your best to the Master,
Naught else is worthy His love;
He gave Himself for your ransom,
Gave up His glory above;
Laid down His life without murmur,
You from sin's ruin to save;
Give Him your heart's adoration,
Give Him the best that you have.
                                   —Howard B. Grose

DAY 4: *Facing the Bible as a Fire*

▶ *Troubleshooting*

The truth of the Bible comes to us as fire. And there are many kinds of fires that it can be to us.

Fire played a vital part in Israelite worship on the altars of incense and burnt offering.

Then the glory of the Lord appeared to all the people, and fire came down from before the LORD and consumed the burnt offering and the fat of the altar.
                                   —Leviticus 9:23–24

Fire was used to symbolize God's glory.

Then I looked, and behold a whirlwind was coming out of the north, a great cloud with raging fire engulfing itself; and brightness was all around it and radiating out of its midst, like the color of amber, out of the midst of the fire.

—Ezekiel 1:4

Fire was used to symbolize God's protective presence.

And Elisha prayer and said, "LORD, I pray, open his eyes that he may see." Then the LORD opened the eyes of the young man, and he saw. And behold, the mountain was full of horses and chariots of fire all around Elisha.

—2 Kings 6:17

Fire describes God's holiness.

For the LORD your God is a consuming fire, a jealous God.

—Deuteronomy 4:24

It is that which purifies and proves.

I will bring one-third through the fire,
Will refine them as silver is refined,
And test them as gold is tested.
They will call on My name,
And I will answer them.
I will say, 'This is My people';
And each one will say, 'The LORD is my God.'

—Zechariah 13:9

It is used to constrain God's messengers.

Then I said, "I will not make mention of Him,
Nor speak any more in His name."
But His word was in my heart like a burning fire
Shut up in my bones;

I was weary of holding it back,
And I could not.

—Jeremiah 20:9

Fire is also used of the Holy Spirit.

Then there appeared to them divided tongues, as of
fire, and one sat on each of them. And they were all
filled with the Holy Spirit.

—Acts 2:3–4

► *Application*

Here we encounter not merely the activity but the intensity of God in fire. And it is a multifaceted intensity, a divine ardor having many expressions:

- Worship
- Revelations of God
- Protection
- Holiness
- Cleansing
- Divine utterances
- The presence of the Holy Spirit

Is there an area in this summary list that catches your attention? Perhaps its the area of cleansing. You may be struggling with a bad habit. Take some time in prayer to tell God about this. Ask him to forgive you and to cleanse you. Use your imagination to see the fire of God consuming that bad habit. Or perhaps it concerns Divine utterances. Has God recently been speaking to you about something, either for you personally or for another person, but for whatever reason you have been holding it back, resisting? Take time in prayer to ask God for his help, and determine that you will obey God's personal word to you.

If you are keeping a spiritual journal, copy the Scripture that most clearly speaks to your situation, and write about the area you've identified where God's word as fire now touches you. Discuss how the fire wants to change you and how you have resisted it. Then write a prayer to God.

If you feel indifferent, or perhaps even uninterested, about any of these areas, maybe the fire is dying out. Take your embers to God, or even your ashes, for he can do miracles even with these.

▶ *Hymn*

GUIDE ME, O THOU GREAT JEHOVAH

Guide me, O Thou great Jehovah,
Pilgrim through this barren land;
I am weak, but Thou art mighty,
Hold me with Thy powerful hand;
Bread of heaven,
Feed me till I want no more;
Bread of heaven,
Feed me till I want no more.

Open now the crystal fountain,
Whence the healing waters flow;
Let the fire and cloudy pillar
Lead me all my journey through;
Strong Deliverer,
Be Thou still my strength and shield;
Strong Deliverer,
Be Thou still my strength and shield.

When I tread the verge of Jordan,
Bid my anxious fears subside;
Bear me through the swelling current,
Land me safe on Canaan's side;
Songs of praises
I will ever give to Thee;
Songs of praises
I will ever give to Thee.
—Peter Williams and William Williams

DAY 5: *Facing the Bible as a Hammer*

▶ *Troubleshooting*

The truth of the Bible may come to us like a hammer.

Is not My word . . . ," says the LORD, "like a hammer that breaks the rock in pieces?
—Jeremiah 23:29

There may be deep-seated attitudes or habits that God may need to break open with his Word. You could identify these areas of your life and have a Bible study concerning them. Let's use the sound Bible study principles as provided in this chapter to highlight one common area that is usually problematic: our attitude toward money.

First, the Bible faces us with reality:

No one can serve two masters. Either he will hate the one and love the other, or he will be devoted to one and despise the other. You cannot serve both God and money.
—Luke 16:13 NIV

There's quite a sting in this statement of Jesus'. So maybe it's just an isolated saying. In which case we would want to look for any passages that may justify and confirm this reality. Here are a few:

The love of money is the root of all kinds of evil, for which some have strayed from the faith in their greediness, and pierced themselves through with many sorrows.
—1 Timothy 6:10

It is easier for a camel to go through the eye of a needle than for a rich man to enter the kingdom of God.
—Matthew 19:24

Woe to you who are rich.

—Luke 6:24

In his book *Money, Sex & Power,* Richard Foster wrote that it is right at this point that we try to tone down Jesus' criticism, but that this is the very thing we must not do if we want it to speak to us.

Our next step, then, is to let the reality change us, which might be hard if we saw only the downside to money. If we could find passages about the upside of money, they might motivate us. One example is in Luke 10 where the Good Samaritan was commended by Jesus for his generous use of money. Another example is in Matthew 26 where Jesus praised a woman for her use of the costly ointment.

How do you feel about money? Do you see only the downside, or can you see the upside as well? How could you go about changing your use of money?

When it's difficult to know how to change, it is helpful to discover a biblical principle that applies to the situation. The one that is perhaps most helpful is that of generosity:

A year ago you were the first ones to give, and you gave because you wanted to. So listen to my advice. I think you should finish what you started. If you give according to what you have, you will prove that you are as eager to give as you were to think about giving. It doesn't matter how much you have. What matters is how much you are willing to give from what you have.

I am not trying to make life easier for others by making life harder for you. But it is only fair for you to share with them when you have so much, and they have so little. Later, when they have more than enough, and you are in need, they can share with you. Then everyone will have a fair share, just as the Scriptures say,

> *"Those who gathered too much*
> *had nothing left.*
> *Those who gathered only a little*
> *had all they needed."*
> —2 Corinthians 8:10–15 CEV

▶ *Application*

Examine your spending and giving patterns in the above light. Does the love of money have too great a lock on your purse strings? How could you begin to apply the biblical principle of generosity as the Word breaks you open in this important area? There may be no easy answer. If so, you may be reading into the Bible only what you want to hear. Be careful of this.

You may find a solution by asking trusted friends how they handle it. Above all, be honest with God as you sort it out in prayer.

▶ *Hymn*

WE GIVE THEE BUT THINE OWN

We give Thee but Thine own,
Whatever the gift may be;
All that we have is Thine alone,
A trust, O Lord, from Thee.

May we Thy bounties thus
As stewards true receive,
And gladly, as Thou blessest us,
To Thee our first fruits give.

The captive to release,
To God the lost to bring,
To teach the way of life and peace,
It is a Christ-like thing.

And we believe Thy word,
Though dim our faith may be;
Whatever for Thine we do, O Lord,
We do it unto Thee.
—William W. How

DAY 6: *Facing the Bible as a Sword*

▶ *Troubleshooting*

The character of the Word of God confronts us like a sword. And though it is two-edged, it is like no human sword. As someone has said, it shares the very attributes of God himself. This means that it is living and active, with a power to do what it sets out to accomplish. And what it will accomplish will be either redemption or judgment, penetrating, as it does, even our most inward and secret thoughts and desires like a dissecting knife. This is the sword that scrutinizes, and before it nothing can be concealed.

> *For the word of God is living and powerful, and sharper than any two-edged sword, piercing even to the division of soul and spirit, and of joints and marrow, and is a discerner of the thoughts and intent of the heart. And there is no creature hidden in His sight, but all things are naked and open to the eyes of Him to whom we must give an account.*
> —Hebrews 4:12–13

▶ *Application*

There used to be a popular game show in America called "I've Got A Secret." A panel of four celebrities would have several minutes to try to guess a contestant's unusual secret. Sometimes they failed. Other times they guessed it.

But everytime the secret was revealed at the end of the game.

At the end of your life, the books will be opened. What will be revealed?

What secret dreams and desires do you have? Which ones are greatly embarrassing in the sense that they are undesirable or even immoral? Let the sword of the Word go to work on you redemptively. Take time to bring any wrong desires to him in prayer. Why not choose to tell your secret and pray for a clean slate?

▶ *Hymn*

THOUGH YOUR SINS BE AS SCARLET

"Though your sins be as scarlet,
They shall be as white as snow;
"Though your sins be as scarlet,
They shall be as white as snow;
Though they be red like crimson,
They shall be as wool!"
"Though your sins be as scarlet,
Though your sins be as scarlet,
They shall be as white as snow,
They shall be as white as snow."

Hear the voice that entreats you,
O return ye unto God!
Hear the voice that entreats you,
O return ye unto God!
He is of great compassion,
And of wondrous love;
Hear the voice that entreats you,
Hear the voice that entreats you,
O return ye unto God!
O return ye unto God!

He'll forgive your transgressions,
And remember them no more;
He'll forgive your transgressions,
And remember them no more;
"Look unto Me, ye people,"
Saith the Lord your God!
He'll forgive your transgressions,
He'll forgive your transgressions,
And remember them no more,
And remember them no more.
—Fanny J. Crosby

DAY 7: *Enjoying the Bible's Sweetness*

▶ *Application*

We have been reflecting on some pretty serious things in this "Take 7 Days" section. But the Christian life is not all work and no joy. Our God is not a cruel taskmaster but a loving Father. Though he disciplines those he loves, he also is the God of all comfort. The Bible can deeply enrich our knowledge of God's comfort whenever the Word comes to us as sweetness and honey.

> *And He said to me, "Son of man, feed your belly, and fill your stomach with this scroll that I will give you." So I ate it, and it was in my mouth like honey and sweetness.*
>
> —Ezekiel 3:3

▶ *Meditation*

The apostle Paul said that "through the . . . comfort of the Scriptures [we] might have hope," (Rom. 15:4). Most Christians have a few biblical verses that are filled with hope and comfort for them. Yet it may have been months since any one of these has been considered. Choose one of your favorites on which to meditate and thank God. Here are a couple of suggestions to provide some ideas.

> *Grace to you and peace from God our Father and the Lord Jesus Christ. Blessed be the God and Father of our Lord Jesus Christ, the Father of all mercies and the God of all comfort, who comforts us in all our tribulation.*
>
> —2 Corinthians 1:2–4

Do you recall a special time when God brought great comfort to you? Did that come from him directly or through a Christian friend or loved one? In your journal write a short "confession of faith" statement to God that acknowledges and affirms how he comforted you. Begin it with, "I believe, God, that you . . . . I thank you for . . . ."

> *Let not your heart be troubled; you believe in God, believe also in Me. In my Father's house are many mansions; if it were not so I would have told you. I go to prepare a place for you. And if I go and prepare a place for you, I will come again and receive you to Myself; that where I am, there you will be also.*
>
> —John 14:1–3

This is a wonderful hope of the glorious future with our Lord. Take some time to write a "poem of praise" that describe what you think it will be like. You can include ideas from other biblical passages about heaven too.

If you have been patiently working through this 7 Day section, take this seventh day as a day of rest. Rejoice over passages of comfort. Cry your eyes out over them. Thank God for them. Share them with someone. Treasure them more deeply. Then rest in them.

Keeping Company with God

"**P**rayer," said Simon Tugwell, "is not another part for us to act, another skill for us to master. . . . It is a relationship, a relationship with God." Praying, then, is living with God, being yourself with God, and letting God be himself with you. When we pray we are giving our attention, however weak, to God, who is always there to give himself to us.

Beginning is often the most difficult part of praying. Our lack of desire or weakness in self-discipline often holds us back, as does a feeling that we don't know how to pray "properly." Or perhaps our image of praying is too closely linked to a particular style or technique we have learned, which may stop us from recognizing others ways of praying. Yet even before we pray, the risen Lord Jesus Christ is praying for us: "It is Christ who died, and furthermore is also risen, who is even at the right hand of God, who also makes intercession for us" (Romans 8:34). Prayer, then, is more about his activity in us than our efforts for him!

As Christians, we recognize God's love and activity in us, and through prayer we enter into the relationship he is forever offering and sustaining in us. This may help us to see prayer for what it really is: an opening of ourselves to the Father who loves and listens, to the Son who intercedes, and to the Spirit who prays within us, drawing us toward God. Our approaches and preferences will vary, and the other chapters in this book will reveal this. Nevertheless, prayer is Almighty God helping us to give ourselves back to him.

Prayer as Personal Pilgrimage

Prayer is part of our life-long pilgrimage of sifting and searching, of asking, seeking, and finding. We show our consent for God's Spirit to express his life in all that we do. When we pray we are letting this happen. Praying as an activity touches every part of us: body, mind, emotions, and spirit. It is an activity through which God our Father can work in us by His Spirit day by day to make us more like his Son Jesus Christ.

Prayer can take a myriad of forms. God is always with us, but we are not always aware of being with him. We may have moments during the day when we ask for help or give thanks for something special. Prayer can be this personal and, in part, unpredictable, happening any place or any time we are open to God. We may hum a hymn, sing a chorus, remember a verse of Scripture, or make a special request. Praying our way through life can be very informal.

Jesus' Example

Jesus himself prayed in many ways and places. He went to the local synagogues to pray with his fellow Jews. He learned from their prayer tradition and through sharing in their religious services. As a result, Jesus would have prayed the psalms and many other sections of scripture, as well as the great prayers of his Hebrew heritage. He probably used a prayer shawl and raised his hands at times. No doubt he prayed standing, kneeling, bowed, or when simply walking along. He prayed publicly and privately. For Jesus, stopping to pray was a way of life, through which he gave himself back to the Father. Giving time to pray deepens our devotion and helps us to find the space, time, posture, words, or silences that we need.

Stopping to Start

Some Christians find it hard to start praying simply because they cannot stop doing everything else. In the bustle of living, stopping can be the hardest thing to do, and eventually our prayer life can wither up and die. Obviously, we need to find ways to stop and pray. This will vary not only from person to person but also during various stages of life. What is helpful to a commuter may not suit a homemaker, truck driver, or college student. We each have to find our own way, and this handbook will introduce you to many possibilities that can be tried. It is important, however, to settle for a basic pattern, because good habits in prayer help us to become more aware of and receptive to the presence of God. And if we review our pattern every few months, that will help us in reaching harmony with what God's Spirit is prompting and shaping within us. The effects of this will spill over into our lives and give us a greater awareness of God. Regular prayer is vital nourishment for spiritual development.

If stopping to pray is difficult, staying in prayer can be just as hard. Our thoughts may wander, and concentration may seem next to impossible. We may be distracted by the activities and noises around us. Inner problems and struggles may also make it hard to stay in prayer. These may surface as part of the process of prayer. But take heart! God is in the recycling business, forming the likeness of Christ out of the disorder and chaos in each of us.

For these reasons our preparations for prayer times are important. They will help us to get beyond these difficulties. Remember too that prayer is *God's* gift to and *his* activity in us. Our part is to make ourselves available to him in an attentive way, learning to listen and offer to God the varied responses that well up within us.

BEGINNINGS

Most of the ways to pray that are touched on here will be developed in more detail in later chapters. The purpose here is to help you to stop and to prepare for staying in a prayer. Sometimes you may experience barrenness, tiredness, or a difficulty settling in and concentrating. Such struggles are common. They are an authentic part of learning to pray. The following approaches have helped many Christians to get beyond their difficulties and distractions in order to stay in prayer.

Finding a Place

Where can you find a quiet place? By having a regular quiet place you will begin to associate being there with praying. By contrast, you can also use the place where you happen to be as a starting point for prayer. You may be sitting on the beach, or waiting for the doctor, or driving for an hour. Learning to be inwardly attentive in your regular place of prayer will help you to be open to God in other places.

Choosing a Time

This is a twofold decision about when and how long you will pray. It may take a while to discover a pattern, so experiment with different times during the day. When can you find ten to twenty minutes without interruptions? Be honest and compassionate with yourself. A few min-

utes is better than none, and with practice you
can work up to longer periods.

Discovering a Posture

Avoid being uncomfortable! With the decline
of the tradition of kneeling in church, many people have adopted the "bowed head crouch,"
which has become an unfortunate norm. Sitting
bent over with head in hands cramps the stom-
ach. This position prevents relaxed breathing,
and unless you are very distressed it is not con-
ducive to ongoing prayer (and even then, not
for long!). Try sitting comfortably in an upright
chair, resting your hands in your lap. Also try
standing, walking, kneeling, or even lying
down.

Accepting God's Presence

Having made some preparations for prayer,
find a way of saying "Here I am, Lord." It can be
a simple statement of your desire to pray, or even
admitting that you do not want to pray but are
willing to be there. If it is a little noisy, create a
bit of quietness by listening to yourself breathe.
You could use the in and out rhythm of your
breathing, imaginatively, to breathe in God's
Spirit and love and to breathe out your anxieties
and concerns. You could try just to be still, accepting God's presence in silence. There is that
popular verse of Psalm 46:10, "Be still, and
know that I am God." Say this verse by stopping
for a few seconds after the second, fourth, and

sixth words. Pausing like this can help emphasize the point of being still. The fact that you are acting out your intention to be open to God is valid in itself, even if you have difficulty focusing on him.

Using Symbols and Repetition

Some people like to use symbols to help them enter into prayer. If you would like to try this but find that you have reservations, start with a symbol which has well-known associations. "*Consider*," as Jesus said, "the lilies of the field" (Matthew 6:28). You could also "consider" a glass of water (thirst), a piece of bread (the body of Christ), a seed pod (fruit), or an empty bowl (hunger). This would not only help you enter into prayer; it would suggest ideas for prayer.

Over a period of time you may want to collect an album of pictures or images which for you are stepping stones into prayer in Jesus' name. Your selection could include prayer cards, postcards, paintings, and pictures of sculptures, as well as scenes of great beauty in the natural world. But do not overlook the more disturbing pictures of human conflict or suffering, which can be helps for praying during times of darkness.

Repeating significant words, phrases, or simple sentences may also enhance prayer. These are ways that some Christians find helpful for moving from the mind to the heart in prayer.

There are many words, names, titles and characteristics, that you can use, such as Emmanuel, Lamb of God, Jesus, Savior, hallelujah, praise the Lord, peace be with you, the Lord is my light, God is love, do not let your hearts be troubled, or Lord, have mercy. Full sentences have been developed from some of these to be used with rhythmic breathing. The Jesus Prayer from the Orthodox Christian tradition is used this way, breathing in and out steadily while quietly repeating: "Lord Jesus Christ, Son of God, have mercy on me, a sinner." Some Christians like to recite lines from worship songs, or the beatitudes from the Sermon on the Mount, or the promise "I am with you always" (Matt. 28:20). Any appropriate short sentence from the Bible can be used to help you center your attention on God.

The Benedictine approach is similar to this. Instead of reading through a whole passage, read biblical phrases or sentences slowly but aloud or in a whisper. Do this with frequent pauses so that the words are *heard* as well as seen and read. Then when a particular word or phrase rings a bell with you, repeat it several times slowly to savor its significance. This can be a good way of reading and praying the Psalms. For example:

Psalm 23, The Lord is my shepherd
Psalm 51, Have mercy on me, O God
Psalm 84, How lovely is your tabernacle
Psalm 103, Bless the LORD, O my soul

Psalm 139, O LORD, You have searched me and known me

Spontaneous Prayer

The ways of praying suggested above encourage a listening disposition and an attentiveness to God. This, however, is not meant to deter the spontaneous praying you may express at other times. You may even find that you are given a way of expressing your prayers that sounds like another language. This is called speaking in tongues and is mentioned in 1 Corinthians 12:10.

Jesus prayed spontaneously and freely. Many Old Testament writers and psalmists also poured out their souls impromptu. They groaned and sighed. They cried out in auguish or with praises. The whole range of emotional experience and ways of using language are found in their prayers.

This kind of praying can lead you naturally into making specific requests for yourself and others. Jesus encouraged his followers to ask God for things.

And I say to you, ask, and it will be given to you; seek, and you will find; knock, and it will be opened to you. For everyone who asks receives, and he who seeks finds, and to him who knocks it will be opened. If a son asks for bread from any father among you, will he give him a stone? Or if he asks for a fish, will he give him a serpent instead of a fish? Or if he asks for an

*egg, will he offer him a scorpion? If you, then,
being evil, know how to give good gifts to your
children, how much more will your heavenly Father give the Holy Spirit to those who ask Him!*
                              —Luke 11:9–13

Simplicity and honestly is the best approach
in "asking prayer." Remember, too, that in all
"asking prayer" the Holy Spirit is at work stimulating and interpreting your longings and concerns to God.

*Likewise the Spirit also helps us in our weak-
nesses. For we do not know what we should pray
for as we ought, but the Spirit Himself makes
intercession for us with groanings which cannot
be uttered. Now He who searches the hearts
knows what the mind of the Spirit is, because
He makes intercession for the saints according to
the will of God.*

                              —Romans 8:26–27

For this reason, the different ways and approaches outlined above can bring a new quality
of discernment into your asking prayers. By first
waiting quietly and listening carefully, your requests afterwards will be more in tune with
God's will and purposes.

Some people find lists of names or topics useful when seeking to pray for others. Using a diary or calendar may be helpful. Writing down
the names of the people is a practical suggestion
that has its roots in the Old Testament. In Exodus
28:29, you can read of how the high priest wore
a breastplate on which the names of the tribes of

Israel were inscribed. Whenever the high priest went into the presence of God, the names symbolized that the twelve tribes were in God's presence too. This is what Jesus is forever doing on our behalf in the presence of God the Father, exposing our needs and disgrace to the Father's almighty love and mercy: "Therefore He is also able to save to the uttermost those who come to God through Him, since He ever lives to make intercession for them" (Hebrews 7:25).

The late Bishop Michael Ramsey used to describe this kind of intercessory prayer (asking on behalf of others) as simply "to be with God with the people on your heart." Some of your concerns may be beyond your capacity to put into words. A scene from a famine, a flood, or an act of terrorism may help bring forth a few words as well as deep emotion. In fact, deep emotion may be all that you can call forth when praying in personal sorrow or for people you love who are ill. "To be there before you, Lord, that's all . . . ," is the way Michel Quoist begins one of his *Prayers of Life*. Your asking may be like that at times. To be there in anguish may be the only kind of appropriate prayer. If so, you can let your emotions spill over into the silent and sovereign love of the crucified God. And by his grace you can later be there again in relief, appreciation, and thanksgiving. Asking, therefore, is not about pleading with an unresponsive God, but entering into the presence of the One who is always working for your good.

> *We know that all things work together for the good to those who love God, to those who are called according to His purpose.*
> —Romans 8:28

A traditional way of praying is to identify the various elements of confession, thanksgiving, adoration, and supplication, and working through each element in prayer. Let each element arise as the Spirit prompts. Some Christians use these elements in any order. Others work through each element as each is evoked by the symbols, prayers or parts of Scripture being used. And still others always begin with "confession" and then proceed into thanksgiving, adoration, supplication or intercession, respectively. What matters most is that you seek to become aware of your relationship with God and let your time with him unfold. Bishop Michael Ramsey put it like this:

To be with God wondering, that is adoration.
To be with God gratefully, that is thanksgiving.
To be with God ashamed, that is confession.
To be with God with others on your heart, that is intercession.

But more than anything else, as Clement of Alexandria said, prayer is keeping company with God. The following exercises will help you do just that.

TAKE SEVEN DAYS . . .

The following exercises are based on praying through some of the great prayers of the Christian faith. The Bible, Jesus, the apostles, and people like St. Francis, St. Ignatius, St. Anslem, St. Augustine and many others have left us concise prayers that encapsulate our longings and fears, our sorrows and praises. These can help us express ourselves in the presence of God. They often put into words what we may be feeling, yet are having difficulty in saying. St. Francis' popular prayer, "Lord, make me an instrument of your peace," is a case in point. Try saying these prayers, or others you may find, by using some of the ideas suggested in the chapter and so enrich your relationship with God.

DAY **1**: *Prayer of Confession*

> Merciful Father, I confess
> My common failings as I live alongside others;
> My lack of understanding,
> My lack of forgiveness,
> My lack of openness,
> My lack of sensitivity.
> I confess the times when I am
> Too eager to be better than others,
> Too rushed to care,
> Too tired to bother,
> Too quick to act from motives other than love.
> Father, forgive me.

▶ *Reflection*

After reading through the prayer once, read it through again, taking each line slowly. Afterward, return to pray through any lines that may have been relevant to you, sensitive to any of your own shortcomings, pausing to ask God for forgiveness. Take your time. There's no hurry. You could then conclude your prayer with:

> O Lord, forgive what I have been,
> Bless what I am,
> Direct what I shall be.

▶ *Memory Prayer*

As a reminder of God's constant love and forgiveness, learn this short saying of St. Augustine's:

> Trust the past to the mercy of God,
> The present to his love,
> The future to his providence.

▶ *Hymn*

MORE HOLINESS GIVE ME

> *More holiness give me,*
> *More striving within;*
> *More patience in suffering,*
> *More sorrow for sin;*
> *More faith in my Saviour,*
> *More sense of His care;*
> *More joy in His service,*
> *More purpose in prayer.*
>
> *More gratitude give me,*
> *More trust in the Lord;*
> *More pride in His glory,*
> *More hope in His Word;*
> *More tears for His sorrows,*
> *More pain at His grief;*
> *More meekness in trial,*
> *More praise for relief.*

More purity give me,
More strength to overcome;
More freedom from earth stains,
More longings for home;
More fit for the kingdom,
More used would I be;
More blessed and holy,
More, Saviour, like Thee.

—Philip P. Bliss

DAY 2: *Prayer of Thanksgiving*

Lord Jesus Christ, I thank you
For all the benefits you have won for me,
For all the pains and insults that you have
   borne for me.
Most merciful redeemer, friend and brother,
May I know you more clearly,
Love you more dearly
And follow you more nearly
Day by day. Amen.

—St. Richard of Chichester

▶ *Reflection*

Find a picture or a symbol that depicts Jesus' sufferings.
Some Bibles provide pictures of this, or you may be able to
recall a scene from a movie or a painting. Take some time
to think about Jesus' pains and insults and the benefits he
won for you.

I gave My back to those who struck Me,
And My cheeks to those who plucked out the
   beard;
I did not hide My face from shame and spitting.

—Isaiah 50:6

And being in agony, He prayed more earnestly. Then His sweat became like great drops of blood falling down to the ground.
          —Luke 22:44

You were not redeemed with corruptible things, like silver or gold, . . . but with the precious blood of Christ, as of a lamb without blemish and without spot.
          —1 Peter 1:18–19

Thank the Lord for specific benefits. If through this exercise you have received some deeper understanding, repeat the above prayer with this new meaning and feeling.

▶ *For Memory*

The following short affirmation embodies three core truths for which we all can be especially thankful. Try to learn it by heart so that you can thank God for these things at any time.

> *Without the* Way,
> *There is no going;*
> *Without the* Truth,
> *There is no knowing;*
> *Without the* Life,
> *There is no living.*
> —Thomas à Kempis

▶ *Hymn*

DRAW THOU MY SOUL, O CHRIST

> *Draw Thou my soul, O Christ,*
> *Closer to Thine;*
> *Breathe into every wish*
> *Thy will divine!*
> *Raise my low self above,*
> *Won by Thy deathless love;*

Ever, O Christ, through mine
Let Thy life shine.

Lead forth my soul, O Christ,
One with Thine own,
Joyful to follow Thee
Through paths unknown!
In Thee my strength renew;
Give me my work to do!
Through me Thy truth be shown,
Thy love made known.

Not for myself alone
May my prayer be;
Lift Thou Thy world, O Christ,
Closer to Thee!
Cleanse it from guilt and wrong;
Teach it salvation's song,
Till earth, as heaven, fulfil
God's holy will.

—Lucy Larcom

DAY 3: *The Lord's Prayer*

Our Father in heaven,
Hallowed be Your name.
Your kingdom come.
Your will be done
On earth as it is in heaven.
Give us day by day our daily bread.
And forgive us our sins,
For we also forgive everyone who is indebted
    to us.
And lead us not into temptation,
But deliver us from the evil one.

—Luke 11:2–4

▶ *Reflection*

It is only too true that we become bored with overused expressions; they seem to have little or nothing to say to us any more. G. K. Chesterton wrote, "Familiarity breeds inattention." This is why many of us now look at the Lord's Prayer without even a second thought. Take some time here to renew your acquaintance with this prayer, to discover ways of freshening it up in your mind. Here is a list of the main characteristics to help get you started. The Lord's Prayer:

- Introduces Christ's disciples into a relationship with the Father similar to his own. "Our" emphasizes the corporate reality of the family of God. "Father" speaks of intimacy, while "in heaven" signals the reverence toward God that, with intimacy, results in a balanced, healthy relationship.

- Reveals that God's name is to be respected and honored (hallowed) because it is holy. "Hallowed be" is a request by us that God's Name be acknowledged, worshipped, and held holy by everyone, everywhere.

- Calls for God to act in such a way as to bring the kingdom into human affairs. "Your will be done" is a call for the beauty and perfection of God's purposes to prevail in the earth.

- Requests daily bread (provision) from God, which has overtones of the bread of life. "Give us . . . daily bread" indicates we are not to be greedy. It is a modest request, consonant with contentment.

- Asks God to forgive us and to preserve us. "Lead us not" and "deliver us from" show a mark of humility. We aren't strong enough to be continually victorious in everything, so we humbly request that God would

spare us from onslaughts and temptation beneath
which we would fall or fail.

▶ *Memory Prayer*

You probably have the Lord's Prayer already committed
to memory. The doxology that follows the Lord's Prayer in
Matthew is not found in Luke. Try the following as a means
of freshening up the prayer. Memorize this short affirmation
of Julian of Norwich and use it as a doxology for Luke's
version above.

> From him we come;
> In him we are enfolded;
> To him we return.

▶ *Hymn*

DEAR LORD AND FATHER OF MANKIND

> *Dear Lord and Father of mankind,*
> *Forgive our foolish ways;*
> *Reclothe us in our rightful mind;*
> *In purer lives Thy service find,*
> *In deeper reverence, praise.*
>
> *Drop Thy still dews of quietness,*
> *Till all our strivings cease;*
> *Take from our souls the strain and stress,*
> *And let our ordered lives confess*
> *The beauty of Thy peace.*
>
> *Breathe through the heats of our desire*
> *Thy coolness and Thy balm;*
> *Let sense be dumb, let flesh retire;*
> *Speak through the earthquake, wind, and fire,*
> *O still small Voice of calm!*

In simple trust like theirs who heard,
Beside the Syrian sea,
The gracious calling of the Lord,
Let us, like them, without a word,
Rise up and follow Thee.
—John G. Whittier

DAY 4: *Prayer of Restful Assurance*

The LORD is my shepherd;
I shall not want.
He makes me to lie down in green pastures;
He leads me beside the still waters.
He restores my soul;
He leads me in the paths of righteousness
For His name's sake.
Yea, though I walk through the valley of the shadow
    of death,
I will fear no evil;
For you are with me;
Your rod and Your staff, they comfort me.
You prepare a table before me in the presence of
    my enemies;
You anoint my head with oil;
My cup runs over.
Surely goodness and mercy shall follow me
All the days of my life;
And I will dwell in the house of the Lord
Forever.
—Psalm 23

▶ *Reflection*

As Hebrews 3—4 indicate, God's rest sometimes escapes
us, but not always. Psalm 23 is a lyrical gem that blends
contrasted imagery; for example, peace and peril. See what

other contrasts you can find. Note them and write them in a prayer to God in your own words to express your trust in God to care for you, whatever happens.

▶ *Memory Prayer*

It's hard to know if St. Patrick was thinking of Psalm 23 when he wrote the following prayer, but he may well have been. Commit it to memory. It is a little longer than the other "memory prayers," yet it is an easy one, and it contains many interesting contrasts like Psalm 23.

> Christ be with me,
> Christ behind me,
> Christ before me,
> Christ beside me,
> Christ to comfort and restore me.
> Christ beneath me,
> Christ above me,
> Christ in quiet,
> Christ in danger.
> Christ in hearts of all who love me.
> Christ in mouth of friend or stranger.

▶ *Hymn*

BLESSED ASSURANCE, JESUS IS MINE

> *Blessed assurance, Jesus is mine!*
> *Oh, what a foretaste of glory divine!*
> *Heir of salvation, purchase of God,*
> *Born of His Spirit, washed in His blood.*
>
> *This is my story, this is my song,*
> *Praising my Saviour all the day long;*
> *This is my story, this is my song,*
> *Praising my Saviour all the day long.*

Perfect submission, perfect delight,
Visions of rapture now burst on my sight:
Angels descending bring from above
Echoes of mercy, whispers of love.

Perfect submission, all is at rest,
I in my Saviour am happy and blest:
Watching and waiting, looking above,
Filled with His goodness, lost in His love.
—Fanny J. Crosby

DAY 5: *Prayer for the Will of God*

Almighty God,
In whom we live and move and have our being,
You have made us for yourself,
So that our hearts are restless
Until they rest in you.
Grant us purity of heart and strength of
    purpose,
That no selfish passion may hinder us
From knowing your will,
No weakness from doing it;
But that in your light we may see clearly,
And in your service find our perfect freedom,
Through Jesus Christ our Lord.
—St. Augustine

▶ *Reflection*

It is said that during the years he was a Christian, St. Augustine's life was filled with a torrent of activity. Maybe one day when he was being deluged he realized the potential for disaster and so said the above prayer! In our day, we are often flooded with activity, and yet much of it may turn out to have been just so much wood, hay, and stubble.

You read through Augustine's prayer; now go back and read through it slowly as a prayer. Pause often so each word and phrase speaks to you, and when you reach a sticking point, take some time to stop there and confess the problem to God. Make it a special purpose of this prayer to ask God to lead you away from superficial busyness into considerate and loving actions.

▶ *Memory Prayer*

Do you know someone who has been seeking the will of God, someone, perhaps, who has asked you to pray with him about this? Here is a way that you could bless the person. Commit the following short prayer to memory, and then the next time you see your friend, take a minute to bless him with the prayer.

> Let Jesus be in your heart,
> Eternity in your spirit,
> The world under your feet,
> The will of God in your actions.
> And let the love of God shine forth from you.
> —St. Catherine of Genoa

▶ *Hymn*

LORD, SPEAK TO ME, THAT I MAY SPEAK

> *Lord, speak to me, that I may speak*
> *In living echoes of Thy tone;*
> *As Thou hast sought, so let me seek*
> *Thy erring children lost and lone.*

Oh, teach me, Lord, that I may teach
The precious things Thou dost impart;
And wing my words, that they may reach
The hidden depths of many a heart.

Oh, fill me with Thy fulness, Lord,
Until my very heart overflow
In kindling thought and glowing word,
Thy love to tell, Thy praise to show.

Oh, use me, Lord, use even me,
Just as Thou wilt, and when, and where;
Until Thy blessed face I see,
Thy rest, Thy joy, Thy glory share.
—Frances R. Havergal

DAY **6**: *Prayer for Rest in Suffering*

▶ *Reflection*

The thought of you stirs us so deeply that we cannot
be content unless we praise you, because you have
made us for yourself and our hearts find no peace until
they rest in you.

—St. Augustine

This confession to God by St. Augustine has been said by many Christians for more than 1500 years. It has been used in many contexts, and yet we may not think of its meaning and message to us in the context of suffering.

Suffering is a pain. It is an unwanted invasion into our lives. Whatever form it takes, and whether or not it is "deserved," suffering has always been felt by God's people. Suffering is hard to deal with, and the sufferers may have misery heaped on misery if they do not know why suffering has come, or if people try to say why, but give superficial answers. When we suffer, we may try to find some peace and rest *from* it, but all we may get is more anxiety and discomfort.

The key challenge is to discover peace and rest *in* our suffering. Suffering forces us to decide *how far* we will live by faith, without understanding it all. True faith does not require an immediate understanding of why God is allowing the suffering. Faith allows us to find peace and rest *in* suffering (in those times we cannot be rid of it) and not merely *in spite of* it. Even as God was deliberately present in the Cross of Christ and in the affliction of St. Paul (2 Corinthians 12:7–9), so God is present with us even in those sufferings that carry Hell's signature. His presence imparts grace and power, mysteriously perhaps, and faithfully continues his work of redeeming—until that great Day. Truly our hearts will find no peace until they rest in God and his promises, especially in the midst of our suffering.

► *Memory Prayer*

Dear Lord, give new meaning to my suffering. Grant me that faith which will help me to rest in you in the midst of it. As I meet you in this newly found rest, I see you with me in my suffering, for you will never leave or forsake me. Grant that I may know your love, here, and discover your redemptive purposes. Give new meaning to my suffering.

> *Come to Me . . . and I will give you rest.*
> —Matthew 11:28

> *Therefore . . . a promise remains of entering His rest.*
> —Hebrews 4:1

▶ *Hymn*

IN HEAVENLY LOVE ABIDING

In heavenly love abiding,
No change my heart shall fear;
And safe is such confiding,
For nothing changes here.
The storm may roar without me,
My heart may low be laid,
But God is round about me,
And can I be dismayed?

Wherever He may guide me,
No want shall turn me back;
My shepherd is beside me,
And nothing can I lack.
His wisdom ever waketh;
His sight is never dim.
He knows the way He taketh,
And I will walk with Him.

Green pastures are before me,
Which yet I have not seen;
Bright skies will soon be o'er me,
Where darkest clouds have been.
My hope I cannot measure;
My path to life is free;
My Savior has my treasure,
And He will walk with me.
                    —Anna L. Waring

DAY 7: *Prayer of the Reconciler and Peacemaker*

Lord, make me an instrument of your peace.
Where there is hatred, let me sow love;
Where there is injury, let there be pardon;

Where there is discord, union;
Where there is doubt, faith;
Where there is despair, hope;
Where there is darkness, light;
Where there is sadness, joy;
For your mercy and your truth's sake.

         —St. Francis of Assisi

▶ *Reflection*

This prayer epitomizes the call of God to be a peacemaker and reconciler. Think about a friend or a loved one who may be struggling with sadness or despair, or who may be in doubt or even darkness. Take time to really try to think of what that must be like. Can you be a peacemaker or reconciler in the situation? Maybe not. But any peacemaking or reconciling that occurs will have been born out of prayer first. Think about the things that would give your friend joy, hope or faith. Then take that before the Lord in prayer. If you cannot be the instrument of peace, pardon or light, ask Jesus to be that to your friend in the circumstances.

▶ *Memory Prayer*

Set our hearts on fire with love to you,
O Christ,
That in the flame we may love you,
And our neighbor as ourselves.

         —Eastern Orthodox prayer

— 4 —
Praying Together

———◆———

Jesus promised that when people gathered together in his name to pray, things would get done: "Again I say to you that if two of you agree on earth concerning anything they ask, it will be done for them by My Father in heaven. For where two or three are gathered in My name, I am there in the midst of them" (Matthew 18:19–20). The disciples took this seriously. The Church was born praying together, and even after Pentecost one of its chief characteristics throughout the book of Acts was corporate prayer.

In fact, if this seems unimportant, we will feel the Lord's rebuke: "Then he came to the disciples and found sleeping, and said to Peter, 'What? Could you not watch with me one hour? Watch and pray lest you enter into temptation. The spirit indeed is willing, but the flesh is weak'"(Matthew 26:40–41). Any group of Christians who want to develop spiritually, whether it's a church, a college fellowship, or just a regular gathering of friends, will want to pray together.

So how do you start? Many Christians will have first experienced group prayer the way I did as a teenager. I started at the Bible study and prayer meeting on Thursday evenings in the back room of our church. After someone had led us in a Bible study or expounded a passage, we would discuss who or what we would pray for and then pray around the circle of the dozen or so who'd turned up. I was always happiest when I was at the start of the circle because there were so many topics to choose from. I dreaded coming after a man we had nicknamed "Rambling Rose," because he would pray for everything on the list and leave us with only a few pathetic petitions to make!

I look back in gratitude for what those meetings taught me. I learned to lift my horizons and expectations of prayer. I began to realize that when God wants to make his presence felt in a group, he often does it when they are praying together. I remember one time when we were praying and nobody wanted to stop. The usual fifteen minutes spread to nearly an hour. Looking back, that was a turning point in the life of our church; the Spirit had decided to blow, just as he did at Pentecost.

These days many churches have decentralized their prayer meetings and made them part of a house group structure. This can make for a more relaxed and experimental approach to prayer, though it does have the disadvantage that the church as a whole doesn't have the same experience of praying together. Churches like this may need to compensate by having an occasional (monthly?) time of prayer together. Or they may want to set aside special times for church-wide prayer, such as when corporate decision-making is in the air. Some kind of prayer vigil might be appropriate on such occasions. Or an entire evening, or a Saturday, could be set aside, in which the time could be divided into half-hour or hour segments, allowing people to come and go. There could be different leaders for different periods, and these could emphasize different aspects of prayer or ways of praying. But don't let it become an endurance test!

However group prayer is structured into church life, we are then faced with the question of deciding the details.

PLANNING GROUP PRAYER

Leadership

Christian leadership is a matter of serving rather than lording it over others:

> Jesus called them to Himself and said, "You know that the rulers of the Gentiles lord it over them, and those who are great exercise authority over them. Yet it shall not be so among you; but whoever desires to be great among you, let him be your servant. And whoever desires to be first among you, let him be your slave—just as the

Son of Man did not come to be served, but to serve.

—Matthew 20:25-28

In leading group prayers, servant leadership *enables* people to pray. It does not inhibit them. It finds ways of involving people without putting them on the spot, though a little tactful coaxing might help! A good leader will want to be clear about what's going on. He will structure the prayer time, but not too tightly, and he will strike a balance between the various elements of prayer, such as worship, confession, and asking. A good leader will also make tactful suggestions so that the inexperienced learn to pray and the stiflingly voluble hold back. A leader may also want to drum up volunteers to lead successive prayer meetings. This can be particularly helpful if there are different traditions represented; that way the group gets the benefit of its variety as well as its unity. And through it all, a leader must be sensitive to the Holy Spirit.

A good leader also needs to be especially sensitive to ticklish situations when they arise. These often call for correction. For example, group prayer may be used, even with good intentions, to embarrass or humiliate someone in the group: "Please help Peter to control his temper." Peter, however, may never have asked for prayer. Sometimes group prayer inadvertently gets into gossip or a breach of confidentiality. Generally a group will grow into what its members feel they can openly share, but presuming on that level of intimacy can be destructive and a backward step. A quiet word by the leader in private is often all that is needed.

Spontaneous Prayer

An initial question is often: "How do we pray? What words do we say?" A common model is spontaneous, or *extempore*, prayer, in which words are thought of on the spot. This keeps the prayer meeting flexible. If someone asks for prayer, we can turn immediately to God with the minimum of fuss. This conversational style is suitable to smallish prayer groups, which are, after all, children talking to their heavenly Father. Yet there is the tendency to get stuck in jargon or a small repertoire of favorite phrases or words, such as using "just" or "Lord" four times in every sentence.

PRAYING SPONTANEOUSLY: SOME GUIDELINES

Addressing God. *The names we use for God are important. The Bible has many different names for God, so don't feel that he always has to be addressed as "Dear Lord" or "Heavenly Father." You could begin a prayer that appeals to God's love, for example, by saying "Loving Lord Jesus." A prayer appealing to God's sovereignty might begin with "Almighty God."*

Pray, don't preach. *Sermonizing merely turns praying into lecturing. Be wise. You are praying on behalf of the group, not preaching.*

Use present-day speech. *God understands contemporary language. Use it. It will help the group's understanding. It's not more spiritual, or more religious, to sound like we are in the court of King James!*

Stick to the point. *Rambling prayers are like badly packed suitcases; it's hard to tell what they contain! Prayers like that are difficult to say "Amen" to.*

Don't be afraid of the quiet. *Don't just pray because no one else is. Try to be sensitive when the Holy Spirit is prompting some time for quiet reflection or petition.*

Avoid recurring words or phrases. *Eliminate needless repetition from your prayer speech. Using words like "Lord," "God," "Heavenly Father," "Jesus," and such on top of one another during a prayer is unnecessary. It is easy to fall into this, and it takes a disciplined mind to stop it. Yet when we do, it has the additional benefit of forcing us to be more creative when we are praying.*

Learning to stop. *Whether praying short or long prayers, try to be sensitive when to stop. This may be best achieved by pacing yourself when praying. There's no need to feel rushed. When you stop, do it in a way that the group knows you have finished. A simple phrase like, "in Jesus' name, amen," is usually sufficient.*

Written Prayers

It may be useful to use a sequence of written prayers, whether from one of the denominational prayer books or from one of the many compilations available. There is sometimes a richness and precision of phrasing here that can elude spontaneous prayer. It can also mean that the silence between prayers is not fraught with the anxiety about what is going to happen or who is going to pray next.

A group may enjoy an entire meeting of written prayers, or combine written and spontaneous prayer. "The Lord's Prayer" is probably the most popular, but the Bible contains a wide variety that can be said. There are also the great prayers of the saints of old. (Several appear in the "Take 7 Days" section of the preceding chapter.) Choruses, worship songs, or phrases from hymns, sung or said, can also be used.

Using Silence

It may seem slightly odd to come together for prayer and then to be completely silent for a while. Yet using silence can be a major step for uniting a group during its prayer time. Silence can be used anytime during a prayer meeting. It can allow time for everyone's thoughts to form. It can help the group become aware of God's presence. A time of silence also allows people to pray silently about matters that cannot be shared openly with the group.

Your group may want to have an entire prayer meeting devoted primarily to silent prayer. The "Julian Groups" in Great Britain do this. They are named after Julian of Norwich, a medieval mystic. The host or leader of the group will often introduce the silent prayer time with a reading or music. There may be some instruction on how to use the silence, and then the group will be silent together for an agreed length of time. The Julian Groups emphasize listening to God, perhaps as one meditates on the reading or the needs of the world, as well as saying prayers in silence. For some, silence is oppressive, even searching. For others, it is a gift from God in the midst of a noisy world.

When praying together in silence there is a sense that the group is listening together to God. This, then, might be a useful strategy for a group or a church looking for corporate guidance or direction. And what to do after the silence is important. People must be given time to come out of it slowly if it has been lengthy. The Society of Friends (Quakers) speak of "talking out of" the silence, sharing words and ideas that were particularly valuable in the silence.

Praying for People in the Group

If the prayer time focuses on the needs of people in the group, it's important to share personal concerns effectively. Every group I've been in has had a different level of "permission" concerning the limits of what we could ask prayer for. It's important to make this as wide as the group's trust in each other will permit. And try not to get stuck praying only about religious concerns or personal crises.

The leader may ask for prayer requests from individuals as a way to lead up to the time for prayer to begin (be careful that the asking time doesn't exceed the prayer time). Everyone in the group should be listening attentively as the prayer requests are being shared. Each person could make a mental note of who they will pray for. Or, after each request, the leader could ask someone to pray for the person, with the group praying silently in agreement. Your group may occasionally want to lay hands on the person being prayed for.

Praying for one another can be done with a symbol, like a lighted candle which is passed from one person to the next. The group would pray for each person who holds the candle, perhaps concluding with a thought about the "light of the world." A rough agreement on timing may be needed, with someone watching the clock for everyone. Using symbols can work surprisingly well.

Another means for discovering ways to pray is to ask one or two people to talk in depth about themselves. They are not to list items for prayer. Rather, they might explain their jobs or what their week was like, or how their families are. They might talk about their goals, their stresses, their joys. As the group listens attentively, this is a good way to prime the prayer pump.

Praying for People Outside the Group

A church prayer meeting will want to pray for its minister, its Sunday school, and so on. A missionary prayer meeting may be held to pray for a country. A prayer group must not get too inward looking. There are times when outside needs are obvious—a friend faces a decision, someone is ill, an earthquake is shown on television, and so on. But our knowledge and concern can be stimulated. Many missionary societies and relief agencies produce cassettes, slides, or videos, which can lead to more informed group prayer. The group does not have to be full of international relations experts to pray for the world, but prayer and knowledge are linked. A group can pray better if it is linked somehow with a particular person or place about which it is praying.

Troubleshooting

Some people in every prayer group find it difficult to pray out loud. Here are some suggestions to help them speak out their prayers:

• Encourage an occasional prayer in which everyone in the group prays several sentences for one topic. Once around the group makes one prayer.

- Have each person pray for a single topic at some length.
- Assign one topic to each person, or have each person "adopt" a long-term prayer topic that he or she will prayer for at each meeting.
- Share stories for prayer out of the newspaper or television news and have each person pray for one.

Family Prayers

As with personal prayer, it is best to set a target for family prayer that can be met each week, rather than being hopelessly ambitious, which may leave the family feeling permanently guilty. A simple pattern is good: a brief Bible reading, prayers of worship, thanks and confession, then prayers for family and friends. It is important for every member of the family to be involved freely rather than to feel browbeaten about it, especially if any came to the table upset. We need to show children that prayer is important, but not in such a heavy way that it turns them off to prayer later on.

One simple way is to say grace before meals. A family that has breakfast on the run, lunch in five different places, and dinner at different times may find it difficult. But Sunday dinner or an evening meal may be a good time to thank God together for all his blessings. With children, or at a special celebration, try going musical, singing a simple chorus or doxology, such as "Praise God from whom all blessings flow." And holding hands around the table can add a special touch.

Prayer need not always involve the whole family. Children at different ages have different capacities, and the one who prays with Mom about his father's interview is doing as important a job as the father praying for his son's injured knee.

Those who are married may find that praying with one's partner can be wonderfully helpful but surprisingly difficult. Many Christian couples find it hard to pray together with regularity. Others have regular times daily or weekly, or they will set aside extended times to pray for special needs. If starting is difficult, start simply. Use the Lord's Prayer, each spouse saying alternate phrases while looking at each other or holding hands. Then pray a short time for obvious needs.

Prayer Partners and Triplets

Some of my most precious experiences in prayer have been with just one other person. When I was a student in college, our Christian fellowship divided up into pairs each term to meet once a week to pray half an hour for our friends and families. Why was it so good? There was a depth of sharing that was inappropriate in a larger group, and we tended to feel easier about confessing doubts and weaknesses.

A variation on this is prayer triplets, which is often used to get people praying for a mission's event. Yet it has much wider possibilities. In its simplest form it involves three people agreeing to pray together regularly, each bringing the names of three people who are not Christians. So the group is praying for nine people, perhaps with the idea of inviting them to an evangelistic event, or simply praying for their conversion to Christ. (There is a book about it: *Three Times Three Equals Twelve*, by Brian Mills.) Obviously the idea is expandable; and, as with a prayer partner, it can be encouraging because you know you are not the only person praying.

Finally, there doesn't have to be a prayer meeting arranged before prayer can be made. There is great virtue in praying whenever it seems appropriate. Recently a Christian couple who were having a hard time asked me and some others to pray for them. I telephoned another friend and told him. He and his wife immediately asked me over to their house so we could pray together. Be sensitive to such impromptu times of prayer.

TAKE SEVEN DAYS . . .

In keeping with the theme of this chapter all of the following exercises are provided for group use.

DAY 1: *Two Kinds of Prayer*

▶ *Scripture*

Also He spoke this parable to some who trusted in themselves that they were righteous, and despised others:

"Two men went up to the temple to pray, one a Pharisee and the other a tax collector. The Pharisee stood and prayed thus with himself. 'God, I thank You that I am not like other men—extortioners, unjust, adulterers, or even as this tax collector. I fast twice a week; I give tithes of all that I possess.'

"And the tax collector, standing afar off, would not so much as raise his eyes to heaven, but beat his breast, saying, 'God, be merciful to me a sinner!'

"I tell you, this man went down to his house justified rather than the other; for everyone who exalts himself will be humbled, and he who humbles himself will be exalted."

—Luke 18:9–14

▶ *Prayer Activity*

The passage is about the Pharisee and the tax collector, and the object is for members of the group to pray for one another as they see themselves in the light of both attitudes.

Begin the prayer activity by having the passage read aloud. Then have the group divide up into pairs. One person will pretend to be a very proud religious leader who, like the Pharisee, seems to be "God's man" and is well respected in the religious community. The other person will adopt the attitude of, let us say, a repentant criminal or a non-religious guy with AIDS. Like the tax collector, he doesn't seem to be "God's man" and is disliked by the community.

You will enter into each role and speak to each other as that person. Have one of you begin by speaking. If you are to portray the prideful attitude, don't project utter obnoxiousness. The Pharisee would not have been seen that way, but instead as a pillar of the community who had rather carefully crossed all the respectable and expected T's and dotted the I's too. His was the "prayer" (if it may be called that) of those who are content that their faithfulness to God has gained them his special favor.

Then it's time for the other person to describe himself. If you are to portray the humble attitude, you acknowledge your sinfulness and your need for God's mercy and forgiveness. You admit that you have been far from God.

After both persons have had ample time, they may want to switch roles. Afterward, it would be good to share the thoughts and feelings each had during the role plays.

So often, we Christians lose the humility our name advertises. This frequently occurs with groups. Can you think of ways in which judgmentalism or a "superior" attitude may be undermining your group's prayers? Close the activity with a time of prayer to ask God to help your group become more humble, especially by holding ever before you the grace by which we all stand before God, grace truly undeserved and . . . amazing.

▶ *Hymn*

AMAZING GRACE

Amazing grace! how sweet the sound,
That saved a wretch like me!
I once was lost, but now am found,
Was blind, but now I see.

'Twas grace that taught my heart to fear,
And grace my fears relieved;
How precious did that grace appear
The hour I first believed!

Through many dangers, toils, and snares,
I have already come;
'Tis grace hath brought me safe thus far,
And grace will lead me home.

When we've been there ten thousand years,
Bright shining as the sun,
We've no less days to sing God's praise
Than when we first begun.
                                        —John Newton

DAY 2: *Remembering People Far Off*

▶ *Scripture*

I thank my God upon every remembrance of you,
always in every prayer of mine making request for you
all with joy, for your fellowship in the gospel from the
first day until now, being confident of this very thing, that
He who has begun a good work in you will complete it
until the day of Jesus Christ; just as it is right for me to
think this of you all, because I have you in my heart,
inasmuch as both in my chains and in the defense and

*confirmation of the gospel, you all are partakers with
me of grace.*

*For God is my witness, how greatly I long for you all
with the affection of Jesus Christ. And this I pray, that
your love may abound still more and more in knowledge
and all discernment, that you may approve the things
that are excellent, that you may be sincere and without
offense till the day of Christ, being filled with the fruits
of righteousness which are by Jesus Christ, to the glory
and praise of God.*

—Philippians 1:3–11

▶ *Prayer Activity*

The apostle Paul has written a letter to Christians whom
he had not seen in a long time. They were special to him,
and it was a letter of thanksgiving and joy for the ways that
the Philippians had helped him. Have everyone in the group
think of people who live far away, perhaps overseas or in
another state, and let it be people who have been a good
influence on them.

Here is a way everyone in the group can send a prayer
letter to God for their far away friends or loved ones. Begin
by having the above passage read aloud. Then go around
the group and have each person pray for a far-away friend
by putting Paul's prayer in his own words, addressing it to
God. Each person may want to stop and highlight one or
two of the verses that seem especially appropriate.

You may long to see this friend, yet your love and affection
for the person can go up to God in prayer as you remember
them in the group. Your love for the person in prayer may
result in your friend's greater love and service to God. This
is what Paul wanted for his friends, and the way in which he
prayed for it is bold and rich.

▶ *Hymn*

WHILE WE PRAY AND WHILE WE PLEAD

While we pray and while we plead,
While you see your soul's deep need,
While our Father calls you home,
Will you not, my brother, come?

Why not now?
Why not now?
Why not come to Jesus now?
Why not now?
Why not now?
Why not come to Jesus now?

You have wandered far away;
Do not risk another day;
Do not turn from God your face,
But today accept His grace.

In the world you've failed to find
Aught of peace for troubled mind;
Come to Christ, on Him believe,
Peace and joy you shall receive.

Come to Christ, confession make;
Come to Christ, and pardon take;
Trust in Him from day to day,
He will keep you all the way
—Daniel W. Whittle

DAY 3: *Remembering the Suffering*

▶ *Scripture*

Grace to you and peace from God our Father and
the Lord Jesus Christ.

Blessed be the God and Father of our Lord Jesus Christ, the Father of mercies and God of all comfort, who comforts us in all our tribulation, that we may be able to comfort those who are in any trouble, with the comfort with which we ourselves are comforted by God. For as the sufferings of Christ abound in us, so our consolation also abounds through Christ.

Now if we are afflicted, it is for your consolation and salvation, which is effective for enduring the same sufferings which we also suffer. Or if we are comforted, it is for your consolation and salvation. And our hope for you is stedfast, because we know that as you are partakers of the sufferings, so also you will partake of the consolation.

And He said to me, "My grace is sufficient for you, for My strength is made perfect in weakness." Therefore most gladly I will rather boast in my infirmities, that the power of Christ may rest upon me.
                                        —2 Corinthians 1:2–7; 12:9

▶ *Prayer Activity*

Here the group will pray for people who are hurting or suffering, be it physical, emotional, or spiritual affliction. The object of this group prayer will not necessarily be for pain and suffering to be removed, but for the person to be comforted by God the Father in the midst of affliction. That is the point of the passages, and it is reinforced by God's revelation that his grace will never be insufficient.

A suggestion, then, is to have the passages read aloud, and then go around the group with each person praying for one or two people. Prayer could be made that the suffering would receive strength, encouragement, and hope. If it is a non-Christian being prayed for, prayer could be said that the person would find God in the midst of the ordeal. Prayer could also be said that the person would have opportunities to be an encouragement to others who suffer similarly.

No one likes to suffer, and this is a very practical way to pray for those who are afflicted. You may never know what their hardships are like, but you can empathize in prayer for God to bring comfort.

▶ *Hymn*

I AM PRAYING FOR YOU

I have a Saviour, He's pleading in glory,
A dear loving Saviour, though earth-friends be few;
And now He is watching in tenderness over me,
And, oh, that my Saviour were your Saviour, too.

For you I am praying,
For you I am praying,
For you I am praying,
I'm praying for you.

I have a Father; to me He has given
A hope for eternity blessed and true;
And soon will He call me to meet Him in heaven,
But, oh, that He'd let me bring you with me, too!

I have a robe: 'tis resplendent in whiteness,
Awaiting in glory my wondering view;
Oh, when I receive it all shining in brightness,
Dear friend, could I see you receiving one, too!

When Christ has found you, tell others the story,
That my loving Saviour is your Saviour, too;
Then pray that your Saviour may bring them to glory,
And prayer will be answered; 'twas answered for you!
—O'Malley Cluff

DAY **4**: *Remembering Christ*

▶ *Scripture*

Therefore if there is any consolation in Christ, if any comfort of love, if any fellowship of the Spirit, if any affection and mercy, fulfill my joy by being like-minded, having the same love, being of one accord, of one mind.

Let *nothing* be done *through selfish ambition or conceit, but in lowliness of mind let each esteem others better than himself. Let each of you look out not only for his own interests, but also for the interests of others.*

Let this mind be in you which was also in Christ Jesus, who, being in the form of God, did not consider it robbery to be equal with God, but made Himself of no reputation, taking the form of a bondservant, and *coming in the likeness of men. And being found in appearance as a man, He humbled Himself and became obedient to* the point of *death, even the death of the cross.*

—Philippians 2:1–8

▶ *Prayer Activity*

First, please read through this entire exercise before you make a decision about it.

The passage teaches that Jesus Christ "made Himself of no reputation." In other words, he emptied himself of many of the privileges that he had as God, in obedience to the Father and in order to serve others. And we are exhorted to be like-minded.

This prayer activity begins by reading the above passage aloud. Everyone in the group is then to take as much time as necessary, within reason, to consider one way to give up a privilege for a certain amount of time in order to use that time in Christian service. Discuss it among yourselves.

Someone may have a favorite night to watch television. Another person may have some hours set aside for playing racketball or golf. Someone else may have several afternoons or evenings booked up with social activities. Another person may spend leisure time reading novels. Have everyone in the group think of ways they could give up such privileges for a week or a month and replace them with activities that take them to minister to others.

Someone may decide that there is some work around the church that could be done. Another person may want to do some hospital visitation or some other kind of volunteer work. Several persons in the group may see that they can band together to go out, perhaps to a shopping mall or airport, to share their faith. Have the group prayerfully brainstorm a list of possibilities. Take plenty of time. Ask the Holy Spirit to focus your minds on the things he would have you to do.

For believers, the voluntary giving up of privileges—done in humility without complaining and in the Name of Jesus—leads to joy when done precisely to serve others, as Philippians 2:1–4 suggests. Jesus himself is our great example of this:

> [*Look*] *unto Jesus, the author and finisher of our faith, who for the joy that was set before Him, endured the cross, despising the shame, and has sat down at the right hand of the throne of God.*
>
> —Hebrews 12:2

Because it is a serious commitment, the group may want to allow a week to think it over and then finalize decisions and plans at the next meeting. Who knows, you may end up giving up a privilege for a more extended length of time once you get into remembering Christ like this.

▶ *Hymn*

MY JESUS, AS THOU WILT

My Jesus, as Thou wilt!
O may Thy will be mine!
Into Thy hand of love
I would my all resign:
Through sorrow or through joy,
Conduct me as Thine own;
And help me still to say,
"My Lord, Thy will be done."

My Jesus, as Thou wilt!
Though seen through many a tear,
Let not my star of hope
Grow dim or disappear:
Since Thou on earth has wept
And sorrowed oft alone,
If I must weep with Thee,
My Lord, Thy will be done.

My Jesus, as Thou wilt!
All shall be well for me;
Each changing future scene
I gladly trust with Thee:
Straight to my home above
I travel calmly on,
And sing, in life or death,
"My Lord, Thy will be done."

—Benjamin Schmolck; Tr. by Jane L. Borthwick

DAY **5**: *Remembering Ourselves*

▶ *Scripture*

> *Therefore we also pray always for you that our God would count you worthy of this calling, and fulfill all the good pleasure of His goodness and the work of faith with power, that the name of our Lord Jesus Christ may be glorified in you, and you in Him, according to the grace of our God and the Lord Jesus Christ.*
> —2 Thessalonians 1:11–12

▶ *Prayer Activity*

This passage is about becoming the kind of children God wants us to be, which is really who we want to be! After the passage has been read and considered by the group, have everyone cite ways in which they are repeatedly disappointed in their performance. It may have to do with one's temper, or a failure to keep promises, or stretching the truth, or any of a number of things. Recurring failures generally tend to make us feel worse than we should about ourselves. It is discouraging to see bad habits or besetting sins return after we have spent a lot of time praying to get rid of them. There's no easy answer to this.

One thing that can be said is that because Christ died a whole man, he redeems the whole person, which includes mind, will, and emotions. Sometimes when we pray for release, we concentrate too much energy on the habit or sin itself. But perhaps the root of change lies in the mind, will, or emotions. One of these areas may be responsible for motivating the habit, sin, or recurring failure. Discuss this in the group, and try to identify a root area.

Afterward, some persons may ask for prayer in a specific area. You can pray with confidence because Christ can redeem the mind, will, and emotions. It is not that you may be changed overnight, but in identifying one of these areas and praying about it, you may find things really begin to change, and you will work with that. There can be freedom for the will (new righteous commitments), a change of mind (new understanding), and appropriate emotions (changed affections with changed allegiances). To keep from discouragment, have the individuals make a commitment to a reasonable follow-through, for example, asking a trusted friend to observe and describe the behavior if it reappears, to support and hold you accountable.

The Living Bible says, "We keep on praying . . . that our God will make you the kind of children he wants to have. . . . Then everyone will be praising the name of the Lord Jesus Christ because of the results they see in you." Certainly that is worth praying about!

▶ *Hymn*

MORE LIKE JESUS WOULD I BE

More like Jesus would I be,
Let my Saviour dwell in me;
Fill my soul with peace and love,
Make me gentle as a dove;
More like Jesus, while I go,
Pilgrim in this world below;
Poor in spirit would I be;
Let my Saviour dwell in me.

If He hears the raven's cry,
If His ever-watchful eye
Marks the sparrows when they fall,
Surely He will hear my call:

He will teach me how to live,
All my sinful thoughts forgive;
Pure in heart I still would be;
Let my Saviour dwell in me.

More like Jesus when I pray,
More like Jesus day by day;
May I rest me by His side,
Where the tranquil waters glide:
Born of Him, through grace renewed,
By His love my will subdued,
Rich in faith I still would be;
Let my Saviour dwell in me.

—Fanny J. Crosby

DAY 6: *Remembering Our Gifts*

▶ *Scripture*

I thank my God always concerning you for the grace of God which was given to you by Christ Jesus, that you were enriched in every thing by Him in all utterance and all knowledge, even as the testimony of Christ was confirmed in you, so that you come short in no gift, eagerly waiting for the revelation of our Lord Jesus Christ.

—1 Corinthians 1:4–7

▶ *Prayer Activity*

After this passage is read aloud, highlight verse seven. Paul has told the Corinthian Christians that they were enriched in spiritual gifts. Sometimes, however, we do not feel like we have much in the way of spiritual gifts. Maybe we do not exercise and so develop them as we ought. Maybe we are not in an environment where they can be sustained, or we do not know how to sustain them. Or maybe we have ignored them.

This prayer activity may call for some soul-searching and confession around the group. The Bible reveals many kinds of gifts. There are gifts of healing, teaching, serving, caring, showing mercy, praying, administrating/facilitating, pastoring, and many others. Have people go around the group and tell what their gifts are. If you are not sure what your's are, ask the group to offer some suggestions as to what they might be. Sometimes "outsiders" see our particular giftings very clearly.

Once all have identified their gifts, take a time for sharing about how you think you are expressing your gifts and how accountable you are being with them before God. Maybe the richness of your gifts has dimmed. If so, for what reason? Maybe you will identify the stronger gifts. Does that mean you have completely ignored serving with the weaker ones? Ask around the group if anyone knows a way you can plug into a certain situation with your gift(s) to stir them up, as the apostle Paul tells Timothy:

> *Do not neglect the gift that is in you.*
> —1 Timothy 4:14

> *Therefore I remind you to stir up the gift of God which is in you.*
> —2 Timothy 1:6

Sometimes we have a gift but we're not in a context in which to express or activate it. It is in plugging ourselves into that context which will not only help us in serving others but also give us a better understanding of the gift. You could close this group prayer activity by praying for those who desire to use their gifts on a more regular basis.

DAY 7: *Receiving Our Resources*

▶ *Scripture*

For this reason I bow my knees to the Father of our Lord Jesus Christ, from whom the whole family in heaven and earth is named, that He would grant you, according to the riches of His glory, to be strengthened with might through His Spirit in the inner man, that Christ may dwell in your hearts through faith; that you, being rooted and grounded in love, may be able to comprehend with all the saints what is the width and length and depth and height to know the love of Christ which passes knowledge; that you may be filled with all the fullness of God.

—Ephesians 3:14–19

▶ *Prayer Activity*

Devote a group prayer time to prayer guided by this prayer of the apostle Paul. Take time to establish the context for the prayer by having the group read Ephesians 1—3:13 out loud. Mention these simple summary statements before the appropriate sections to help members follow the flow of thought in this majestic epistle.

Ephesians 1:1–14: Because believers are positioned *in Christ,* they have already received "every spiritual blessing" (including being chosen, adopted, redeemed, and included in Christ's inheritance).

Ephesians 1:15–23: The apostle prays that believers will know what all they have been given in Christ.

Ephesians 2:1–22: Believers were spiritually dead, but

have been made alive by God's mercy with Christ, and all—Jew and Gentile—have been joined together in one holy temple in the Lord.

Ephesians 3:1–13: Paul has been gifted by God to be a special minister to Gentiles, to help them become fellow heirs along with Jewish believers.

Then have the group read the prayer of 3:14–19, looking for all the things Paul prays for (at least 5; more may be inferred).

List and discuss what you have found. Then do one or more of the following:

1. Have the group identify the one request for which it sees the greatest need, and have the group pray about it.

2. Have members each identify one request as most needed personally, then mention it to the group. The group can then pray for each person's request. Members should be specific to help the group pray effectively. They could use a starter phrase to help them express their needs. For example, "I need to be 'strengthened with might through His Spirit in the inner man' for . . . ." (Members here insert the challenge, difficulty, or anxiety-inducing situation they are facing, for which they desire God to strengthen them.

   Other starter phrases: "I/we want to . . . ."

   • "have deeper assurance that Christ dwells in my/our hearts when . . . occurs."

   • "experience the motivation and security provided by being 'rooted and grounded in love' in (name areas of life or relationships or situations in which one is motivated by fear or anger, etc.)."

   • "experience Christ's love when I'm feeling or experiencing . . . ."

3. Have the group pray for the granting of each request

you listed, with an emphasis on these as requests to be granted to the *group,* not just to individuals. The "you's" of the prayer are all plural. Paul is writing to *churches,* not to individuals as individuals.

— 5 —

Devotion in the Dark

---◆---

Christians believe that God is good, and that he is love. Yet just as belief in God has become highly questionable for many Jews because of the Holocaust, so, too, killer earthquakes and other calamities cause some Christians to question whether God is good and loving.

Someone drops into deep depression or goes through an unwanted divorce. Someone is dealing with secret wounds or the death of a vision. Even more seriously, a young couple's child is killed in an accident, or a spouse is struck down with cancer. A family faces a suicide, or a child is born with a debilitating disease.

Events like these can shake one's faith and raise questions we never thought we would ask: How could God do this to me? How could he let it happen? I don't think God really cares. Is God getting back at me for something? Why should I keep believing now? Why should I serve him any more?

And with such questions come a whirlwind of emotions that we may not be prepared to wrestle with: anger, despair, hopelessness, depression, and even violence or rage. Tragic events also bring degrees of physical, mental, emotional or spiritual collapse and restructuring. It is in such dark episodes that faith can be born, strengthened, weakened, or abandoned. We grow or become stunted. We mature or wither. We are met and carried by God's compassion, or we shrivel up with bitterness.

Facing Earthquake Questions

Some people would have us ignore killer earthquake questions, as if those who dare to grapple with them are weak in the faith. Yet if we should find ourselves with questions like these, to dismiss them is merely to evade them. There are several ways we can tackle these questions and the sufferings that produced them.

One way is to admit what the questions assume about God. For example, "God will always find a way to get back at me. You know, an eye for an eye and all that." Yet do we really believe that our Father is dedicated to vindictiveness? We can also look at what the questions assume and expect about ourselves. For example, "I don't deserve this. I expected better than this from God." Here, blame is laid squarely on God; or else one supposes that "bad" people might deserve this, but not me. Either assumption, however, could easily be presumption, which adds to the pain of any event:

*Keep back Your servant also from
    presumptuous sins;
Let them not have dominion over me.
Then I shall be blameless.*
                        —Psalm 19:13

The legitimacy of these assumptions can be seen when they are faced honestly, humbly, and redemptively. We face such assumptions when we detect that they may be couched in the indignation, wounded pride, or self-pity that we feel. If we can let these feelings lead us to confess our ignorance and to pray for forgiveness, welling bitterness will be replaced by God's compassion. In turn, we then may be able to explore the conviction that God is good, and that he is love, within the process of our pain and sufferings. Amazingly, it is through this interplay of our suffering and our certainty of God's goodness and love that faith is *strengthened*—even when we feel it may be weakening.

Another way to authentic devotion in the dark is to seek out those who have experienced the darkness and come through it the better for it. One Christian man, for example, has been able to use the lessons he learned from God as a result of his divorce to help save a friend's marriage. This is a redemptive use of the man's sufferings. Other Christians are helped by reading the Psalms or the book of Job. Despite the fact that God seemed to be his sworn enemy and that his "friends" tried to dump a load of sins on him,

Job wanted to come to grips with the real God during his intense sufferings. He was dead honest with God. And his persistence paid off. This is faith in action.

The Power Struggle Within

If we took this discussion a step or two deeper, we would see that God frequently works within our pain and suffering, whether it is our own fault or not, to help us see whom or what we really worship. Some fortunate souls may find that they are worshipping God (you can pray for the rest of us!). Others, however, when they catch their breath, may unmask an idol or two because pain and suffering really exposes things and lays them bare. Adversity gives an opportunity for the Holy Spirit to "bring to light the hidden things of darkness and reveal the counsels of the hearts" (1 Corinthians 4:6), with us fully attentive.

Often our conceptions of God need correction, and idols of the heart need to be forsaken. And yet we may have held on to these things so tightly and closely for so long that only during a crisis do they surface and become recognized for what they are. If so, God is unmasking the idols so that we may get free of their power over certain areas of our lives.

Deep affliction, therefore, often faces us with a power struggle over who will be Lord in these areas. The more our suffering engages us with

God, the more profound the confrontation with any idols within us. The ultimate question of suffering, then, is often, Whom do we really want to be Lord—God? or ourselves or some other idol? The struggle is often fierce. Yet because it centers on the vital issues of power and control, it is a key to much spiritual development and coming closer to God.

Few Christians are able to navigate through such depths of exposure to the truth on their own. Most people ought to seek wisely for help and guidance from their ministers or trusted counselors, because things can easily get too confused. When you think you may be going out of your mind, or when you think that nobody has ever experienced this before, or when you think that nobody could understand, it is time to talk to someone who can help. When the truth surfaces in the darkness, we may be forced to admit that we have a fundamental misapprehension of who God is or a self-protecting ignorance of that idol hidden within. The crisis can produce fruit, however, and a potential break*down* can become a break*through*. Yet this rarely occurs apart from trusted help and guidance.

Identifying Some Idols

Power and control are prized in our cultures. Yet they are the very features of our self-determination which God requires us to surrender that we may be able to abandon ourselves more fully to *his* power and lordship. When God uses suffering as part of this process, it is a painful experience. And, yet, it throws into sharp focus the question of what is really true, and, hence, in the end, of who is Lord.

One area in which God seems to be exposing idols today is that of *health* or *beauty*. Both are too highly esteemed today, even by many Christians. A sudden illness or a physical handicap can throw such a value system into confusion. *Wealth* or *prosperity* is another idolatry. Bankruptcy or loss of a job can be an intense time of soul-searching that can, under the light of the Holy Spirit, disclose ungodly motivation.

Divorce is another, often excruciating, time of soul-searching. We can become bitter as a result of it, and so perhaps go through it again, and even again. Or we can let the anguish speak like God's megaphone, helping us identify our responsibility. And this is usually the result of something having been wrong within us long *before* the marriage took place.

After his divorce, Frank (not his real name) discovered that long before he got married he had never submitted his relationships with Christian women to the Lord. In his hands, under his control, Frank got into a bad marriage. And it cost him. He did not want the Lord to disciple him in that area of his life because it would touch him too deeply, too person-

ally. Today, however, Frank would tell you about
the foolishness of such idolatry and the suffering it caused several dear friends and loved
ones.

We could think also of an unplanned or even
an unwanted pregnancy. This could be viewed
as a disastrous intrusion on a woman's privacy,
well-being, or "rights" over her own body. It
could be seen as an "accident" easily remedied
by abortion. Or it may be received as an invitation to hand over control to God for the rest of
two lives that will now be entirely different because the pregnancy will be carried to term.

Whatever we may be suffering, however dark
it may be for a season, we have to learn that we
cannot control God and that he is always driving
for more depth of commitment, freely given, to
him. It is the greatest of illusions to see ourselves
one day sitting back somehow fully in control.
Crisis will usually shatter the illusion that we
can be self-sufficient, self-controlled. And how
we respond to crisis, pain, and suffering is the
key. In fact, our highest activity during such periods will be *how* we respond to God.

If there is nothing else to be learned, there is
this high honor: a deeper understanding of the
Incarnation. It is only when we are assaulted,
assailed, ignored, wounded, misunderstood, or
hurt by others that we know what it is like to be
unwanted, unneeded, despised, valueless, un-
appreciated, or undesired. It is then that the In-

carnation becomes more real, more accessible, humanly speaking. When events seem to be destroying the last remnants of what gave meaning and order to our lives, *that* may be the moment in which Christ bursts through all our defenses to make himself known. This is salvation. And, actually, it is what we hoped and longed for all along. We just never knew it would be like this. God loves us to the last prop.

Landmarks in the Darkness

When things are very dark sometimes all we can do is stop and wait it out. It's so dark or foggy that the map no longer makes sense. But while we are waiting it out, it can be very helpful to recall where we have been, to touch base with our Christian milestones, and so encourage our faith.

Some Christians find it beneficial to recall their conversion experience, or perhaps their recommitment to Christ, or their baptismal promises. Others find it good to meditate on a favorite verse from the Bible. Music can be especially instrumental in bringing comfort during times of depression. A favorite song or hymn has been known to pull people through.

Others may find it valuable to recall Christ's sufferings and the glory that followed. Others find it a blessing simply to take it by faith that God is *always* with them: "For He Himself has said, 'I will never leave you nor forsake you'" (Hebrews 13:5). And there may be some circumstances in which you feel under demonic oppression or attack. Even if you are not sure, call together your minister and some trusted friends for a time of prayer concerning this.

During spiritual darkness or physical and emotional sufferings, you will experience many things being shaken, "that the things which cannot be shaken may remain" (Hebrews 12:27). When you touch base with these Christian milestones you will find that they are among those things which cannot be shaken.

Below are Scriptures that may be helpful as landmarks. But first, a quick word to say that the last thing the severely afflicted needs or wants is platitudes. Several years ago a family was in shock due to the suicide of one of the sons. An aunt tried comforting one member of the family by hugging him and saying, "Praise the Lord. It's okay. Praise the Lord. Praise the Lord." She said this repeatedly. At such a time of grief, though the aunt meant well, "Praise the Lord" became an offensive and cheap blasphemy. If you find the verses below to be like that, simply pass them by for now. Yet many Christians have been helped by their relevance, and it is with this in mind that they are offered.

> *Surely the Lord is in this place, and I did not know it.*
>
> —Genesis 28:16

If I say, "Surely the darkness shall fall on me,"
Even the night shall be light about me;
Indeed, the darkness shall not hide from You,
But the night shines as the day;

The darkness and the light are both alike to You.
—Psalm 139:11–12

Being confident of this very thing, that He who has begun a good work in you will complete it until the day of Jesus Christ.
—Philippians 1:6

Your life is hidden with Christ in God.
—Colossians 3:3

Jesus came and stood in the midst, and said to them, "Peace be with you."
—John 20:19

For I am persuaded that neither death nor life, nor angels nor principalities nor powers, nor things present nor things to come, nor height nor depth, nor any other created thing, shall be able to separate us from the love of God which is in Christ Jesus our Lord.
—Romans 8:38–39

These things I have spoken to you, that in Me you may have peace. In the world you will have tribulation; but be of good cheer, I have overcome the world.
—John 16:33

Short prayers can be valuable to offer when words fail us. Again, if these seem like platitudes, simply ignore them for now. Yet, even though at first sight they may seem like whistling in the dark, later they may hold keys to sanity and triumph.

Lord, save us! We are perishing!
—Matthew 8:25

Lord, I believe; help my unbelief!
—Mark 9:24

Come, Lord Jesus!
—Revelation 22:20

Out of the depths I have cried to You, O LORD;
Lord, hear my voice!
Let your ears be attentive
To the voice of my supplications.
I wait for the LORD, my soul waits,
And in His word I do hope.
For with the LORD there is mercy,
And with Him is abundant redemption.
—Psalm 130:1–2, 5, 7

- Lord Jesus Christ, Son of God, have mercy on me.
- Be present, O merciful Jesus, and be made known to me in . . . .
- Lord, it is dark. Be my light.
- I do not understand,
      but I desire truth;
  I do not see,
      but I desire sight;
  I do not know,
      but I desire to be known.
- Lord, come close.
  Though I fear your coming close,
  Though I fear your being here,
  Come near.

In *The Problem of Pain,* C. S. Lewis wrote that when Man fell into sin he became ill-adapted to the universe. His point was that the Fall set in motion a virtually unlimited potential for catastrophes, big or small. These were not planned by God, but they have everything to do with his help to make things right. The reality of pain and suffering, therefore, is now a fact of life. But God himself suffered in the Incarnation and crucifixion so that he might meet us with comfort, even though our earthquake questions remain unanswered for the time being—maybe for the rest of our lives.

TAKE SEVEN DAYS...

DAY 1: *Meditation on the Absence of God's Presence*

▶ *Scripture*

My God, My God, why have You forsaken Me?
Why are You so far from helping Me,
And from the words of My groaning?
O My God, I cry in the daytime, but You do not hear;
And in the night season, and am not silent.
But You are holy,
Enthroned in the praises of Israel.
Our fathers trusted in You;
They trusted, and You delivered them.
They cried to You, and were delivered;
They trusted in You, and were not ashamed.
But I am a worm, and no man;

A reproach of men, and despised by the people.
All those who see Me ridicule Me;
They shoot out the lip, they shake the head, saying,
"He trusted in the LORD, let Him rescue Him;
Let Him deliver Him, since He delights in Him!"
But You are He who took Me out of the womb;
You made Me trust while on My mother's breasts.
I was cast upon You from birth.
From My mother's womb
You have been My God.
Be not far from Me,
For trouble is near;
For there is none to help.
Many bulls have surrounded Me;
Strong bulls of Bashan have encircled Me.
They gape at Me with their mouths,
Like a raging and roaring lion.
I am poured out like water,
And all My bones are out of joint;
My heart is like wax;
It has melted within Me.
My strength is dried up like a potsherd,
And My tongue clings to My jaws;
You have brought Me to the dust of death.
For dogs have surrounded Me;
The congregation of the wicked has enclosed Me.
They pierced My hands and My feet;
I can count all My bones.
The look and stare at Me.
They divide My garments among them,
And for My clothing they cast lots.
But You, O LORD, do not be far from Me;
O My Strength, hasten to help Me!
Deliver Me from the sword,

My precious life from the power of the dog.
Save Me from the lion's mouth
And from the horns of the wild oxen!
You have answered Me.
I will declare Your name to My brethren;
In the midst of the assembly I will praise You.
You who fear the LORD, praise Him!
All you descendants of Jacob, glorify Him,
And fear Him, all you offspring of Israel!
For He has not despised nor abhorred the affliction of
   the afflicted;
Nor has He hidden His face from Him;
But when He cried to Him, He heard.
My praise shall be of You in the great assembly;
I will pay My vows before those who fear Him.
The poor shall eat and be satisfied;
Those who seek Him will praise the LORD.
Let your heart live forever!
All the ends of the world
Shall remember and turn to the LORD,
And all the families of the nations
Shall worship before You.
For the kingdom is the LORD's,
And He rules over the nations.
All the prosperous of the earth
Shall eat and worship;
All those who go down to the dust
Shall bow before Him,
Even he who cannot keep himself alive.
A posterity shall serve Him.
It will be recounted of the Lord to the next generation,
They will come and declare His righteousness to a
   people who will be born,
That He has done this.

—Psalm 22

▶ *Insight*

Psalm 22 is the supreme example of what it is like to lose the presence of God. Its opening words were quoted by our Lord on the Cross. God had forsaken him, and from that point the sufferer sinks into ever increasing depths of despair. His bodily condition, his emotional experience; none of it speaks of a knowledge of the presence of God. The intense anguish builds and lasts; until, suddenly, as is seen in the last phrase of verse twenty-one, there is a cry of immeasurable relief. God has broken his silence, and the remainder of the Psalm is that of praise and thanksgiving.

▶ *Meditation*

Divide the Psalm into two parts, the second half beginning with the phrase "You have answered me" in verse twenty-one. Take the meditation in these two parts. The first is about an eclipse of hope. Why Christians at times have to endure this may not be answerable immediately. But we can be sure of one thing: it will be only that—an eclipse, however long it lasts. The presence of God will return, and with it hope. This is the second part of the meditation.

In the first part, take comfort in that Christ made continual supplication but went unanswered. See how he is cast back on his former beliefs and is ridiculed. Notice how his relationships are misunderstood. But in all this, consider how he trusts anyway. In the second half of the meditation, even if this is far from you at present, take heart that God broke through to the sufferer. And when God did, it was so real that great assurance and testimony breaks out of the psalmist's heart. Notice that such salvation stimulates him to give praise both among the brethren and to the world.

On a piece of paper, or in your spiritual diary, write about a period in which you experienced an eclipse of hope. Include ideas about how you felt about unanswered prayer, what kind of anguish you faced, how long it lasted, why it might have happened. You could also include what helped you through. Perhaps it was an unexpected provision of love or practical means. Maybe it was leaning on favorite verses. But don't forget to write about what it felt like when the sun returned! You may want to try your hand at writing a few verses of a praise poem about it.

Why? To non-Christians, such depth of suffering and a willingness to trust anyway must seem like the worst sort of delusion. Yet this is a work of God's grace, and it will certainly one day redound to God's glory. Jesus Christ "by the grace of God [tasted] death for everyone" (Heb. 2:9). If God had enough grace for that, he will have enough for the sufferings we face, and with it the return of hope.

▶ *Hymn*

IT IS WELL WITH MY SOUL

When peace like a river attendeth my way,
When sorrows like sea-billows roll;
Whatever my lot, Thou hast taught me to say,
"It is well, it is well with my soul."

It is well with my soul,
It is well, it is well with my soul.

Though Satan should buffet, though trials should come,
Let this blest assurance control,
That Christ has regarded my helpless estate,
And hath shed His own blood for my soul.

My sin—O, the bliss of this glorious thought,
My sin—not in part but the whole,

Is nailed to the cross and I bear it no more,
Praise the Lord, praise the Lord, O my soul!

And, Lord, haste the day when
the faith shall be sight,
The clouds be rolled back as a scroll,
The trump shall resound and the Lord shall descend,
"Even so"—it is well with my soul.
                                    —Horatio G. Spafford

DAY 2: *Meditation on Deep Grief over Personal Sin*

▶ *Scripture*

Have mercy upon me, O God,
According to Your lovingkindness;
According to the multitude of Your tender
mercies,
Blot out my transgressions.
Wash me thoroughly from my iniquity,
And cleanse me from my sin.
For I acknowledge my transgressions,
And my sin is always before me.
Against You, You only, have I sinned,
And done this evil in Your sight—
That You may be found just when You speak,
And blameless when You judge.
Behold, I was brought forth in iniquity,
And in sin my mother conceived me.
Behold, You desire truth in the inward parts,
And in the hidden part You will make me to
know wisdom.
Purge me with hyssop, and I shall be clean;

Wash me, and I shall be whiter than snow.
Make me hear joy and gladness,
That the bones You have broken may rejoice.
Hide Your face from my sins,
And blot out all my iniquities.
Create in me a clean heart, O God,
And renew a steadfast spirit within me.
Do not cast me away from Your presence,
And do not take Your Holy Spirit from me.
Restore to me the joy of Your salvation,
And uphold me by Your generous Spirit.
Then I will teach transgressors Your ways,
And sinners shall be converted to You.
Deliver me from the guilt of bloodshed,
O God,
The God of my salvation,
And my tongue shall sing aloud of Your
*   righteousness.*
O Lord, open my lips,
And my mouth shall show forth Your praise.
For You do not desire sacrifice, or else I
*   would give it;*
You do not delight in burnt offering.
The sacrifices of God are a broken spirit,
A broken and a contrite heart—
These, O God, You will not despise.
Do good in Your good pleasure to Zion;
Build the walls of Jerusalem.
Then You shall be pleased with the sacrifices
*   of righteousness,*
With burnt offering and whole burnt offering;
Then they shall offer bulls on Your altar.
*   —Psalm 51*

▶ *Insight*

Psalm 51 surrounds the anguish King David felt over his sins with Bathsheba and against Uriah. Here is a heart broken by guilt and overwhelmed by shame. Here is a person who is willing to repent and come to complete cleansing no matter what the cost. And here is a God who answers.

▶ *Meditation*

No Christian likes to be dealt with by God over his sins. And, yet, this is a vital part of spiritual growth. As you read through the Psalm prayerfully, notice the personal accountability words: "my transgressions," "my iniquity," "my sin." This is God's conviction, and David cannot rest until full confession has been made.

Take as much time as you need to make your full confession. If you are alone in prayer, use your imagination to help you see that you are giving over that sin to God. See Jesus on the Cross with the sin, where he forgave it. Then notice that sin is ultimately against God, verse four. This, too, needs confession.

Yet within this is the appeal to God's mercy and lovingkindness, which motivates the psalmist to pray for complete cleansing and renewal. Spend time with these verses, appealing to God in your own words and way. Plead with God for a restoration of joy and relationship. Cast yourself upon God who alone can save you from your sins and make you holy. *Own* your sins, but then through forgiveness let them go to God. Take some time in closing to rest in God's forgiveness and praise him for Calvary.

Why? That the repentant may experience the joy of forgiveness. Immediately after David made his confession to Nathan, he was declared forgiven. But the wonder of such amazing grace had yet to well up in joy in David's heart. The deep dealings of God over our sins are necessary that we may walk more continually in that joy.

▶ *Hymn*

ROCK OF AGES

Rock of ages, cleft for me,
Let me hide myself in thee;
Let the water and the blood
From thy side, a healing flood,
Be of sin the double cure,
Cleanse me from its guilt and power.

Should my tears forever flow,
Should my zeal no languor know,
All for sin could not atone:
Thou must save, and thou alone;
In my hand no price I bring,
Simply to thy cross I cling.

While I draw this fleeting breath,
When mine eyelids close in death,
When I rise to worlds unknown
And behold thee on thy throne,
Rock of ages, cleft for me,
Let me hide myself in thee.
—Augustus Montague Toplady

DAY 3: *Meditation on the Grievous Misunderstanding of Friends*

▶ *Scripture*

Then Job answered and said:
"No doubt you are the people,
And wisdom will die with you!

But I have understanding as well as you;
I am not inferior to you.
Indeed, who does not know such things as these?
"I am one mocked by his friends,
Who called on God, and He answered him,
The just and blameless who is ridiculed.
A lamp is despised in the thought of one who is at
    ease;
It is made ready for those whose feet slip.
The tents of robbers prosper,
And those who provoke God are secure—
In what God provides by His hand.

"Behold, my eye has seen all this,
My ear has heard and understood it.
What you know, I also know;
I am not inferior to you.
But I would speak to the Almighty,
And I desire to reason with God.
But you forgers of lies,
You are all worthless physicians.
Oh, that you would be silent,
And it would be your wisdom!
Now hear my reasoning,
And heed the pleadings of my lips.
Will you speak wickedly for God,
And talk deceitfully for Him?
Will you show partiality for Him?
Will you contend for God?
Will it be well when He searches you out?
Or can you mock Him as one mocks a man?
He will surely rebuke you
If you secretly show partiality.
Will not His excellence make you afraid,

And the dread of Him fall upon you?
Your platitudes are proverbs of ashes,
Your defenses are defenses of clay.
                    —Job 12:1–6; 13:1–12

▶ Insight

The book of Job is largely about four friends who seek to comfort Job in his intense sufferings, yet after several days they only add to his affliction when attempting to answer the question of why he is suffering. All of their answers would be right in various situations, but not in Job's, for neither they nor he had any knowledge of what had happened behind-the-scenes, as recorded in Chapters 1 and 2. Thus a key verse in the book is God's opening statement out of the whirlwind: "Who is this who darkens counsel by words without knowledge?" (38:2).

One can feel God's hot challenge to such presumption as Job tries to give an answer for what has occurred without a clue as to what set the events in motion. Even among close friends misunderstandings like this can occur over events like divorce, separation, suicide, and a fatal accident. They may not know, and you may not yet know, what combination of causes produced the suffering. Yet God will know.

▶ Meditation

This meditation is long, but well worth it. Take the time to get alone and read through the entire book of Job. It will take about one hour. Pay attention to the misunderstandings of Job's friends. They accuse him of everything from blatant sin to presumption to hypocrisy to pride.

You may suffer from grievous misunderstandings. What have your friends misunderstood? Forgive them for this.

Close the book of Job and make your appeal to God alone. Make it seriously and bodly. God is not going to be shocked by your response. You are hurting. Yet he alone has a knowledge of the situation. And he is waiting to hear from you. When he does, you will hear from him.

Why? Perhaps an over-emphasis on theology, psychology, or other "ologies" has made us chiefly dependent on rational thinking for all of our answers. Friends (we must be wise not to turn ourselves into ones like these) may not be able to live peacefully without a definitive answer, however ill-advised, to our situations and circumstances. Yet the book of Job is a striking illustration of the inadequacy of human reason to pin a thing down. God, however, will be able to pin it down. He knows what occurred in the first two chapters. Turn to him to find out.

▶ *Hymn*

COME, YE DISCONSOLATE

Come, ye disconsolate, wherever ye languish,
Come to the mercy-seat, fervently kneel:
Here bring your wounded hearts, here tell your
anguish;
Earth has no sorrow that heaven cannot heal.

Joy of the desolate, light of the straying,
Hope of the penitent, fadeless and pure!
Here speaks the Comforter, tenderly saying,
"Earth has no sorrow that heaven cannot cure."

Here see the Bread of life; see waters flowing
Forth from the throne of God, pure from above:
Come to the feast of love; come, ever knowing
Earth has no sorrow but heaven can remove.
—Thomas Moore and Thomas Hastings

DAY 4: *Meditation When Part of You Is Dying*

▶ *Scripture*

Now a certain man was sick, Lazarus of Bethany, the town of Mary and her sister Martha. It was that Mary who anointed the Lord with fragrant oil and wiped His feet with her hair, whose brother Lazarus was sick. Therefore the sisters sent to Him, saying, "Lord, behold, he whom You love is sick."

When Jesus heard that, He said, "This sickness is not unto death, but for the glory of God, that the Son of God may be glorified through it."

Now Jesus loved Martha and her sister and Lazarus. So, when He heard that he was sick, He stayed two more days in the place where He was. Then after this He said to the disciples, "Let us go to Judea again."

The disciples said to Him, "Rabbi, lately the Jews sought to stone You, and are You going there again?"

Jesus answered, "Are there not twelve hours in the day? If anyone walks in the day, he does not stumble, because he sees the light of this world. But if one walks in the night, he stumbles, because the light is not in him." These things He said, and after that He said to them, "Our friend Lazarus sleeps, but I go that I may wake him up."

Then His disciples said, "Lord, if he sleeps he will get well." However, Jesus spoke of his death, but they thought that He was speaking about taking rest in sleep.

Then Jesus said to them plainly, "Lazarus is dead. And I am glad for your sakes that I was not there, that you may believe. Nevertheless let us go to him."

Then Thomas, who is called the Twin, said to his fellow disciples, "Let us also go, that we may die with

Him." So when Jesus came, He found that he had already been in the tomb four days.

Now Bethany was near Jerusalem, about two miles away. And many of the Jews had joined the women around Martha and Mary, to comfort them concerning their brother. Then Martha, as soon as she heard that Jesus was coming, went and met Him, but Mary was sitting in the house.

Now Martha said to Jesus, "Lord, if You had been here, my brother would not have died. But even now I know that whatever You ask of God, God will give You."

Jesus said to her, "Your brother will rise again." Martha said to Him, "I know that he will rise again in the resurrection at the last day."

Jesus said to her, "I am the resurrection and the life. He who believes in Me, though he may die, he shall live. And whoever lives and believes in Me shall never die. Do you believe this?"

She said to Him, "Yes, Lord, I believe that You are the Christ, the Son of God, who is to come into the world."

And when she had said these things, she went her way and secretly called Mary her sister, saying, "The Teacher has come and is calling for you." As soon as she heard that, she arose quickly and came to Him.

Now Jesus had not yet come into the town, but was in the place where Martha met Him.

Then the Jews who were with her in the house, and comforting her, when they saw that Mary rose up quickly and went out, followed her, saying, "She is going to the tomb to weep there."

Then, when Mary came to where Jesus was, and saw Him, she fell down at His feet, saying to Him, "Lord, if You had been here, my brother would not have died."

Therefore, when Jesus saw her weeping, and the

Jews who came with her weeping, He groaned in the spirit and was troubled. And He said, "Where have you laid him?"

They said to Him, "Lord, come and see."

Jesus wept. Then the Jews said, "See how He loved him!" And some of them said, "Could not this Man, who opened the eyes of the blind, also have kept this man from dying?"

Then Jesus, again groaning in Himself, came to the tomb. It was a cave, and a stone lay against it. Jesus said, "Take away the stone."

Martha, the sister of him who was dead, said to Him, "Lord, by this time there is a stench, for he has been dead four days."

Jesus said to her, "Did I not say to you that if you would believe you would see the glory of God?" Then they took away the stone from the place where the dead man was lying. And Jesus lifted up His eyes and said, "Father, I thank You that You have heard Me. And I know that You always hear Me, but because of the people who are standing by I said this, that they may believe that You sent Me."

Now when He had said these things, He cried with a loud voice, "Lazarus, come forth!" And he who had died came out bound hand and foot with graveclothes, and his face was wrapped with a cloth. Jesus said to them, "Loose him, and let him go."

Then many of the Jews who had come to Mary, and had seen the things Jesus did, believed in Him.

—John 11:1–45

▶ *Insight*

The death is not for your undoing but for God's glory, and any "delay" must be seen as God's concern and love for you. It is not a lack of care or concern. And one of the highest purposes for the delay is "that you may believe" (v. 15).

▶ *Meditation*

After reading this amazing passage, take time to sort out just what it is that has died in you. Make clear the identity of what has died. Jesus is deeply moved by this death, even though, like the disciples and Mary and Martha, you may not be too sure about this at first.

Take time, then, to tell God that you accept his timing for resurrection. Pray for that resurrection. And then get ready for the vivid drama that unfolds when life swallows up death.

Why? You do not even have to have faith for this one! After all, how much faith did Lazarus have in the tomb? This is God's sovereign choice of you for blessing, and many people will hear about it and come to see: "Now a great many of the Jews knew that He was there; and they came, not for Jesus' sake only, but that they might also see Lazarus, whom He had raised from the dead" (John 12:9). Indeed, resurrection life is a truly amazing thing to see.

DAY 5: *Meditation on the Weight of Caring for*
            Others

▶ *Scripture*

> Then they came to a place which was named Gethsemane; and He said to His disciples, "Sit here while I pray."
> And He took Peter, James, and John with Him, and He began to be troubled and deeply distressed. Then

He said to them, "My soul is exceedingly sorrowful, even to death. Stay here and watch."

He went a little farther, and fell on the ground, and prayed that if it were possible, the hour might pass from Him. And He said, "Abba, Father, all things are possible for You. Take this cup away from Me; nevertheless, not what I will, but what You will."

—Mark 14:32–36

▶ Insight

This passage marks the paragon of the cost of serving others. Jesus' agony is compounded by a process of clarification that reveals just what it is going to cost him to serve others. It is plain (from the long time it takes him to pray that the cup may pass from him) that he does not like what he sees. Nevertheless, at the end of the process, the depth and height of realistic self-understanding before God is confessed when Jesus prays, "Nevertheless, not what I will, but what You will" (v. 36).

▶ Meditation

Some of us are involved in long-term care of others, not as a paying job but as an inescapable part of life. We take care of a handicapped child, a spouse with a debilitating disease, or an aged parent. It weighs us down. There's no "time out" from it. The cost of such human service is daunting, perhaps even sorrowful. You wish. . . .

As you read through this passage in Mark's gospel, take time to remind God that you are accepting his will. "Come bodly to the throne of grace," where you will "obtain mercy and find grace to help in the time of need" (Heb. 4:16). We may not experience the ultimate anguish that was Christ's, but we shall be placing ourselves in the company of Jesus, who identified with us fully.

▶ *Hymn*

BLEST BE THE TIE THAT BINDS

Blest be the tie that binds
Our hearts in Jesus' love:
The fellowship of Christian minds
Is like to that above.

Before our Father's throne
We pour united prayers;
Our fears, our hopes, our aims are one;
Our comforts and our cares.

We share our mutual woes,
Our mutual burdens bear;
And often for each other flows
The sympathizing tear.
—John Fawcett

DAY **6**: *Meditation on Suffering for Well-doing*

▶ *Scripture*

But even if you should suffer for righteousness'
sake, you are blessed. "And do not be afraid of their
threats, nor be troubled." But sanctify the Lord God
in your hearts, and always be ready to give a defense
to everyone who asks you a reason for the hope that is
in you, with meekness and fear; having a good con-
science, that when they defame you as evildoers, those
who revile your good conduct in Christ may be
ashamed.

For it is better, if it is the will of God, to suffer for
doing good than for doing evil. For Christ also suffered
once for sins, the just for the unjust, that He might bring

*us to God, being put to death in the flesh but made
alive by the Spirit.*

*Therefore, since Christ suffered for us in the flesh,
arm yourselves also with the same mind, for he who
has suffered in the flesh has ceased from sin, that he
no longer should live the rest of his time in the flesh for
the lusts of men, but for the will of God.*
—1 Peter 3:14–18; 4:1–2

▶ Insight

Suffering for well-doing may be the hardest act of Christian obedience, especially today, in an age that teaches us to cling to our rights for all we're worth. "I don't have to suffer like that! I've got my rights! And if you persist in making me suffer like that, I'll see you in court!" And once again we come face to face with the conflict between holding on to our rights and fulfilling our responsibilities to obey God.

▶ Meditation

Consider the times that you have been treated unjustly at work by your employer and felt you had a right to quit your job. Or, perhaps you are married to a non-Christian and it is generally difficult for you to respond to him or her as Christ would because you are not being treated fairly. Or maybe you have been back-stabbed by someone in the congregation whom you had helped. These and a hundred other injustices are the reason for the above passages.

This kind of suffering on the part of an innocent Christian can only be responded to in kind as the example of Christ teaches us. Otherwise, God will be dealing with us for our disobedience here. But if we follow Christ's example, we will be more closely united with him in this high form of obedience. Take some time to pray, first, with thanksgiving that you are suffering for doing good rather than for doing evil. And then ask God for the strength of character to help you continue following the example of Christ in this.

We may also reflect on the undeserved sufferings of Christians in China or Pakistan or other difficult countries. We may find ourselves grateful that we have shared with them in the fellowship of Christ and his sufferings.

▶ *Hymn*

FAITH OF OUR FATHERS

Faith of our fathers! living still—
In spite of dungeon, fire, and sword:
O how our hearts beat high with joy,
Whenever we hear that glorious word:

Faith of our fathers, holy faith!
We will be true to thee till death.

Our fathers, chained in prisons dark,
Were still in heart and conscience free:
And truly blest would be our fate,
If we, like them, should die for thee.

Faith of our fathers! faith and prayer
Shall win all nations unto thee;
And through the truth that comes from God,
Mankind shall then indeed be free.

Faith of our fathers! We will love
Both friend and foe in all our strife:
And preach thee, too, as love knows how,
By kindly deeds and virtuous life.
　　　　　　　　　　—Frederick William Faber

DAY 7: *Meditation on the Hope of Future Glory*

▶ *Scripture*

Now after six days Jesus took Peter, James, and John, and led them up on a high mountain apart by themselves; and He was transfigured before them. His clothes became shining, exceedingly white, like snow, such as no launderer on earth can whiten them. And Elijah appeared to them with Moses, and they were talking with Jesus.

Then Peter answered and said to Jesus, "Rabbi, it is good for us to be here; and let us make three tabernacles: one for You, one for Moses, and one for Elijah"— because he did not know what to say, for they were greatly afraid. And a cloud came and overshadowed them; and a voice came out of the cloud, saying, "This is My beloved Son. Hear Him!"

Suddenly, when they had looked around, they saw no one anymore, but only Jesus with themselves.

But we all, with unveiled face, beholding as in a mirror the glory of the Lord, are being transformed into the same image from glory to glory, just as by the Spirit of the Lord.

—Mark 9:2–8; 2 Corinthians 3:18

▶ *Insight*

Christ's light is greater than our darkness, and one day we will be transfigured by Christ. This word "transfigured" in Mark 9:2 is used only in two other places. It is found in Romans 12:2, where it is translated as "transformed" (by the renewing of your mind); and again as "transformed" in 2 Corinthians 3:18. The context is the product of a sinless and perfected humanity, which may have been what Moses and Elijah were to represent, as they stood talking with Jesus on the mountain.

▶ *Meditation*

We have been considering some pretty heavy things in the above exercises. Yet for the Christian they are not without a purpose, an end. And that purpose is the end for which all things exist. And that end is not an event, or an ideal, or even heaven. It is a Person.

This is the point of it all. It is what the Bible means when it says that "all things work together for good to those who love God, to those who are called according to His purpose" (Rom. 8:28). That purpose is a Person, Jesus Christ, and when we are finally with him we shall be "conformed to [his] image" and "glorified" (Rom. 8:29–30). A new creation. A member of sinless and perfected humanity.

And that—after all—is worth waiting for. It may not answer all of our earthquake questions; it may not deliver us from suffering. But these things will pale in comparison to the glory that shall follow.

Sometimes we don't finish certain projects simply because we have not set ourselves energetically enough to reach the end. Take several minutes alone in prayer for meditation. Close your eyes and imagine that you are looking at Mount Everest. Nothing is going to move that! It's firm and solid. With that thought in mind, tell God you want to be that "solid" in your following after him until the end, to reach the end who is Jesus Christ. Explain to him why you may have been vacillating and ask for great grace to finish the course, to be as "firm" as the mountain in your resolve.

Why? Why? Why? Sometimes the philosopher rages in us all. Sometimes he cannot be silenced. Sometimes we're afraid to ask, to doubt. Yet there may be more healthy faith in honest doubt than in pretending we don't have troubling questions. And then there are the years when no answers may be forthcoming.

Let us, therefore, take courage and comfort in the assurance and end of our faith:

> *Behold, I tell you a mystery: We shall not all sleep, but we shall be changed—in a moment, in the twinkling of an eye, at the last trumpet. For the trumpet will sound, and the dead will be raised incorruptible, and we shall be changed. Then shall be brought to pass the saying that is written: "Death is swallowed up in victory."*
>
> *"O Death, where is your sting?*
> *O Hades, where is your victory?"*
>
> *But thanks be to God, who gives us the victory through our Lord Jesus Christ. Therefore, my beloved brethren, be steadfast, immovable, always abounding in the work of the Lord, knowing that your labor is not in vain in the Lord.*
>
> —1 Corinthians 15:51–52, 54–55, 57-58

▶ *Hymn*

WHEN WE ALL GET TO HEAVEN

Sing the wondrous love of Jesus,
Sing His mercy and His grace;
In the mansions bright and blessed
He'll prepare for us a place.

When we all get to heaven,
What a day of rejoicing that will be!
When we all see Jesus,
We'll sing and shout the victory.

While we walk the pilgrim pathway
Clouds will overspread the sky;
But when traveling days are over,
Not a shadow, not a sigh.

Let us then be true and faithful,
Trusting, serving every day;
Just one glimpse of Him in glory
Will the toils of life repay.

Onward to the prize before us!
Soon His beauty we'll behold;
Soon the pearly gates will open,
We shall tread the streets of gold.
—Eliza E. Hewitt

— 6 —

Imagination and Spirituality

— ◆ —

There is a scene in the film "Nicholas and Alexandra" where the deposed czar is standing on the back of the train that was taking him to prison and execution. Czar Nicholas turned to his guard and asked, "Was it because I was cruel and a bad ruler that the people hated me?" His guard replied, "No, it wasn't so much because you were bad. It was because you did not have any imagination. You just did not see the damage you were doing."

"Imagination" is the ability to see the significance of things, whether present or absent. It is also the ability to use material forms and figures (such as paintings and photographs) as symbols of the things they represent, such as art used to inspire worship. Imagination is also used with "memory" to locate and develop feelings and images of things and events that no longer exist.

Our imaginations, then, give us the capacity

to explore reality in many ways and to develop our sense of the wonder of God and his creation.

God's Gift of Imagination

Imagine God using his imagination!

> Then God said, "Let the earth bring forth grass, the herb that yields seed, and the fruit tree that yields according to its kind."
>
> Then God said, "Let the waters abound with the abundance of living creatures, and let the birds fly above the earth."
>
> Then God said, "Let the earth bring forth the living creature according to its kind: cattle and creeping thing and beast of the earth."
> —Genesis 1:11, 20, 24

This is only a part of the kaleidoscope of color and life that God created. We have this saying that "God created out of nothing." But think of what must have been going on in his mind before the jellyfish or the cardinal or the giraffe appeared. What an imagination! And then God said, "Let us make man in Our image" (Genesis 1:26). It should come as no surprise, then, that we too have imaginations. People by nature are creative, able to express a riot of gifts and skills. Thus "imagination" is part of what it means to be human *and* to be spiritual.

We begin to use our imaginations in childhood, playing games like "house," "war," "tea party," or "Robin Hood." These are ways of identifying with and understanding our parents and life's larger events. They are times of story-telling and living through the excitement and adventures of our heros. Play is a creative moment for inventing with our minds; it is a vehicle of discovery and learning as we learn to include others in our make-believe world.

We can take new steps forward spiritually as we rediscover some of the imaginative processes we knew as children. This is not about imagining make-believe. It is about a redemptive use of our imaginations to help us reach spiritual maturity. This would include using our imaginations to increase our awareness of who we are and of what it means to belong to God and the church. Our imaginations can also be used in the processes whereby we receive healings and attain vision. All of this, and more, is part of spiritual development. "Imagination" is sometimes a missing, or at least a deficient, dimension in the process.

Sharing Our Imaginations

All art forms are vehicles of expression for our minds, and they are powerful ways for sharing imagination. Art represents reality as the artist sees it. We are being invited to share the work, to appreciate its significance, to draw our own conclusions. The message may be something beautiful, or it may present a challenge or critical comment. Therefore a painting of a pastoral scene or a photograph of a war-torn people stir powerful emotions in different directions.

Symbols also help us share thoughts and feelings. Some symbols are universally recognized, such as a wedding ring or a black dress for mourning. Usually we are not affected superficially by such symbols, but we are able to understand from them immediately more deeply what is going on and thereby behave with appropriate feelings, thoughts, and responses.

For the Christian, the cross is a symbol of Christ's death and resurrection. It represents the forgiveness of our sins. When we focus on the cross we don't stop at the superficial level of the symbol; our imaginations enable us to enter into the meaning it represents. Other symbols are not static but dynamic, in that they are a kind of human drama. Two examples are the laying on of hands and the anointing with oil for healing. Here, our actual contact with the symbols is part of our obedience, and it helps our concentration. Nevertheless, symbols are not ends in themselves, as though they held magic powers. Instead, they "kick us into life" by our imagination, connecting us spiritually with what God has done and is doing.

The Prophets and Jesus

The prophets provide many examples of God's messages by the use of symbols. Consider how Isaiah, by walking naked through the streets of Jerusalem, riveted the imagination of the wayward nation Israel. It was a compelling prophetic challenge to them to turn from their disastrous policies and be obedient to Yahweh. When Jeremiah meditated upon the potter at his wheel he gained insight into how God could remold an intransigent people. Ezekiel played siege games with an imaginary Jerusalem, using the shavings from his own hair, to speak powerfully to his audience about the consequences of disobedience. In Acts 21:10–11, we read of the prophet Agabus who, far from merely telling Paul of the captivity that lay ahead for him, wrapped himself in the apostle's leather belt, and the imagery spoke for itself.

These examples show how prophetic impact was heightened by the use of symbols, which appealed to the imagination and allowed people to reflect upon the divine messages they represented. It is important to note that the use of those symbols was not divorced from the facts. This combination of word and symbol is seen strikingly in the ministry of Jesus.

Almost the whole of Jesus' ministry is an appeal to the imagination. His teaching employed a wealth of imagery and story. When speaking about his work, he pictured himself as "the gate," "the good shepherd," and "the true vine." Rather than give doctrinal definitions of salvation, he told parables. Jesus gave no lecture on heaven, instead he filled the imagination of his disciples with pictures of the pearl of great price or the fisherman dragging in a full net at the end of a working day. He gave us ideas of a great house with room for the faithful and a banquet for those of all classes who simply had time for the master's words. (This is not to say that he did not also teach systematically, as the Sermon on the Mount illustrates.)

Jesus also appealed to the childlike qualities within his disciples if they were to make progress on their spiritual journey: "Assuredly, I say to you, unless you are converted and become as little children, you will by no means enter the kingdom of heaven" (Matthew 18:3). Even though this is a pointed reference to conversion, surely Jesus is also challenging his followers to recapture a childlike sense of wonder: to keep their imaginations alive!

By using pictures, stories and symbols, Jesus invited his listeners to identify more fully with the issues at stake. Imagination engaged their thoughts and feelings. How many of Jesus' listeners would have laughed at the idea of a beam sticking out of someone's eye? Until suddenly they saw themselves! How many would have felt justified at the prodigal son's predicament? Until Jesus developed the part of his father's forgiveness. Imagination offers us an opportunity to understand as Jesus' listeners understood. It offers us the potential for understanding with the heart as well as the head.

Imagination at Work

Icons

One of the most exquisite art forms throughout Church history has been icons. These visual images were chiefly developed by the eastern church. Each painting was to be a work of faith and prayer and closely examined to ensure that it was doctrinally acceptable. The individual character of the artist (or group of artist monks) was not to show in the work, in order to underline the primacy of divine authority. The aim was to keep the human personality in the background as much as possible, out of deference to the Creator himself. Standardized goldleaf backgrounds and stylized two-dimensional features were used in order to focus one's attention on the sacred mystery represented, rather than on the representation itself. So an icon is a work of art that points not to the artist but to God.

Part of the way icons work is through symbolism. We may need the key to unlock the meaning hidden in the symbols, to learn the language the artist is speaking. For example, in the Mother of God odigitria icon, Mary points to her child: a symbol that Jesus is "the way, the truth and the life." Jesus holds the scroll of the Law in his left hand and gives a sign of blessing with his right: symbols that Jesus is both the just judge and merciful savior. Similarly, the letters within Jesus's halo mean "He who is" and proclaim his divinity. Coupled with his depiction as human we have a powerful symbol of Jesus also as fully divine.

Icons, therefore, demand a particular way of looking. And we are not to worship the image but the God to whom the image points. So an icon is not so much to be looked at as looked *through*. This may explain the common practice of portraying the eyes of Christ as expression-less. The onlooker is invited to travel through the vacant regard of the image to God.

Looking through an icon can be a step in worship. For example, if the picture was of Mary and Jesus, then the worshipper was to look through the eyes of the mother and enter into her feelings of wonder and privilege at being the mother of Christ. Her special grace and station would be perceived and the individual would for a moment touch the mystery of the Incarnation. This would bring him to a deeper and fuller worship of God. If the one's focus were upon Jesus, then the worshipper might enter into the subject of God's wondrous gift of his Son for sinners. So the icon was used by one's imagination as an initial stepping stone for meditation upon the mystery of God. And this was not meant to be merely a cerebral exercise but that which engaged the whole person.

Dreams

Dreams make use of the imagination, and in the Bible we see that God used dreams to communicate with people. Through the message of a dream, Joseph, Mary, and the infant Jesus were saved from the murderous hands of Herod. Through the interpretation of dreams, Joseph equipped the Egyptians to prepare for seven years of famine. God can use our dreams to communicate with us. Interestingly, the Hebrew term for dreaming includes the idea of "recovery," in the sense of making whole or healthy. Dreaming, then, may be good for us.

Our dreams sometimes reflect how we feel about certain things, and if so we would want to pay attention to those feelings. Some dreams may mirror our "unfinished business," and then there are nightmares or recurring dreams that disturb us. The symbols and pictures in these kinds of dreams may be worth trying to clarify.

For example, I counseled a woman who had recurring dreams of a little girl in a soiled dress who was being kept forcibly on a man's lap. The prayer-approach I used with this dream was to ask the question that God asked Adam, "Where are you?" (Gen. 3:9). What followed was a meditation on the woman's feelings about the dreams, which were those of helplessness and feeling dirty and guilty. These were then offered to Christ, and as we continued the process a moment of clarity came when the woman was able to share that for years she had been repressing feelings of guilt because she had been sexually abused. She had not told anyone for fear of exposure and rejection. It became clear that she was the little girl of the dream, and the final stage in the meditation released her from a lifetime of guilt and insecurity and renewed her marriage.

Healing Memories

All of us have memories, and no matter how old they may be, there are times when something may trigger one of them. These may be pleasant or painful. The ministry of inner healing, or healing the memories, attempts to bring the healing power of Jesus into the area of crippling memories through a process of mental and emotional reconstruction of an event under the guidance of the Holy Spirit.

One example of how this might work could be seen in a person who suffers from depression, fear, or anxiety. This person would first find someone to pray with. He would then begin the prayer time by focusing on Jesus, perhaps by meditating on a verse like, "The LORD is my helper; I will not fear. What can man do to me?" (Hebrews 13:6). He may find it helpful to picture Jesus demonstrating this truth. The next step would be to invite Jesus to come to minister to the hurt feelings and depression. And if possible this may include thinking of the actual event that relates to the hurt feelings and depression. The person may also try to verbalize his feelings.

The person will try to stay focused chiefly on Jesus all the while, so that after the memory has been clarified, prayer for healing can take place. And in many, if not most, cases this will include forgiving whoever caused the injury.

A final step may be to offer God thanksgiving for healing and for new insights gained. Celebration often followed healing in the stories the Bible records. Joseph threw his arms around Benjamin and wept as he shared how God had given him a new perspective on his years of slavery. The father of the prodigal killed the fatted calf and threw a party when his lost son came home. The two disciples on the road to Emmaus went dashing back to Jerusalem to tell the other disciples that Jesus had changed their thinking about what had happened at Calvary.

Naturally the new outlook and healing needs to be worked out and applied by choice and faith. And it is not unusual for there to be challenges to that. But the love of Jesus has brought release, and we need to apply our faith to the new ground gained.

The Possibilities

In Genesis 6:5, God declared that "every imagination of the thoughts of [man's] heart was only evil all the time." This is quite an indictment. And it is instructive that most of the biblical references to the imagination are in the context of idolatry. Even today in Christendom there have been unfortunate abuses and even nonbiblical uses of the imagination. People have fallen prey to worshiping images themselves, or assigning a magical power to symbols. Others have slipped up by thinking that the Jesus we imagine in our minds is the real Jesus. And another error has been to invite "Jesus" into the past to alter it. The past, however, cannot be altered, which is why it has to be forgiven.

This is not the book to explore all that dealing with past wounds entails. Yet two things need to be said here. One is that there is a proper, that is to say a biblical, use of our imaginations. More and more we need to be discovering what this is. And, second, any readers who feel uncomfortable about exploring further possibilities for using their imaginations probably should not. It's not wrong to feel that way.

Yet what an invitation it is from God to dare to imagine what blessings he has in store for us. It seems that not even our wildest dreams can fully grasp this:

> *Eye has not seen, nor ear heard,*
> *Nor have entered into the heart of man*
> *The things which God has prepared for those*
> *who love Him.*
>
> —1 Corinthians 2:9

One of the delights of rediscovering a biblical use of the imagination is that it continually holds out the possibility of something new. We cannot finally catalog all the ways in which God can use our imaginations to take us deeper into him. For "he is able to do exceedingly abundantly above all that we ask or think" (Eph. 3:20). *Think about it!*

TAKE SEVEN DAYS . . .

DAY 1: *On the Beach with Jesus*

▶ *Meditation*

This activity is based on Peter's encounter with Jesus on the shore of the Sea of Tiberias. It invites you to experience what the encounter meant for Peter and to see what that may mean for you. It also provides an opportunity for you to offer a gift to Jesus and to receive something from him.

Start by opening your Bible to John 21:1–17. Then spend a minute or so relaxing in a comfortable position. Read the passage slowly and imagine yourself alongside Peter in the boat.

> *After these things Jesus showed Himself again to the disciples at the Sea of Tiberias, and in this way He showed Himself: Simon Peter, Thomas called the Twin, Nathanael of Cana in Galilee, the sons of Zebedee, and two others of His disciples were together.*
>
> *Simon Peter said to them, "I am going fishing." They said to him, "We are going with you also." They went out and immediately got into the boat, and that night they caught nothing.*
>
> *But when the morning had now come, Jesus stood on the shore; yet the disciples did not know that it was Jesus. Then Jesus said to them, "Children, have you any food?" They answered Him, "No."*
>
> *And He said to them, "Cast the net on the right side of the boat, and you will find some." So they cast, and now they were not able to draw it in because of the multitude of fish.*
>
> *Therefore that disciple whom Jesus loved said to Peter, "It is the Lord!" Now when Simon Peter heard that it was the Lord, he put on his outer garment (for he had removed it), and plunged into the sea. But the other disciples came in the little boat (for they were not far from land, but about two hundred cubits), dragging the net with fish.*
>
> *Then, as soon as they had come to land, they saw a fire of coals there, and fish laid on it, and bread.*
>
> *Jesus said to them, "Bring some of the fish which you have just caught."*

Simon Peter went up and dragged the net to land, full of large fish, one hundred and fifty-three; and although there were so many, the net was not broken.

Jesus said to them, "Come and eat breakfast." Yet none of the disciples dared ask Him, "Who are You?" knowing that it was the Lord. Jesus then came and took the bread and gave it to them, and likewise the fish. This is now the third time Jesus showed Himself to His disciples after He was raised from the dead.

So when they had eaten breakfast, Jesus said to Simon Peter, "Simon, son of Jonah, do you love Me more than these?" He said to Him, "Yes, Lord; You know that I love You." He said to him, "Feed My lambs."

He said to him again a second time, "Simon, son of Jonah, do you love Me?" He said to Him, "Yes, Lord; You know that I love You." He said to him, "Tend My sheep."

He said to him the third time, "Simon, son of Jonah, do you love Me?" Peter was grieved because He said to him the third time, "Do you love Me?" And he said to Him, "Lord, You know all things; You know that I love You." Jesus said to him, "Feed my sheep."

—John 21:1–17

You probably have a number of things on your mind, even, perhaps, like Peter you may be thinking about how terrible your work day was. Now you see the shore nearby, and Jesus is waiting for you on the beach.

See yourself leaping like Peter into the water to reach Jesus. How does it feel to be pushing through the water? Is there some resistance? As you reach shore, allow the importance of the moment to sink in. You're meeting with Jesus. He is waiting for you.

How does Jesus greet you? Is it as he greets Peter, asking for something? If so, what gift can you offer Jesus? Notice that the reason Jesus desires your gift is to use it with his own provisions (v. 9). Think about how Jesus will use your gift.

Soon it will be time to leave this shore. Before you leave, what is Jesus saying to you? For Peter it was a challenge. For you it may be that, or it may be a word of comfort, healing, or direction. As you close the exercise, take time to think about how you will use what Jesus has given you. As you come out of your imagination and into the place you are in, close the meditation with a prayer of thanks.

On a sheet of paper, or in your journal, write down your impressions from Jesus. If it was a word of comfort, did a passage of Scripture come to mind? If so, record that, and you will have it to refer to as a word of comfort anytime in the future. Was it a word of direction or perhaps reproof? You can use your journal to record it as a means to holding yourself accountable.

▶ *Hymn*

SOMETHING FOR THEE

Saviour, Thy dying love
Thou gavest me,
Nor should I aught withhold,
Dear Lord, from Thee:
In love my soul would bow,
My heart fulfill its vow;
Some offering bring Thee now,
Something for Thee.

At the blest mercy seat,
Pleading for me,
My feeble faith looks up,
Jesus, to Thee:
Help me the cross to bear,
Thy wondrous love declare,

> *Some song to raise, or prayer,*
> *Something for Thee.*
>
> *Give me a faithful heart,*
> *Likeness to Thee,*
> *That each departing day*
> *Henceforth may see*
> *Some work of love begun,*
> *Some deed of kindness done,*
> *Some wanderer sought and won,*
> *Something for Thee.*
>
> *All that I am and have,*
> *Thy gifts so free,*
> *In joy, in grief, through life,*
> *Dear Lord, for Thee!*
> *And when Thy face I see,*
> *My ransomed soul shall be,*
> *Through all eternity,*
> *Something for Thee.*
>   —Sylvanus D. Phelps

DAY 2: *In the Arms of Father God*

▶ *Meditation*

It is not uncommon for Christians to draw their understandings of the Father primarily from how their human fathers behaved toward them. This may not be a bad idea; unless, as in not a few cases, one's father is not a good role model.

Imagine your heavenly Father's love. After a suitable period of silence, imagine yourself as a very young child being held securely and lovingly in your heavenly Father's arms. You're vulnerable, but he's strong and dependable. Imagine his protective care. If this is difficult, perhaps there remains some hurt or unforgiveness in your heart towards your human father. Take some time with your heavenly Father to share this, and to ask for forgiveness and healing. Close by rejoicing that your heavenly Father has got you and your world in his hand. You are safe: "No one is able to snatch them out of My Father's hand," (John 10:29).

Find a quiet spot where you can write a letter to Father God. If you are struggling with accepting him as a loving Father, make that the subject of the letter. If you are overwhelmed with him as Father, make that the subject. If you are puzzled about some of the ways he acts as Father, tell him about that. Be honest, and whatever subject you would like to talk to him about, use that as the subject.

Here are some ideas you may want to consider when writing. You are in a wonderfully unique situation as a Christian. According to Jesus himself, in John 8:44, not everyone has God as Father, unfortunately. You can thank God in your letter that you are a child of his and that your "sonship" is based on Jesus' relation to the Father:

> *Go to My brethren and say to them, 'I am ascending to My Father and your Father.'*
>
> —John 20:17

Thank him in writing, too, that because you are a child you are an heir with Jesus Christ. Doesn't that excite you! Think of it:

> *The Spirit Himself bears witness with our spirit that we are the children of God, and if children, then heirs— heirs of God and joint heirs with Christ, if indeed we suffer with Him, that we may also be glorified with Him.*
>
> —Romans 8:16–17

Or, you could include in your thanksgiving an appreciation of the many other loving and tender aspects of Father
God, such as his watchful care, his rich provisions, his faithfulness, or even that he disciplines those that he loves. However you choose to write it, a letter is a very personal way
to say thank you to Father God.

DAY 3: *Practicing the Presence of Christ*

▶ *Meditation*

God is always present with us, but we are not always
aware of him. Our lives and minds get preoccupied with so
much that drives out a consciousness of God for extended
periods of time. Yet we have a definite role to play with our
wills and attitudes in acknowledging and seeking fellowship
with the God who *is* present.

This is an exercise in which you become aware of the
presence of God throughout your day. This does not usually
come easily and so may take some practice. It does not
matter whether you are at home, at work, or someplace else.
The idea is to create a kind of space in your imagination in
which to experience and feel the presence of Christ in the
many activities of the day. For example, if you're busy preparing a meal or driving a car, your mind will drift off into any
number of unimportant thoughts. When you catch yourself
doing this, stop those thoughts and begin thinking about
the God who is present with you in the kitchen or the car. A
simple prayer or moment of thanksgiving to him would be
nice.

The idea is to cultivate a continual awareness of God
through Jesus Christ in your daily activities. Maybe you're
at work and in a tough situation for an hour or two, a setting
in which you would normally strive through without a thought
about God. Stop a moment. Take a walk alone down a hall-

way or find an empty spot like a bathroom, where you can take a few minutes to say a simple prayer acknowledging that God is with you in the fire. There may even be a setting in which you suddenly become aware of God's presence and it brings conviction. How will you deal with that?

After you have practiced the presence of God for a day or two, make some notes about what this was like. You may want to share the experience with some friends. Or you may want to write in your journal about the contrast between "normal" days and those you spent becoming more aware of God's presence. The long-range goal would be that your days would become increasingly filled with a conscious awareness of God.

▶ *Hymn*

NEAR TO THE HEART OF GOD

There is a place of quiet rest
Near to the heart of God,
A place where sin cannot molest,
Near to the heart of God.

O Jesus, blest Redeemer,
Sent from the heart of God,
Hold us who wait before Thee
Near to the heart of God.

There is a place of comfort sweet
Near to the heart of God,
A place where we our Savior meet,
Near to the heart of God.

There is a place of full release
Near to the heart of God,
A place where all is joy and peace,
Near to the heart of God.
—Cleland B. McAfee

DAY 4: *Discovering the Meanings of Dreams*

▶ *Exercise*

The following are several initial steps for recording and understanding some of your dreams. While many dreams will be unimportant, others are worth trying to understand. They may help you to have a better awareness of yourself, especially your thoughts and feelings. They may even help you to discover a message from God.

1. Pray before you go to sleep that God will help you remember any significant dreams. Commit your sleep to him.

> *And it shall come to pass in the last*
> *   days, says God,*
> *That I will pour out of My spirit on all*
> *   flesh;*
> *Your sons and your daughters shall*
> *   prophesy,*
> *Your young men shall see visions,*
> *Your old men shall dream dreams.*
> *   —Acts 2:17*

2. Keep pen, paper, and a small light nearby.
3. When you awaken from a dream, or in the morning, immediately write down as much of the dream as you can. At the least, jot the details in their sequence.
4. Write down as many associations to your dream as you can, such as links with the real world or present events.
5. Add whatever feelings you can, either those in the dream or those you feel about events in the dream. For example, when such and such occurred, I felt

like _____. Your associations with current events and activities and your feelings may be keys to understanding what the dream is saying.

6. Take some time, either during the night or in the morning, to write down what the dream appears to be saying. This may not be the whole story, or even part of the story, but it is important to get started with trying to come to some understanding.

7. Now you can take time to pray and bring the dream and all it contains, as well as your associations, feelings, and ideas, to the Lord. Simply ask Jesus to help you to understand. Insight may not come immediately. If that is the case, then try to keep the dream in your prayers during the next several days.

8. You may not receive understanding of the dream as a whole. The Lord may give you insight about certain elements of the dream.

9. If you gain an understanding of a dream that requires some action on your part, take time to follow through. Perhaps it is a challenge or conviction of sin. Take time to work this through with Jesus.

10. If you have gone through steps one to seven and still have no understanding about the dream, you're not alone. This occurs more often than people are willing to admit. The best thing to do, then, is probably just to give the dream and all your thoughts about it to the Lord and forget about it. He knows that you have tried to gain understanding, and he is quite capable of bringing any understanding that may be necessary at a later date. In the meantime, the worst thing you can do is to work yourself up into a nervous state by trying to pry out of a dream meanings that are not forthcoming.

DAY 5: *Forgiving Close Friends or Spouse*

▶ *Exercise*

In relationships between spouses and among close friends, a person may have a hard time practicing forgiveness because frequency of contact often includes the same frequent offenses. The friend or spouse has not had enough time to get the offensive behavior out of his or her "system," and in the meantime you have to be forgiving. And it grates on you, just as it did on Peter:

> *Then Peter came to Him and said, "Lord, how often shall my brother sin against me, and I forgive him? Up to seven times?" Jesus said to him, "I do not say to you, up to seven times, but up to seventy times seven."*
> —Matthew 18:21–22

In this prayer activity, find a place where you can be alone. Now take some time with your eyes closed to use your imagination to see the person who needs to be forgiven. Think about the specific thing that you need to forgive. What is the main issue? Why is it a sin? What needs may motivate this person's offensive behavior?

While thinking about this, place your hands open on your lap, palms up. With your eyes still closed, place the person's sin(s) against you in your hands and lift it up to God with forgiveness in your heart toward the person. Invite Jesus to help you if necessary. And when you are doing this, remember that there are two other hands in your life. These are the bloody nail pierced hands of Jesus, and they are part of the purchase of forgiveness. As you lift your hands to God, remember those nail-pierced hands that were lifted up for you. Not only that *you* may be forgiven but that you may be able to forgive others as well. Even 490 times. And pray that God will help you better understand what needs are yet unmet in this person and how God can use you to help those be met.

Close the prayer activity by thanking the Lord for his shed blood, and for renewed grace to enjoy once again the presence of your friend or spouse.

► *Hymn*

DEPTH OF MERCY! CAN THERE BE

Depth of mercy! can there be
Mercy still reserved for me?
Can my God His wrath forbear,
And the chief of sinners spare?

I have long withstood His grace;
Long provoked Him to His face;
Would not hear His gracious calls;
Grieved him by a thousand falls.

Jesus, answer from above:
Is not all Thy nature love?
Wilt Thou not the wrong forget?
Lo, I fall before Thy feet.

Now incline me to repent;
Let me now my fall lament;
Deeply my revolt deplore,
Weep, believe, and sin no more.

—Charles Wesley

DAY **6**: *The Healing Square*

► *Exercise*

This prayer activity will help you focus on how others have hurt you and how to receive healing.

1. Take a blank sheet of paper and draw a large square on it.
2. Slowly and prayerfully look back on your life to discover any times that may still be painful to you.
3. Write within the square the names or initials of people who were instrumental in bringing these hurts and pains to you.
4. Put a circle around the names or initials of those who are not close to you now as a result of this.
5. Choose one of these people to pray for. Tell Jesus how you feel about him or her, and be as honest as you can.
6. As you pray, try to see why that person hurt you. When you can, put a horizontal line through the name.
7. Now tell Jesus that you forgive the person. Do this as sincerely as you can. When you have forgiven, draw a vertical line through the midpoint of the horizontal line. By the Cross the offender is forgiven and reconciliation takes place.

   Therefore as the elect of God, holy and beloved, put on tender mercies, kindness, humility, meekness, longsuffering; bearing with one another, and forgiving one another, if anyone has a complaint against another, even as Christ forgave you.
   —Colossians 3:12–13

8. Often, we have been a part of the problem that caused the offenses. If this is true for you with person "X", put an x through the name. Then take time to ask God to forgive you for your part.
9. Now comes the hard part. Ask God to show you if you need to initiate contact with the person to ask forgiveness for your part. If so, ask God also for an appropriate means by which to do this.
10. Close this prayer activity in your own way. And be wise to follow through on it if necessary. (Note: the

"Healing Square" exercise can also be applied on yourself when you are trying to work through offenses you have caused others.)

▶ *Hymn*

I WOULD BE TRUE

I would be true, for there are those who trust me;
I would be pure, for there are those who care;
I would be strong, for there is much to suffer;
I would be brave, for there is much to dare,
I would be brave, for there is much to dare.

I would be friend of all—the foe, the friendless;
I would be giving, and forget the gift;
I would be humble, for I know my weakness;
I would look up, and laugh, and love, and lift,
I would look up, and laugh, and love, and lift.

I would be learning, day by day, the lessons
My heavenly Father gives me in his Word;
I would be quick to hear his lightest whisper,
And prompt and glad to do the things I've heard,
And prompt and glad to do the things I've heard.
—Howard Arnold Walter

DAY 7: *Breaking Through Hindering Circumstances*

▶ *Exercise*

Whoever has served Jesus for any length of time has discovered situations in which fulfilling his commands seem difficult if not impossible. Often there is some blockage in personal development causing this. Read Matthew 17:14–21 to see some disciples who faced this. The Lord had sent them to accomplish certain tasks, and yet one of those was hindered due to a lack in their personal growth: they did not take time in fasting and prayer.

> *And when they had come to the multitude, a man came to Him, kneeling down to Him and saying, "Lord, have mercy on my son, for he is an epileptic and suffers severely; for he often falls into the fire and often into the water. So I brought him to your disciples, but they could not cure him."*
>
> *Then Jesus answered and said, "O faithless and perverse generation, how long shall I be with you? How long shall I bear with you? Bring him here to Me." And Jesus rebuked the demon, and it came out of him; and the child was cured from that very hour.*
>
> *Then the disciples came to Jesus privately and said, "Why could we not cast it out?" So Jesus said to them, "Because of your unbelief; for assuredly, I say to you, if you have faith as a mustard seed, you will say to this mountain, 'Move from here to there,' and it will move; and nothing will be impossible for you. However, this kind does not go out except by prayer and fasting."*
>
> —Matthew 17:14–21

What was the last time Jesus required obedience of you that you could not perform? Take time in prayer to ask Jesus why that occurred. To discover this, you may want to place yourself imaginatively back in the situation. Invite Jesus into the moment to reveal the problem(s). It is usually a blindspot on our parts, just as it was with the disciples in the above passage.

Be careful, though, that your problem, also like the disciples, is not that of unbelief. Ask Jesus to show you if it is. And if so, repent.

Sometimes it is far too late to return to a former failed obedience, but at other times it is the Lord's will that we do.

Close this prayer activity by asking the Lord to show you what he would have you to do. And ask him to add to your faith and to remove any blockages in your growth.

▶ *Hymn*

TRUST AND OBEY

When we walk with the Lord in the light of His Word,
What a glory He sheds on our way!
While we do His good will He abides with us still,
And with all who will trust and obey.

Trust and obey, for there's no other way
To be happy in Jesus,
But to trust and obey.

Not a shadow can rise, not a cloud in the skies,
But His smile quickly drives it away;
Not a doubt nor a fear, not a sigh nor a tear,
Can abide while we trust and obey.

Not a burden we bear, not a sorrow we share,
But our toil He doth richly repay;
Not a grief nor a loss, not a frown nor a cross,
But is blest if we trust and obey.

But we never can prove the delights of His love
Until all on the altar we lay;
For the favor He shows and the joy He bestows
Are for them who will trust and obey.

Then in fellowship sweet we will sit at His feet,
Or we'll walk by His side in the way;
What He says we will do, where He sends
we will go—
Never fear, only trust and obey.

—John Stammis

— 7 —
Physical Spirituality

———————◆———————

Many Christians believe that to be spiritual they must keep their bodies out of the picture, or subdue them as much as possible. Yet this is not a biblical perspective. In this chapter we will explore why this misunderstanding exists and the role our bodies have in our spirituality.

Understanding Body and Spirit

The first thing which needs to be said is that when God created the human body he pronounced it "good":

> And the LORD God formed man of the dust of the ground, and breathed into his nostrils the breath of life; and man became a living being.
>
> —Genesis 2:7

> Then God saw everything that He had made, and indeed it was very good.
>
> —Genesis 1:31

Even this side of the Garden incident, the "goodness" of the human body has not been lost. Yes, it is affected by the Fall, but it is not intrinsi-

cally evil. Otherwise, it could not be redeemed.
Yet passages such Romans 8:28 speak of the redemption of our bodies. In the meantime, because God made them "good," our bodies are never out of the picture of our spirituality. In fact, our bodies are involved in all our worship, prayers, and responses to God. Some of the ways we worship, pray, and respond have become so automatic that we hardly think of them as "using our bodies"; for instance, kneeling to pray or raising hands to worship, and especially using the mouth to speak.

All human spirituality is by design to some extent physical. This can add a source of tremendous spiritual richness and vitality to your life. Or it can hinder spiritual growth. For instance, if you pray at the end of the day, or in the early morning, and your body is tired or sleepy, then prayer will be superficial and unsatisfying.

Body and Spirit Influence Each Other

What one does physically has an influence on the person's spiritual state. A Christian's lifestyle should not be one of bodily overindulgence or neglect. Excessive eating, drinking, or smoking, the abuse of drugs, immorality, or lack of exercise are likely to hinder spiritual growth. This is not honoring God with our bodies:

Do you not know that your body is the temple of the Holy Spirit who is in you, whom you have from God, and you are not your own? For you

*were bought at a price; therefore glorify God in
your body.*

—1 Corinthians 6:19–20

Just as the body affects the spirit, you can often
discern things about a person by seeing the effects of spiritual things on the body. An extreme
example is demonic possession, when satanic
forces may control a person's movements and
speech. And Paul writes about the harmful influence of spiritual sin on the physical body: "For
he who eats and drinks [the Lord's Supper] in
an unworthy manner eats and drinks judgment
to himself, not discerning the Lord's body. For
this reason many are weak and sick among you,
and many sleep" (1 Corinthians 11:29–30).

Sin can have a great and long-standing effect
on the body. I have prayed with people who have
harbored resentment or hatred for years and then
finally forgave those who wronged them. These
persons discovered that release from the spiritual bondage of bitterness, anger and unforgiveness healed physical symptoms such as
migraines, twitches, high blood pressure, ar-
thritis, and paralysis. On a more upbeat note, as
a final example of the way the spirit affects the
body, I remember a small child who pointed at
an elderly, humble, and deeply prayerful member of our church and whispered to me, "I bet
she's a Christian, 'cos she looks all sort of nice
and shiny!"

Historical Roots of a Wrong View

Obviously, then, our bodies play a role larger than we may have thought in spirituality. This was the Hebrew view, as well as that of Jesus and the New Testament writers. Unfortunately, other early Christian thinkers and writers were increasingly influenced by Platonic philosophy and Gnosticism. Both were dualistic in nature, teaching that body and spirit were two separate entities and that the former was evil and the latter good. The spirit was seen as caged temporarily within the decaying evil matter of a physical body. Thus, to be truly "spiritual" one sought release from the evil matter of the body. When this false belief infiltrated Christianity it led people in one of two opposite distortions. Some people whipped and punished their bodies in an attempt to subdue and weaken this imprisoning cage and so set the spirit free. Others concluded that spirit was so infinitely superior to physical matter that it could not become unspiritual no matter what physical excesses they indulged.

Finding the Right View

Because far too much Christian thinking today remains influenced by the above dualisms, let's look more closely at the Bible for the right view of our bodies.

It is amazing that the central beliefs of the Christian faith and God's greatest acts in creation and redemption include the human body significantly. We have already noted that when God created us in his image, male and female, this included physical bodies which were "good." In the Incarnation, God in Christ became flesh in Mary's womb. He was not a divine Spirit temporarily inhabiting an independent physical body (another error within Gnosticism), but he actually became human. He experienced the delights, frustrations, and hurts of being physical. In his crucifixion, Christ's body was battered and wounded for us. Yet none of this made him "less spiritual." In fact, the central act of worship for Christians down the centuries and across the world has focused on sharing Christ's body and blood. What could be more spiritual? And yet it is a physical memorial! And in his resurrection, Christ was raised from the dead completely, body and all. Thus we who follow Christ believe in the resurrection of the body. This earthly body will be transformed into a heavenly body. But it will still be a body and its purpose will be the same: to be an essential part of what makes me me, through which I will be able to rejoice and enjoy and glorify God.

In the Old Testament, the physical body is appreciated with wonder as God's gift:

> *For You formed my inward parts;*
> *You covered me in my mother's womb.*
> *I will praise you, for I am fearfully and*
>   *wonderfully made;*
> *Marvelous are Your works.*
>   —Psalm 139:13–14

The Song of Solomon is full of frank and simple enjoyment of the beloved's physical beauty and of pleasure in the use of the senses. And also in the Old Testament, God's people frequently used their bodies to express themselves in prayer and worship. Here are several examples:

- Singing

> Sing praise to the LORD, you saints
>   of His,
> And give thanks at the remembrance
>   of His holy name.
>
> —Psalm 30:4

> Sing to the LORD,
> For He has done excellent things;
> This is known in all the earth.
>   —Isaiah 12:5

- Making Music

> And the priests attended to their services; the Levites also with instruments of the music of the Lord, which King David had made to praise the Lord . . . . The priests sounded trumpets . . . while all Israel stood.
>
> —2 Chronicles 7:6

- Clapping and Shouting

> Oh, clap your hands, all you peoples!
> Shout to God with the voice of triumph!
>   —Psalm 47:1

- Leaping and Dancing

> Then David danced before the Lord with all his might; and David was wearing a linen ephod. Michal, Saul's daughter, looked through

*a window and saw King David leaping and
whirling before the LORD.*

—2 Samuel 6:14, 16

• Prostration

*This was the appearance of the likeness of
the glory of the LORD. So when I saw it, I fell
on my face.*

—Ezekiel 1:28

• Fasting, Sackcloth and Ashes

*Then I set my face toward the Lord God to
make request by prayer, with fasting, sackcloth, and ashes.*

—Daniel 9:3

In the New Testament, the positive Jewish understanding of the body's place in spirituality
was carried into the early Christian church. Paul
expressed it clearly: "I urge you, brothers, in
view of God's mercy, to offer your bodies as living sacrifices, holy and pleasing to God—this is
your spiritual act of worship" (Romans 12:1 NIV).
The whole person, body and spirit, is involved
in the offering of worship. The physical offering
is spiritual worship.

The early Christians followed a messiah who
had come not just to preach a spiritual gospel
but to show his Father's love and power by making the blind see, the deaf hear, and the lame
leap for joy. Jesus cared for and ministered to
both body and spirit. He was not a body-denying
ascetic.

Unfortunately, centuries of confusion have ex-
isted in the Church by contrasting the Greek

word *sarx* (literally "flesh") with "the spirit."
Until recently English translations of the Bible
have set "flesh" in conflict with "spirit":

> *For I know that in me (that is, in my flesh)*
> *nothing good dwells.*
>
> —Romans 7:18

> *For those who live according to the flesh set*
> *their minds on the things of the flesh, but those*
> *who live according to the Spirit, the things of the*
> *Spirit.*
>
> —Romans 8:5

> *So then, those who are in the flesh cannot*
> *please God. But you are not in the flesh but in*
> *the Spirit, if indeed the Spirit of God dwells in*
> *you.*
>
> —Romans 8:8–9

However, by *sarx* Paul did not mean "the physical body." A more accurate meaning is rendered
by the NIV translation: "the sinful nature." What
conflicts with the spirit is not the body but our
sinful, selfish, disobedient human nature that
repeatedly turns its back on God.

Using the Body in Prayer and Worship

With the basics of a biblical foundation we can
now explore a range of ideas and suggestions
for putting all this into practice. Many ways for
using the body in prayer and worship have been
noted above, and these may be put into practice
either individually or in group settings, in
homes or churches.

One of the ways we have not discussed is using the body silently. Psalm 46:10 tells us to "be still, and know that I am God." Using the body in prayer and worship, then, does not necessarily mean making movement and noise. An excellent piece of advice comes from St. Francis de Sales: "Half an hour's listening is essential except when you are very busy. Then a full hour is needed."

To use the body silently, one needs to be quiet and relaxed, and yet alert. If you have difficulty relaxing, lie down on the floor on your back and take several minutes to relax your leg and arm muscles. One way to accomplish this may be to tighten each one for several seconds and then release it. And to remain alert, simply do not try this when you are tired.

Keep your breathing even and gentle. Posture is important also, especially if you are going to be in prayer for a long time. A prayer stool, which is used when kneeling, may be helpful. A prayer stool is easy to make. All you need is a strong smooth plank about eighteen inches long and four inches wide. It needs to be supported at each end about five inches off the floor (like a mini-bench). Kneel down and place the stool behind you so that it arches across your ankles. When you rest back on the stool you are in a kneeling posture. This is a good position for remaining alert and relaxed for extended periods. And if you place a cushion on it, it's even more comfortable.

At times it may be helpful to use postures to

express certain feelings. You could kneel to express penitence, dance or leap to express joy, or cup your hands together and lift them upward to express giving or receiving from God. Sometimes postures can be useful for changing one's feelings. For example, if I know that I should repent of something but do not want to, I make myself kneel in a crouched-up position, which gradually works to help me feel more penitent. If I want to praise God but am feeling fed up or depressed, I move around with my arms and head raised and I try to sing. It seems as if these deliberate physical acts of obedience are part of what it means to offer my body as a living sacrifice, and God seems to honor it.

When it comes to leaping, dancing, and shouting, you may feel self-conscious and a little silly at first, especially in a group. Yet if you persevere in this it can become quite liberating. In an earlier chapter we noted Jesus' command to become like children. Now children certainly know how to express joy, excitement, love, and other emotions physically! Or think of people watching their favorite sport's event. Should we adults, then, not have moments when we get similarly excited about our awesome God?

And then there are those Christians who have been given the spiritual gift of speaking in tongues, and who find it a blessed way to pray or worship. It seems to help them focus their concentration on God. Praying or worshipping in tongues is not an uncontrollable ecstatic utterance. It is simply speaking to God in a language given by the Holy Spirit that the Christian does not understand.

Discovering that the physical body can be an asset to spirituality is one thing; applying this knowledge is a lifetime task. This chapter has been meant to get the reader started. Try out some of the things you have discovered above, or take time with the exercises that follow here. In trying things out you will discover what suits you. And you will be creating contexts for fresh experiences with God through Jesus Christ.

TAKE SEVEN DAYS . . .

That God, all Spirit, should have such an affection, such a love to this body, this earthly body, this deserves wonder. The Father was pleased to breathe into this body, at first, in the Creation; the Son was pleased to assume this body himself, after, in the Redemption; the Holy Ghost is pleased to consecrate this body, and make it His temple, by His sanctification.

—John Donne

DAY 1: *Using Sight and Smell*

▶ *Activity*

We generally take our sight for granted, but what would it be like to be blind? One way to appreciate thanking God for eyesight is first to take several minutes walking around with eyes shut tight. Afterward, think about how all of your daily activities would be affected if you were blind.

Now take time to thank God for being able to see. And if you know someone who has very poor eyesight or who is blind, take some time to pray for him or her.

Another way to use eyesight in prayer is to look thoughtfully at an object that represents the thing for which you are praying. This may give you some additional insight for praying. For example, by setting a small leafy branch from a tree in front of you, you may be able to pray with more concentration about the injustices surrounding the wanton destruction of the world's rain forests. Or, if you have a map of the city or country to look at as you prayed for a missionary friend there, you might find new ideas by which to pray for that area.

Have you ever been on a sniffing expedition? People who live or work in crowded cities may take issue with that! But the idea is not only about pleasant smells. It is simply to regain a consciousness of the things that are there to be smelled. This can be as easy as walking around the house to concentrate on how many things you can smell. After you have rediscovered odors and scents, take time to thank God for the sense of smell.

If you want a real challenge, go to a local rubbish dump; walk through it, seeing and smelling what has been broken and rejected and become unusable. Later, take time to pray about situations in which people have been abused, or even used up and "trashed." Pray for the "human rejects" and those who are wasting their lives. God, remember, has a special place in his heart for outcasts.

▶ *Hymn*

OPEN MY EYES THAT I MAY SEE

Open my eyes that I may see ·
Glimpses of truth Thou hast for me·

Place in my hands the wonderful key
That shall unclasp, and set me free:
Silently now I wait for Thee,
Ready, my God, Thy will to see;
Open my eyes, illumine me, Spirit divine!

Open my ears that I may hear
Voices of truth Thou sendest clear;
And while the wave-notes fall on my ear,
Everything false will disappear:
Silently now I wait for Thee,
Ready, my God, Thy will to see;
Open my ears, illumine me, Spirit divine!

Open my mouth and let me bear
Gladly the warm truth everywhere;
Open my heart, and let me prepare
Love with Thy children thus to share:
Silently now I wait for Thee,
Ready, my God, Thy will to see;
Open my heart, illumine me, Spirit divine!
—Clara H. Scott

DAY 2: *Using Touch and Taste*

▶ *Activity*

The object here is to become more conscious of the amazing sensitivity of your skin. Try feeling things with your eyes closed, exploring the different textures of cloth, fruit, walls, feathers, metal, and so on. The next time you hold hands with the two persons on either side of you during a prayer meeting, notice the differences of their skins' surfaces. What does that tell you about each person? How could such knowledge be used in prayer?

Holding the hand or hugging a bereaved or lonely person will probably comfort him much more than words could do. And rubbing a tense person's shoulders or back may bring much more relief from tension or stress than prayer could do. This is love in action. Is that an unspiritual thing to do?

The next time you have a family meal or a "love feast" at church, ask the participants not to take for granted the various tastes of the meal. Then take time afterward to thank God as a group for all the foods that are available, which he has provided.

Eating together is an ancient biblical expression of shared faith. Here is an idea for your prayer group. Arrange one meeting in which each person brings an item of food that reveals or expresses something about him or her. Someone may bring a fast-food meal to represent that his life is too fast-paced. Another person may bring a prepared dish to share about her cultural background. After people have shared and the meal has been eaten, use the remainder of the fellowship to pray for any special reasons or needs that have arisen out of the sharing.

For example, one person may have brought home-made soup because she is dieting. She could share why she is dieting. Perhaps it's due to a doctor's advice. If so, the group could pray for her health. Another person may not have eaten any of the desserts because she is diabetic, and this could be a matter for prayer. The person who brought the fast-food meal may not realize the extreme amounts of cholesterol or fats that he is dumping into his system. A person in the group who has medical knowledge could describe the problems here (for the entire group). The one who brought a cultural dish may need prayer about her family's resistance to Christianity. Your group will discover many ways to share, discuss, and pray.

DAY **3**: *"Sensing" the Lord's Prayer*

▶ *Activity*

This is a simple exercise in which you will add movements to phrases of The Lord's Prayer to express some meaning behind the truths. And during each movement you will pause briefly to consider each truth represented. You may think of your own ways to do this, and it can be done with other prayers as well. The following are suggestions to get you going. A phrase will be cited first and then the suggested movement and meditation.

- *Our Father in heaven*
  Head bowed and palms together, then slowly raise both (and your attention) to God. Recall that this is where the Father is and that Jesus is at his right hand.

- *Hallowed be Your name*
  Spread your arms out in front of you to indicate your openness to God. Think about his holiness and about how much of your life you have opened to it.

- *Your kingdom come*
  Lower your arms to waist level. Take a minute to pray about God's rule in your life.

- *Your will be done*
  Make fists and raise your arms extended at your sides. Think of one way in which the world is closed to God's rule.

- *On earth as it is in heaven*
  Open both fists and turn one palm toward heaven and one toward earth. Pray for God's will to come from heaven into the earth in the area where you have noted that it is closed.

- *Give us day by day our daily bread*
  Bring hands slowly together and cup them palms up at your waist. Tell God you are willing to receive on a regular basis whatever he has for you.

- *And forgive us our sins*
  Bow your head and cover your face with both hands. This represents shame and penitence. If there is an area of your life that needs confession, take time for it here.

- *For we also forgive everyone who is indebted to us*
  Rest your arms at your sides. Is there anyone you need to forgive? If so, while you forgive them in your heart, lift both hands out in front of you to represent the offering and giving of your forgiveness to the person.

- *And do not lead us into temptation*
  Stretch one of your arms across your face, palm outward, in a defensive gesture. Stretch the other arm out at your side, raising your palm up to God. Ask him to lead you swiftly away from any temptation you may be facing.

- *But deliver us from the evil one*
  Close this prayer activity by using your arms in front of you to make a cross. Have your palms fully open. Look at the palm that is pointed upward, and then at the palm that is pointed horizontally. Thank God that Christ came down from heaven to deliver us from evil by the Cross.

▶ *Hymn*

SWEET HOUR OF PRAYER

Sweet hour of prayer, sweet hour of prayer,
That calls me from a world of care,
And bids me at my Father's throne,

Make all my wants and wishes known!
In seasons of distress and grief,
My soul has often found relief,
And oft escaped the tempter's snare
By thy return, sweet hour of prayer.

Sweet hour of prayer, sweet hour of prayer,
The joys I feel, the bliss I share
Of those whose anxious spirits burn
With strong desires for thy return!
With such I hasten to the place
Where God my Saviour shows His face,
And gladly take my station there,
And wait for thee, sweet hour of prayer.

Sweet hour of prayer, sweet hour of prayer,
Thy wings shall my petition bear
To Him, whose truth and faithfulness
Engage the waiting soul to bless:
And since He bids me seek His face,
Believe His word, and trust His grace,
I'll cast on Him my every care,
And wait for thee, sweet hour of prayer.
            —William W. Walford

DAY 4: *Taking a Prayer Walk*

▶ *Activity*

A Christian man tells the story of how he got caught in the trap of thinking he had to pray in only one way, for that was the only way God heard him. Or so he thought. He did not think he could "connect" with God apart from kneeling. Yet after several years of this, the day came when God challenged him. He began to see that he had made prayer into one "technique" that he was unwilling to live without. *What if I couldn't kneel,* he thought? His wife really experienced the presence of God during prayer walks, but he always found it boring and "dry" when he tried them.

He suddenly realized that it did not matter what his feelings were when he prayed and that God would hear his prayers however he prayed. He broke out of the habit of kneeling during prayer times and took prayer walks. This has not only freed him of being locked into a technique, but it has opened to him a whole new perspective of prayer and God.

Prayer walks can be done almost anywhere. They can be done alone or in a group. They can be done for short or extended periods of time. If they are done in a group, the group can remain together or break up into pairs or individuals who then regroup at a set time and place to discuss how they prayed and what occurred

▶ *Scripture*

In the beginning God created the heavens and the earth. The earth was without form, and void; and darkness was on the face of the deep. And the Spirit of God was hovering over the face of the waters.

Then God said, "Let there be light"; and there was light. And God saw the light, that it was good; and God divided the light from the darkness. God called the light Day, and darkness He called Night. So the evening and the morning were the first day.

Then God said, "Let there be a firmament in the midst of the waters, and let it divide the waters from the waters." Thus God made the firmament, and divided the waters which were under the firmament from the waters which were above the firmament; and it was so. And God called the firmament Heaven. So the evening and the morning were the second day.

Then God said, "Let the waters under the heavens

be gathered together into one place, and let the dry land *appear*"; and it was so. And God called the dry land *Earth*, and the gathering together of the waters He called *Seas*. And God saw that it was good.

Then God said, "Let the earth bring forth grass, the herb that *yields seed*, and the fruit tree that *yields fruit according to its kind*, whose seed is in itself, on the earth"; and it was so. And the earth brought forth grass, the herb that *yields seed according to its kind*, and the tree that *yields fruit*, whose seed is in itself according to its kind. And God saw that it was good. So the evening and the morning were the third day.

Then God said, "Let there be lights in the firmament of the heavens to divide the day from the night; and let them be for signs and seasons, and for days and years; "and let them be for lights in the firmament of the heavens to give light on the earth"; and it was so.

Then God made two great lights: the greater light to rule the day, and the lesser light to rule the night. He made the stars also. God set them in the firmament of the heavens to give light on the earth, and to rule over the day and over the night, and to divide the light from the darkness. And God saw that it was good. So the evening and the morning were the fourth day.

Then God said, "Let the waters abound with an abundance of living creatures, and let birds fly above the earth across the face of the firmament of the heavens." So God created great sea creatures and every living thing that moves, with which the water abounded, according to their kind, and every winged bird according to its kind. And God saw that it was good. And God blessed them, saying, "Be fruitful and multiply, and fill the waters in the seas, and let birds multiply on the earth." So the evening and the morning were the fifth day.

Then God said, "Let the earth bring forth the living creature according to its kind: cattle and creeping thing and beast of the earth, each according to its kind"; and it was so. And God made the beast of the earth according to its kind, cattle according to its kind, and everything that creeps on the earth according to its kind. And God saw that it was good.

Then God said, "Let Us make man in Our image, according to Our likeness; let them have dominion over the fish of the sea, over the birds of the air, and over the cattle, over all the earth and over every creeping thing that creeps on the earth." So God created man in His own image; in the image of God He created him; male and female He created them. Then God blessed them, and God said to them, "Be fruitful and multiply; fill the earth and subdue it; have dominion over the fish of the sea, over the birds of the air, and over every living thing that moves on the earth."

And God said, "See, I have given you every herb that yields seed which is on the face of all the earth, and every tree whose fruit yields seed; to you it shall be for food. Also, to every beast of the earth, to every bird of the air, and to everything that creeps on the earth, in which there is life, I have given every green herb for food"; and it was so.

Then God saw everything that He had made, and indeed it was very good. So the evening and the morning were the sixth day.

—Genesis 1:1–31

The Sunset Praise-Walk. Choose a place where you can walk outside for forty-five minutes. It doesn't matter if people are around or not. It could be a country lane, city streets, a suburban area, or just about anywhere outside.

Look at the above passage as a thematically arranged description of various aspects, dimensions, and things of

Creation. Before you begin the Sunset Praise-Walk, make a mental or written note of the things of Creation you are most likely to see, feel, or experience. On the walk you will make brief stops to thank and praise God for several things you see or experience. For example, you could spend a few moments in praise to express gladness to God about something's beauty or usefulness. You could thank him that it is so different from something you saw a few minutes earlier.

Two of the very first "things" you'll see and feel are "light" and "earth." Shortly afterward the sun will be setting and you will be in the darkness that God also created. Thank him for that, and for the transition from day to night, and why that is important, e.g. for rest and recovery. The stars and moon may now be out. It all looks so different than it did a half hour ago. This could be a metaphor that God is not static and that he changes things. What one thing have you been wanting God to change? Take a moment of praise to acknowledge that he can change it.

At another spot you may stop to feel the soil, hear a dog bark, or listen to the wind. You may even stop to talk to someone. As you walk on, thank God for creating that person and say a prayer for him or her.

When you arrive back home, re-read the above passage in a new light. You may want to record your reflections on paper. (This kind of activity can also be turned into a Sunrise Praise-Walk.)

On the walls of most Catholic churches are a series of paintings or carvings depicting the story of Good Friday. These are called "Stations of the Cross." Walking meditatively through these scenes, pausing for about five minutes at each one, can be a good devotional aid.

A prayer walk through the streets of a city should be able to trigger several areas for prayer that you may never have considered. A prayer walk through the countryside or considered. A prayer walk through the countryside or wooded area should be able to provide you with interesting and fresh ways of appreciating God at work in nature. It may spark you to pray for farmers or the ecology. As Brother Lawrence suggested in his book *The Practice of the Presence of God,* God can be experienced and prayer can be made anywhere.

DAY 5: *The Bread from Heaven*

▶ *Activity*

This spiritual exercise can be done on your own or with a group. You will need coarse brown bread or rolls and a Bible. Time permitting, bake your own as part of the meditation.

As you read through John 6:22–59, take time to look at that coarse bread in your hands. Really feel it and smell it as you read through the passage.

> *On the following day, when the people who were standing on the other side of the sea saw that there was no other boat there, except that one which His disciples had entered, and that Jesus had not entered the boat with His disciples, but His disciples had gone away alone—however, other boats came from Tiberias, near the place where they ate bread after the Lord had given thanks—when the people therefore saw that Jesus was not there, nor His disciples, they also got into boats and came to Capernaum, seeking Jesus.*
>
> *And when they found Him on the other side of the sea, they said to Him, "Rabbi, when did You come here?"*
>
> *Jesus answered them and said, "Most assuredly, I*

say to you, you seek Me, not because you saw the signs, but because you ate of the loaves and were filled. Do not labor for the food which perishes, but for the food which endures to everlasting life, which the Son of Man will give you, because God the Father has set His seal on Him."

Then they said to Him, "What shall we do, that we may work the works of God?"

Jesus answered and said to them, "This is the work of God, that you believe in Him whom He sent."

Therefore they said to Him, "What sign will You perform then, that we may see it and believe You? What work will You do? Our fathers ate the manna in the desert; and it is written, 'He gave them bread from heaven to eat.'"

Then Jesus said to them, "Most assuredly, I say to you, Moses did not give you the bread from heaven, but My Father gives you the true bread from heaven. For the bread of God is He who comes down from heaven and gives life to the world."

Then they said to Him, "Lord give us this bread always."

And Jesus said to them, "I am the bread of life, He who comes to Me shall never hunger, and he who believes in Me shall never thirst. But I said to you that you have seen Me and yet do not believe.

"All that the Father gives Me will come to Me, and the one who comes to Me I will by no means cast out. For I have come down from heaven, not to do My own will, but the will of Him who sent Me.

"This is the will of the Father who sent Me, that of all He has given Me I should lose nothing, but should raise it up at the last day. And this is the will of Him who sent Me, that everyone who sees the Son and

believes in Him may have everlasting life; and I will raise him up at the last day."

The Jews then complained about Him, because He said, "I am the bread which came down from heaven." And they said, "Is not this Jesus, the son of Joseph, whose father and mother we know? How is it then that He says, 'I have come down from heaven'?"

Jesus therefore answered and said to them, "Do not murmur among yourselves. No one can come to Me unless the Father who sent Me draws him; and I will raise him up at the last day. It is written in the prophets, 'And they shall all be taught by God.' Therefore everyone who has heard and learned from the Father comes to Me. Not that anyone has seen the Father, except He who is from God; He has seen the Father.

"Most assuredly, I say to you, he who believes in Me has everlasting life. I am the bread of life. Your fathers ate the manna in the wilderness, and are dead. This is the bread which comes down from heaven, that one may eat of it and not die. I am the living bread which came down from heaven. If anyone eats of this bread, he will live forever; and the bread that I shall give is My flesh, which I shall give for the life of the world."

The Jews therefore quarreled among themselves, saying "How can this Man give us His flesh to eat?"

Then Jesus said to them, "Most assuredly, I say to you, unless you eat the flesh of the Son of Man and drink His blood, you have no life in you. Whoever eats My flesh and drinks My blood has eternal life, and I will raise him up at the last day. For My flesh is food indeed, and My blood is drink indeed. He who eats My flesh and drinks My blood abides in Me, and I in him. As the living Father sent Me, and I live because of the Father, so he who feeds on Me will live because of Me.

"This is the bread which came down from heaven—not as your fathers ate the manna, and are dead. He who eats this bread will live forever." These things He said in the synagogue as He taught in Capernaum.
—John 6:22–59

Now take time to reflect on verse 35: "I am the bread of life." You can gain a deeper appreciation of what it cost for Jesus to become the bread of life by thinking about what went in to making the coarse bread. For example, to have flour, grains had to be crushed and ground. Think of Christ in Gethsemane, which means "oil press." Think of him being broken on the Cross.

When thinking of yourself, recall that yeast goes into making bread. Jesus likened the leaven (yeast) in bread to false doctrine: "Then they understood that He did not tell them to beware of the leaven of bread, but of the doctrine of the Pharisees and Sadducees" (Matt. 16:12). The apostle Paul likened it to malice and wickedness: "Therefore purge out the old leaven, that you may be a new lump, since you truly are unleavened. Let us keep the feast, not with old leaven, nor with the leaven of malice and wickedness, but with the unleavened bread of sincerity and truth," (1 Corinthians 5:7–8). These are strong words from both our Lord and Paul. Take time to consider if there is any way in which they apply to you.

Salt is also used in the making of this coarse bread. Jesus tells us that we "are the salt of the earth; but if the salt loses its flavor, how shall it be seasoned? It is then good for nothing but to be thrown out and trampled underfoot by men" (Matt. 5:13). More strong words. Are you seasoning those around you with your words and lifestyle?

And dough has to be kneaded. How does God pummel you into shape? Do you know that this is to help you grow spiritually, to remove spiritual flab or stodginess?

To conclude this activity, take time to break the bread,

and to chew and eat it. Read verse thirty-five while you are doing this, and ask God to help you become life to others.

▶ *Hymn*

BREAK THOU THE BREAD OF LIFE

Break Thou the bread of life,
Dear Lord, to me,
As Thou didst break the loaves
Beside the sea;
Beyond the sacred page
I seek Thee, Lord,
My spirit pants for Thee,
O living Word.

Bless Thou the truth, dear Lord,
To me, to me,
As Thou didst bless the bread
By Galilee;
Then shall all bondage cease,
All fetters fall;
And I shall find my peace,
My All in all.

Thou art the bread of life,
O Lord, to me,
Thy holy Word the truth
That saveth me;
Give me to eat and live
With Thee above;
Teach me to love Thy truth,
For Thou art love.

O send Thy Spirit, Lord,
Now unto me,
That He may touch my eyes
And make me see:

Show me the truth concealed
Within Thy Word,
And in Thy Book revealed
I see the Lord.
—Mary A. Lathbury and Alexander Groves

DAY **6**: *The Vinedresser*

▶ *Activity*

For this exercise you will need to find a vine, rose bush, fruit tree, or some other kind of flowering shrub. After you have carefully read John 15:1–17, look closely at the shrub or tree and try to use what you see in prayer or meditation.

"I am the true vine, and My Father is the vinedresser. Every branch in Me that does not bear fruit He takes away; and every branch that bears fruit He prunes, that it may bear more fruit. You are already clean because of the word which I have spoken to you.

"Abide in Me, and I in you. As the branch cannot bear fruit of itself, unless it abides in the vine, neither can you, unless you abide in Me. I am the vine, you are the branches. He who abides in Me, and I in him, bears much fruit; for without Me you can do nothing. If anyone does not abide in Me, he is cast out as a branch and is withered; and they gather them and throw them into the fire, and they are burned.

"If you abide in Me, and My words abide in you, you will ask what you desire, and it shall be done for you. By this My Father is glorified, that you bear much fruit; so you will be My disciples.

"As the Father loved Me, I also have loved you; abide in My love. If you keep My commandments, you will abide in My love, just as I have kept My Father's com-

mandments and abide in His love. These things I have spoken to you, that My joy may remain in you, and that your joy may be full.

"This is My commandment, that you love one another as I have loved you. Greater love has no one than this, than to lay down one's life for his friends. You are My friends if you do whatever I command you.

"No longer do I call you servants, for a servant does not know what his master is doing; but I have called you friends, for all things that I heard from My Father I have made known to you.

"You did not choose Me, but I chose you and appointed you that you should go and bear fruit, and that your fruit should remain, that whatever you ask the Father in My name He may give you. These things I command you, that you love one another.

—John 15:1–17

Do you see any dead wood? Touch it. Break it off. Notice how brittle it is. Is there any "dead wood" in your life that God needs to prune? If so, take time in prayer about this, reflecting on verses 1–3.

Look also at the flowering parts. How much fruit do you think God sees in your life? Is it small and undeveloped? Is it fresh and well-kept? Is it starting to rot or wither due to misuse or lack of use? Take time in prayer.

Recite verse five several times and especially consider the phrase "without Me you can do nothing." Ask yourself how fully you believe this. There may be a relation between that and the bearing of fruit which remains, according to verse sixteen. Maybe the soil of your believing is not as full of faith as you thought. Look at and feel the soil in which the shrub in planted. It's probably moist and mulched and filled with everything suitable for full growth. Close this prayer time by recommitting your life to God in this vital area.

▶ *Hymn*

I AM THE VINE

"I am the vine and ye are the branches,"
Bear precious fruit for Jesus today;
Branches in Him no fruit ever bearing,
Jesus hath said, "He taketh away."

"I am the vine and ye are the branches;
I am the vine, be faithful and true;
Ask what ye will, your prayer shall be granted,
The Father loved me, so I have loved you."

"Now ye are clean through words I have spoken,
Living in Me, much fruit ye shall bear;
Dwelling in you, My promise unbroken,
Glory in heaven with Me ye shall share."

Yes, by your fruits the world is to know you,
Walking in love as children of day;
Follow your Guide, He passeth before you,
Leading to realms of glorious day.
—Knowles Shaw

DAY 7: *Go Enjoy Something*

▶ *Activity*

First Timothy 6:17 says, "Trust . . . in the living God, who gives us richly all things to enjoy." Go enjoy something. And *thank God for it.* It's simple, and it's spiritual.

▶ *Hymn*

LET EVERY HEART REJOICE AND SING

Let every heart rejoice and sing,
Let choral anthems rise;

Ye aged men, and children, bring
To God your sacrifice.

For He is good, the Lord is good,
And kind are all His ways;
With songs and honors sounding loud,
The Lord Jehovah praise.
While the rocks and the rills,
While the vales and the hills,
A glorious anthem raise;
Let each prolong the grateful song,
And the God of our fathers praise,
And the God of our fathers praise.

He bids the sun to rise and set;
In heaven His power is known;
And earth subdued to Him, shall yet
Bow low before His throne.
                        —Henry S. Washburne

— 8 —

Deeper into Scripture

———— ◆ ————

Throughout this book we have been getting acquainted with various ways to use the Bible for spiritual growth. This chapter takes us a little deeper into the exploration to see if we can learn ways to get even more out of the Bible, and so discover more of God in our growth.

Four Ways to Handle the Bible

We will be looking chiefly at meditation and contemplation, but it may be helpful to begin by noting these in comparison to Bible study and biblical criticism.

- Bible study is what it says. You study the text of the Bible as it stands in order to discover what it says about an event, a word, a person, a subject, a doctrine, and so forth. You use various helps: reference Bibles, Bible dictionaries, concordances, and commentaries. This task leads to greater understanding and often to action.

- Biblical criticism (it need not be destructive!) means going behind the text to ask questions. How did it come about? What happened at Jericho and Ai? What is the relationship between the Kings and Chronicles? We can look for the original reading and meaning of the Greek and Hebrew text by using the literary, theological, archaeological, and linguistic skills of detailed articles in journals, commentaries, and scholarly books.

- Meditation, like Bible study, begins with the text as it is, taking it as the word of God, and then we seek prayerfully and consciously to be shaped and molded by it. Although meditation and Bible study are different, we cannot make too sharp a distinction; the one flows naturally into the other. Meditation helps the Bible to get "under your skin" so that you can live, breathe, and feel God better, and so mature with greater assurance.

- Contemplation is much more a steady, or fixed, and deliberate looking to God in Jesus Christ. It has set aside questions and debate for vision, praise, adoration, and self-giving. It is the look of love. And just as Bible study can flow naturally into meditation, so meditation can flow naturally into contemplation.

We need to use the Bible in a variety of ways. We need the approach of study and criticism, but we need to meditate and contemplate on the wonder of God too. If we're all meditation and no study we may lose the historical and objective realities of the Bible and drift into a make-believe world. If we're all study and no meditation we may be merely dry academics who have little intimacy with the Lord who inspired the text. According to our Lord, some people fall prey to this:

> You search the Scriptures, for in them you think you have eternal life; and these are they which testify of Me. But you are not willing to come to me that you may have life.
> —John 5:39–40

Applying Each Method

Let's look at the variety and balance needed when using the Bible by seeing how four different sets of eyes might view Mark 14:1–11. This is the story of the woman who anointed Jesus' head with expensive perfumed ointment.

- The Bible student will place the story in its context of the last week of Jesus' life, noting the preparation for Jesus' burial, the expensiveness of the ointment, and the comments of the disciples. This is the stance of the cameraman, who notes every detail of the scene.

- The biblical critic will want to know about the relationship between the different gospel accounts. He will compare Mark 14, Luke 7, and John 12. He will ask who the woman was and where the event took place. He will look for nuances in the accounts. Here is the investigative reporter.

- The meditator uses imagination more creatively to enter into the story and identify with the woman's sacrificial devotion, or the disciples' resentment, or Jesus' appreciation, or the whole interlock of relationships. Our role is reflective. We are like artists.

- The person who contemplates will identify with the woman of whom Mark writes and lavish all of herself on Jesus Christ with extravagant love. This is a worshipper.

Meditation and Contemplation

Here are several contexts in which Christians find it helpful in their spiritual growth to practice meditation or contemplation.

Liturgy

Much church liturgy, such as the form of words used in certain prayers, can be a scriptural meditation. We can learn to savor and appreciate the prayers and open ourselves to its depths of meaning. Using liturgy as a basis for meditating on Scripture has a long history. Tradition has it that St. Augustine and St. Ambrose composed the *Te Deum* ("You are God and we praise you. You are the Lord and we acclaim you . . .") under the inspiration of the Holy Spirit and from their store of memorized Scripture—over 1600 years ago!

We've Got Rhythm!

Repeating Scripture rhythmically is a way both to memorize and reflect on a subject. Monks and nuns did this in times past as they walked their cloisters. The practice was known as "rumination," from the same root as our word "ruminating," meaning both "to chew the cud" and "to meditate." Now you don't need a cloister to walk around! Just take a single verse or a few words to mull over.

Singing

Many of the new songs and choruses that have entered church life in the last several years are, like much liturgy, close to, or even straight from, Scripture. When you've got a scriptural song or chorus in your head it can be a perfect opportunity for meditation. But in your enthusiasm for new music, don't forget that poets and hymn writers have been doing this for centuries, for millennia. Don't cut yourself off from the scriptural hymns of past ages.

Write It Down

Writing Scripture can help us, as does the previous approach, to take it in slowly, meditatively, and so get more out of each word, phrase, or sentence. Try a psalm to see how this works. If you have skill in calligraphy (literally "beautiful writing") you may be able to produce something for display. The process of producing it will allow you to meditate on the text.

Picture It

The Bible contains many word-pictures, and sometimes our meditation on a text can be aided by pictures or scenes themselves. This can work two ways. We may be struck by a picture or scene and link it with a Bible passage, or we may start with the Bible and find a picture or scene to embellish it.

If you see a postcard or picture that moves you, take a minute or two to consider what aspects of it are touching. Then see if you can let the picture lead you into a reflection on a particular biblical passage. For instance, a news item about a disaster at sea may bring to your mind the story of Jesus in the boat with the disciples during the storm. The sight of a funeral may remind you of the story of Lazarus. A homeless person may remind you of Jesus saying that he had nowhere to lay his head.

Recurring Symbols

Keep an eye open for the many repeated "everyday symbols" in the Bible. Rivers, trees, stones, fire, bread, huge buildings, tiny rooms, the kitchen, shoes, clothes, and others can help you build up a rich canvas of meditational insights on the basis of a few simple items.

You could keep a notebook for listing all the different contexts in which each word appears and what part it plays in the event or situation. After you get several references to one word, you would then become aware of the different nuances, characteristics, or features of the "thing." A concordance is quite handy if you find a favorite word you want to meditate on. There is much more to be gleaned from the everyday symbols of Scripture than may at first be thought.

Adults Only?

Meditation sounds like a very "grown–up" activity. But remember God's command to Israelite parents:

> These commandments that I give you today are to be upon your hearts. Impress them on your children. Talk about them when you sit at home. . . .
>
> —Deuteronomy 6:6–7 NIV

Children as young as three can begin to learn Scripture, and enjoy it! They can dwell on it long before they know what "meditate" means. Often, of course, it's children who teach adults: "From the lips of children and infants you have ordained praise" (Psalm 8:2). Here are a several suggestions for helping "impress" Scripture on children:

- Take one verse and learn it with the child phrase by phrase. It could be selected to coincide with the church season or a family situation.
- When you discuss what it means, listen to the child's wisdom.
- Make up a simple tune with the words. Singing the verse will help make an "impression."
- Write out the verse in pencil so that the child can go over the lettering with felt pens or draw borders or pictures to illustrate the text. (Older children, of course, will not need as much help.)

The key to meditation or contemplation, whether we are on our own or in a group, whether we're nine or ninety years old, is that it is a discipline which is developed by practice. Find out what suits you and try to stick with it. Grow into it and with it. And try not to limit yourself to only one way or you may get stuck in a rut.

We often think we have to have lots of time in order to meditate. This can be a matter of temperament. Some people do take longer to prepare themselves for prayer and meditation, where others can quickly jump in. Meditation, however, is more a matter of quality than quantity. Even a busy mother can keep a Bible open in the kitchen to select a verse and return to it occasionally during the day. As we reflect on a few passages, phrases, or verses, they will eventually shape our waking, sleeping, living, thinking, and feeling.

Somehow we must find a way of remembering God that will actually last through the day. We need a kind of "memory" of God hour by hour that will influence our hearts and our most unpremediated and spontaneous activities and behavior. This is what meditation is supposed to achieve. It is not primarily a matter of spending a certain period of time every now and then having beautiful thoughts. It is about building up a Christian memory that will aid our personal development instinctively. Building up a Christian memory like this will take time. It is a big mistake to look always for immediate results. But in time, a Christian memory like this will greatly help us deal with the road ahead. Meditation can be seen as a kind of rehearsal for the unknown future, and the more diverse the material one has stored away, the better prepared one will be.

The Old Testament is just as rich for imaginative meditation as the New. During a desperate period of financial shortage when ends didn't meet for months, I found the book of Deuteronomy the very food of life as I walked with the Israelites in the desert, feeling with them the scorching heat and the sand between my toes, seeing the unending horizon in the heat haze. I knew the fear of perhaps never getting out alive. I was aware of the lurking dangers of scorpions and snakes, sensing the cracking throat of desperate thirst and the misery of having left behind enjoyable food and comforts. Then God's promises and basic provisions impressed themselves deeply upon me and the Presence stood with me in my kitchen like the pillar of cloud and fire. Outwardly, circumstances didn't change; but inwardly I did.

Meditation is more than acquiring knowledge. It is the forming of a mentality.

TAKE SEVEN DAYS . . .

DAY 1: *Meditation with Short Biblical Books*

▶ *Idea*

Short books of the Bible lend themselves to being reread several times. For example, if you take one month, you could read a short book many times from beginning to end to subconsciously absorb all of its ins and outs. Or you could spend extended periods of time with individual verses, consciously immersing yourself in them. And the way to begin would be to use a reference Bible or commentary to discover the book's main and sub-themes, the purpose of the book, where it was written from and to whom, and so forth.

Here is an approach from the book of First Peter to offer some ideas for getting into any short book.

• *Discover the purpose.*
    It is generally recognized that First Peter was written to scattered groups of Christians who probably were fairly new to the faith.

- *Themes.*

  Peter instructed these Christians in the practicalities of living the faith. He also warned them how to deal with suffering and trials.

- *Tracing.*

  As you read through the book the first time, make a note of recurring themes, for example, suffering, salvation, submission, hope, and behavior. In subsequent readings, trace each theme, even backwards.

- *Follow-up themes.*

  As you're tracing themes, one or two may strike you as especially relevant. Remember, you're not in a hurry, here, to see how fast you can get things done. So if a theme "hits" you, you will probably want to stop and take time with it. Perhaps to memorize the verse or compare it with others.

- *Write it out.*

  Some Christians find it helpful to write thematic verses out on a small card to carry around in a pocket or purse for consideration throughout the day.

- *Pray a verse.*

  Turn some verses into prayer or praise throughout the day. This is a good way to let the truth of it sink in to become more instinctive.

- *Express feelings.*

  Some people might find that 2:13 or 3:1 makes them angry or frustrated! "Therefore submit yourselves to every ordinance of man for the Lord's sake, whether to the king as supreme." "Wives, likewise, *be* submissive to your own husbands, that even if some do not obey the word, they, without a word, may be won by the conduct of their wives." Others might get excited over 1:23: "having been born again, not of corruptible seed but incorruptible, through the word of God which lives and abides forever." Let God know what you are thinking and feeling about such passages. Turn the moment into prayer. Why do you feel like this? Try to explain it to God.

- *Be honest.*

Sometimes we brush past passages that we are not too sure about. This is a kind of automatic response; we tend to dismiss what we don't really "feel good" about. But here we're talking about the Bible. Maybe we are brushing off a passage because we don't really believe it. Be honest with yourself. Ask yourself if you really believe all the passages in the book. Which ones give you trouble? Take those in prayer to ask God why, and to change the way you think about them.

- *Include children.*

First Peter has verses about children. If you can include children in this meditation, make up a tune with them about these verses.

However you go about meditating on a short book, walk through it in humility of mind. Let it come on board to shape, or reshape, your life.

DAY 2: *Stressing Successive Words*

▶ *Idea*

This approach to absorbing Scripture moves the stress, or accent, from word to word throughout a verse. This can assist you in exploring a meaning more deeply, either with familiar passages or with those that don't really "speak" to you.

Here is a way into a familiar verse to help it become fresh again. It will offer several principles to use on any verse wherein you want to shift the accent of words.

Matthew 11:28:

Come to me . . . I will give you rest.

Come—the simple invitation; am I resisting?

To—the direction toward which someone is calling.

Me—it turns out to be Jesus calling; he is the object of the invitation.

I—a reaffirmation of who is calling; and *who* is calling?

Will—intention and certainty, which implies capacity and ability.

Give—you are going to be made a present of something.

You—being singled out; what do you think about that?

Rest—the provision disclosed; relief, freedom, peace is waiting.

While stressing each word, meditate for a minute or two on each idea represented. The phrase that has been chosen out of Matthew 11:28 makes a complete thought. How does that thought move you? What kind of rest do you desire, mental, physical, emotional? Close the exercise, whether with this one or those of your own choosing, with a prayer to wrap up the meditation with a personal appeal to God.

▶ *Hymn*

JESUS WILL GIVE YOU REST

Will you come, will you come, with your poor broken heart,
Burdened and sin oppressed?
Lay it down at the feet of your Savior and Lord,
Jesus will give you rest.

> *O happy rest, sweet, happy rest!*
> *Jesus will give you rest;*
> *O why don't you come in simple, trusting faith?*
> *Jesus will give you rest.*
>
> *Will you come, will you come? there is mercy for you,*
> *Balm for your aching breast;*
> *Only come as you are, and believe on His name,*
> *Jesus will give you rest.*
>
> *Will you come, will you come? you have nothing to pay;*
> *Jesus, who loves you best, . . .*
> *By His death on the cross purchased life for your soul,*
> *Jesus will give you rest.*
>
> *Will you come, will you come? how He pleads with you now!*
> *Fly to His loving breast,*
> *And whatever your sin or your sorrow may be,*
> *Jesus will give you rest.*
> —Fanny J. Crosby

DAY 3: *Imaginative Study*

▶ Idea

This meditative exercise is a kind of role play that allows you to enter imaginatively into a biblical event. You should read what a reference Bible or commentary has to say about the scene first, before doing the exercise. This will give you many more ideas about the context and the characters. Here is an imaginative use of Deuteronomy Chapter 8 to get you started.

- You're back in time several thousand years as part of the Israelite multitude which is about to enter the fertile promised land of Canaan. Your wilderness experience is ending. But it is important to remember where you have come from and where you are going, and *why:* Because of the LORD God.

- What do you look like? How are you dressed?

- What role do you want to play? Are you single or married? Do you have children? What is your role, or position, in this great congregation of God's chosen people?

- Now read through the passage as if you were listening to Moses.

- Go back over the passage to highlight the verses that seemed especially relevant to you. There are many key truths, such as obedience, humility, provision, and discipline. Do any of these relate to you today as a member of your church?

- The wilderness was a terrible place (v. 15). Can you imagine it? Better still, can you imagine God's provision even in such a place? How does God provide for you?

- If you want to do this with several friends, you could at this point discuss among yourselves what it feels like to be living in the ancient past and to have God provide for you. He certainly wouldn't provide you with a car or a computer! Yet what would he have provided? Banter such ideas around the group.

Close the exercise by returning in your mind to the present, and then thank God for your life today and all his provisions. Pray, too, about any other ideas or concerns that have arisen due to your meditation.

DAY 4: *Thematic Study*

▶ *Idea*

In this exercise you would use a concordance to build up a series of verses on a chosen theme. Think of a theme that would be relevant to your life. You could take a time of Bible study on, say, day one, to look up the verses that contain the words of your theme and then to write each one in a notebook.

Beginning on day two, you could start with a meditation and prayer about each verse. Note how the words are used in various contexts, especially the ones that apply to your situation. Look at the surrounding verses to see how they increase your understanding of the chosen theme. You may want to stay with a single line or two, perhaps memorize it, to help digest it and make it your own.

Here are a few verses on the theme of "trust," in which an objective was to find one word to conceptualize the truth of the verse and write it alongside in the notebook.

> *Though He slay me, yet will I trust Him.*
> —Job 13:15

KEY CONCEPT: SELF-SACRIFICE.

> *Those who trust in the LORD*
> *Are like Mount Zion,*
> *Which cannot be moved, but abides forever.*
> —Psalm 125:1

KEY CONCEPT: STABILITY.

> *Trust in the LORD with all your heart,*
> *Do not lean on your own understanding.*
> —Proverbs 3:5

KEY CONCEPT: COMPLETE (TRUST).

This is what the Sovereign LORD, the
Holy One of Israel, says,
"In repentance and rest is your salvation,
in quietness and trust is your strength."
—Isaiah 30:15

KEY CONCEPT: RESTFUL (TRUST).

Blessed is the man who trusts in the LORD,
And whose hope is on the LORD.
For he shall be like a tree planted by the
waters.
—Jeremiah 17:7–8

KEY CONCEPT: NOURISHED.

From word, to phrase, to verse, to context, to key point for you, seek understanding from God as to how it applies. In the case of "trust," can I affirm I am trusting as deeply as Job? Do I feel the stability of trust? How does it nourish me? Take some time for confession and prayer where necessary. If you do several of these kinds of exercises over the course of a few months, you are well on your way to building up a Christian memory.

▶ *Hymn*

TAKE MY LIFE AND LET IT BE

Take my life and let it be
Consecrated, Lord, to Thee;
Take my moments and my days
Let them flow in ceaseless praise,
Let them flow in ceaseless praise.

Take my hands and let them move
At the impulse of Thy love;
Take my feet and let them be
Swift and beautiful for Thee,
Swift and beautiful for Thee.

Take my voice and let me sing
Always, only, for my King;
Take my lips and let them be
Filled with messages from Thee,
Filled with messages from Thee.

Take my silver and my gold—
Not a mite would I withhold;
Take my intellect and use
Every power as Thou shalt choose,
Every power as Thou shalt choose.

Take my will and make it Thine
It shall be no longer mine;
Take my heart—it is Thine own,
It shall be Thy royal throne,
It shall be Thy royal throne.

Take my love—my Lord, I pour
At Thy feet its treasure store;
Take myself—and I will be
Ever, only, all for Thee,
Ever, only, all for Thee.
—Frances Ridley Havergal

DAY 5: *That's Greek to Me?*

▶ *Idea*

Parts of the Old Testament seem irrelevant or incomprehensible to modern Christians. And, yet, perhaps there is a creative way to discover some gems for today. What sections of the Old Testament seem foreign to you (besides the genealogies!)? Again, a Bible concordance and commentary are good places to start to open up these sections. Here are some thoughts about the "Tabernacle," from Exodus 26 to start you off.

- Take time to read through the chapter once.

- What would it have been like to be one of the workers building the Tabernacle? For instance, imagine making, molding, or carving those hundreds of fussy, ornate bits! But this cannot possibly have any bearing on my life, can it? Well, maybe it sheds some light on how the little details of our lives ought to serve to glorify God.

- Why is so much space given to these details? The frequent repetition of minute items such as "five curtains," "fifty loops," "double over the sixth curtain," "four cubits," "rams skins dyed red," "forty sockets of silver," and so on, what's the point for today? Perhaps as we dwell on the repetition of the little things we will catch a vision of the splendor of the entire Tabernacle. How much space and frequency is given by you to God for the small details of your life?

- Read the passages that reveal the beautiful colors, patterns and shapes of the Tabernacle. Reflect about what this would be like if it were seen in the Church by the world. There're a lot of problems, here, aren't there? Take some time to pray about these.

- If you look up related passages, you find that the Tabernacle was movable and that God dwelt in a certain area of it, the Most Holy Place. John tells us that "the Word became flesh and dwelt [tabernacled] among us" (John 1:14). Spend some time comparing between the two.

As you close the meditation, find one truth that sticks to you. In this passage that may be v. 30: "And you shall raise up the tabernacle according to its pattern which you were shown on the mount." Several times Moses repeated this to the builders. They were not to change one small detail of the plans that Moses had received from God on Mount Sinai. This was because it all foreshadowed the coming Messiah, and to alter even the smallest detail of God's plans would be to give a false picture of him. Maybe this is why God is concerned about the small details in our lives, and maybe we have several that, unfortunately, are giving a false picture of the Messiah to the world. Prayer, here, could be the start of changing that.

DAY 6: *Discovery through Symbolic Action*

▶ *Idea*

Meditative discoveries do not have to be acquired through sitting still, relaxing, closing our eyes, being quiet, and using our imaginations in a kind of "story land." Participation in a symbolic action can be just as enlightening. The Lord's Table, for example, speaks volumes to many Christians.

Here is one to try with a group (include children too). In John 13:1–17, we read about Jesus washing his disciples' feet. We've all heard that this is a lesson about Christian service, and it is. But if we take verses thirteen and sixteen as a key point, suddenly the symbolism becomes a picture of how Jesus turns the disciples' ideas about "rights" and "authority" on their heads.

> *Now before the Feast of the Passover, when Jesus knew that His hour had come that He should depart from this world to the Father, having loved His own who were in the world, He loved them to the end.*
> *And supper being ended, the devil having already put it into the heart of Judas Iscariot, Simon's son, to betray Him, Jesus, knowing that the Father had given*

all things into His hands, and that He had come from God and was going to God, rose from supper and laid aside his garments, took a towel and girded Himself.

After that, He poured water into a basin and began to wash the disciples' feet, and to wipe them with the towel with which He was girded. Then He came to Simon Peter. And Peter said to Him, "Lord, are You washing my feet?"

Jesus answered and said to him, "What I am doing you do not understand now, but you will know after this."

Peter said to Him, "You shall never wash my feet!" Jesus answered him, "If I do not wash you, you have no part with Me."

Simon Peter said to Him, "Lord, not my feet only, but also my hands and my head!"

Jesus said to him, "He who is bathed needs only to wash his feet, but is completely clean; and you are clean, but not all of you." For He knew who would betray Him; therefore He said, "You are not all clean."

So when He had washed their feet, taken His garments, and sat down again, He said to them, "Do you know what I have done to you? You call Me Teacher and Lord, and you say well, for so I am. If I then, your Lord and Teacher, have washed your feet, you also ought to wash one another's feet. For I have given you an example, that you should do as I have done to you. Most assuredly, I say to you, a servant is not greater than his master; nor is he who is sent greater than he who sent him. If you know these things, blessed are you if you do them.

—John 13:1–17

Think about Jesus' lesson as you wash each other's feet.

You'll need a sponge, or a cloth, a large pan that can

hold a few inches of water, and drying towels. Have everyone remove their shoes and socks. Split the group in half, and have each person in one half pick someone in the other half whose feet he will wash. Reverse the procedure after the first half has finished.

While the washing is taking place, have someone read aloud, slowly, through John 13:1–17. It would probably be best if everyone were fairly quiet at this point, so as to let the reading and the washing break in and stir up. Be thinking about your key in verses thirteen to sixteen. It is really about humility. And the greatest act of humility was about to take place on the Cross. Be thinking about this kind of *service.*

While the second half of the group is having its feet washed, notice the feelings, emotions, and thoughts that this foot washing is stirring up. For some, this activity will have moved far beyond mere symbolism. This symbolic act will provide many things to pray about after everyone's feet have been washed and dried.

Before you pray, however, take time to discuss among yourselves how you felt, what happened, why it affected you, and so forth. And when you do pray, make a commitment to become more like Jesus in your view of "rights" and "authority."

▶ *Hymn*

LORD, WE COME BEFORE YOU NOW

Lord, we come before Thee now;
At Thy feet we humbly bow;
O do not our suit disdain!
Shall we seek Thee, Lord, in vain?
Shall we seek Thee, Lord, in vain?

Lord, on Thee our souls depend;
In compassion now descend,
Fill our hearts with Thy rich grace,

Tune our lips to sing Thee praise,
Tune our lips to sing Thee praise.

In Thine own appointed way,
Now we seek Thee; here we stay;
Lord, we know not how to go,
Till a blessing Thou bestow,
Till a blessing Thou bestow.

Grant that all may seek and find
Thee a God supremely kind;
Heal the sick; the captive free;
Let us all rejoice in Thee,
Let us all rejoice in Thee.
—W. Hammond

DAY 7: *Contemplation*

▶ *Idea*

Many biblical passages provide contexts for contemplation and worship of God through Jesus Christ. One suggestion is to sit down with your Bible and a concordance and choose twelve such passages. You could either reference the passages on a sheet of paper that you will keep in your Bible or take time to write them out in a notebook for use. The idea is to contemplate on God once a month using one of the chosen passages. Here is one to get you going.

He has delivered us from the power of darkness and conveyed us into the kingdom of the Son of His love, in whom we have redemption through His blood, the forgiveness of sins. He is the image of the invisible God, the firstborn over all creation. For by Him all things were created that are in heaven and that are on earth, visible

*and invisible, whether thrones or dominions or princi-
palities or powers.*

*All things were created through Him and for Him.
And He is before all things, and in Him all things consist.*

*And He is the head of the body, the church, who is
the beginning, the firstborn from the dead, that in all
things He may have preeminence. For it pleased the
Father that in Him all fullness should dwell, and by Him
to reconcile all things to Himself, by Him, whether things
on earth or things in heaven, having made peace
through the blood of His cross.*

—Colossians 1:13–20

This passage gives a profound view of Jesus Christ, God
the Son. It is full of deep significance, which makes it an
excellent passage for contemplation of God. It shows that
the Son is the image of his loving Father, that Jesus Christ
is the image of the invisible God, that in him all things were
created, that he is the fullness of God, and many other wor-
shipful connotations.

Read the passage slowly a few times. Look at Jesus.
Consider just who he is. Think about what he has done. If
your attention wanders, simply catch yourself whenever
you're distracted and discipline your imagination to return
to the contemplation of God.

When you find yourself really getting into the passage,
talk to Jesus. Tell him of your love. This is not really a time
to be asking things from him; rather, to be simply sharing
your love with him, to be more deeply in his presence. Share
with him out of the above passage. Pick out ideas for which
you will thank him, such as for creating the things of earth
and heaven or for being the head of the church.

To close the contemplation, notice that this passage is
enclosed between two verses which speak of redemption.
Redemption cost God. It was a sacrifice. Now take a minute
to read Revelation 5. A Lamb, representing divine self-

sacrifice, sits on the throne of the universe, ruling. This is the God we contemplate:

And I saw in the right hand of Him who sat on the throne a scroll written inside and on the back sealed with seven seals.

Then I saw a strong angel proclaiming with a loud voice, "Who is worthy to open the scroll and to loose its seals?" And no one in heaven or on the earth or under the earth was able to open the scroll, or to look at it. So I wept much, because no one was found worthy to open the scroll, or to look at it.

But one of the elders said to me, "Do not weep. Behold, the Lion of the tribe of Judah, the Root of David, has prevailed to open the scroll and to loose its seven seals."

And I looked, and behold, in the midst of the throne and of the four living creatures, and in the midst of the elders, stood a Lamb as though it had been slain, having seven horns and seven eyes, which are the seven Spirits of God sent out into all the earth. Then He came and took the scroll out of the right hand of Him who sat on the throne.

Now when He had taken the scroll, the four living creatures and the twenty-four elders fell down before the Lamb, each having a harp, and golden bowls full of incense, which are the prayers of the saints. And they sang a new song, saying:

"You are worthy to take the scroll,
And to open its seals;
For you were slain,
And have redeemed us to God by Your blood
Out of every tribe and tongue and people and
    nation,

And have made us kings and priests to our God;
And we shall reign on the earth."

Then I looked, and I heard the voice of many angels around the throne, the living creatures, and the elders; and the number of them was ten thousand times ten thousand, and thousands of thousands, saying with a loud voice:

> *"Worthy is the Lamb who was slain*
> *To receive power and riches and wisdom,*
> *And strength and honor and glory and*
>   *blessing!"*

And every creature which is in heaven and on the earth and under the earth and such as are in the sea, and all that are in them, I heard saying:

> *'Blessing and honor and glory and power*
> *Be to Him who sits on the throne,*
> *And to the Lamb, forever and ever!"*

Then the four living creatures said, "Amen!" And the twenty-four elders fell down and worshiped Him who lives forever and ever.

—Revelation 5

▶ *Hymn*

ALL HAIL THE POWER OF JESUS' NAME

All hail the power of Jesus' name!
Let angels prostrate fall;
Bring forth the royal diadem,
And crown Him Lord of all;
Bring forth the royal diadem,
And crown Him Lord of all!

Ye chosen seed of Israel's race,
Ye ransomed from the fall,

Hail Him who saves you by His grace,
And crown Him Lord of all;
Hail Him who saves you by His grace,
And crown Him Lord of all!

Let every kindred, every tribe,
On this terrestrial ball,
To Him all majesty ascribe,
And crown Him Lord of all;
To Him all majesty ascribe,
And crown Him Lord of all!

O that with yonder sacred throng
We at His feet may fall!
We'll join the everlasting song,
And crown Him Lord of all;
We'll join the everlasting song,
And crown Him Lord of all!

—Edward Perronet

Wisdom for Living

—————◆—————

What motivates people to read books? If they are going on vacation, they may like detective thrillers so that they can pit their brains and curiosity against Sherlock Holmes or Hercule Poirot. Others may have a fascination about people and so prefer biographies. Other people may read to improve their knowledge of cooking, or cars, or classical music. In each case the motivation will be obvious.

What reason could we have for reading the Bible? Paul's second letter to Timothy provides as succinct a reason as any:

> *All Scripture is given by inspiration of God, and is profitable for doctrine, for reproof, for correction, for instruction in righteousness, that the man of God may be complete, thoroughly equipped for every good work.*
> —2 Timothy 3:16–17

We need to be sure that that is actually what we want, or Bible reading will be a chore to be got through as quickly as possible. And this may be one reason why some of us find reading the Bible difficult to get around to. Sloth, or laziness, to some extent may be another reason. Sin, too, may be a reason. D. L. Moody wrote on the flyleaf of his Bible: "This book keeps me from sin. Sin keeps me from this book."

Satan will also try to hinder us from studying the Bible. Note how he tempted our first parents in the Garden of Eden. Adam and Eve clearly understood what was permitted and what was forbidden. Yet three times the serpent challenged them concerning the veracity of God's word.

- He tempted them to *doubt* God's word: "Has God indeed said, 'You shall not eat of every tree of the garden'?" (Genesis 3:1).

- He encouraged them to *disregard* God's word: "You will not surely die" (Genesis 3:4).

- He pushed them to *disobey* God's word: "God knows that in the day you eat of it . . . you will be like God" (Genesis 3:5).

Jesus warned us in John 8:44–46 that the devil's ways do not change: "You are of your father the devil, and the desires of your father you want to do. He was a murderer from the beginning, and does not stand in the truth, because there is no truth in him. When he speaks a lie, he speaks from his own resources, for he is a liar and the father of it. But because I tell the truth, you do not believe Me. Which of you convicts Me of sin? And if I tell the truth, why do you not believe Me?" (John 8:44–46). So we can expect the devil to tempt *us* to doubt, disbelieve, and disobey. But whatever reasons we may have for not spending time with the Bible, maybe we can find some positive encouragement to help motivate us to read it.

Motivations

The passage from Second Timothy, above, is chiefly about deepening one's obedience to God as a result of being challenged by the Scripture. The thought of "obedience," however, may settle on our shoulders like an oppressive weight. Let's see if there is a way to correct that.

- Obedience brings God's blessings.

> *Blessed is the man*
> *Who walks not in the counsel of the*
> *   ungodly,*
> *Nor stands in the path of sinners,*
> *Nor sits in the seat of the scornful;*
> *But his delight is in the law of the* LORD,
> *And in His law he meditates day and*
> *   night.*
> *He shall be like a tree planted by the*
> *   rivers of water,*
> *That brings forth its fruit in its season,*
> *Whose leaf also shall not wither;*
> *And whatever he does shall prosper.*
> *   —Psalm 1:1–3*

- Obedience brings true freedom.

> *Then Jesus said to those Jews who believed*
> *in Him, "If you abide in My word, you are*
> *my disciples indeed. And you shall know the*
> *truth, and the truth shall make you free."*
> *   —John 8:31–32*

- Obedience brings assurance of salvation.

Add to your faith virtue, to virtue knowledge, to knowledge self-control, to self-control perserverance, to perseverance godliness, to godliness brotherly kindness, to brotherly kindness love. For if all these things are yours and abound, you will be neither barren nor unfruitful in the knowledge of our Lord Jesus Christ. For he who lacks these things is short-sighted, even to blindness, and has forgotten that he was cleansed from his old sins. Therefore, brethren, be even more diligent to make your call and election sure, for if you do these things you will never stumble; for so an entrance will be supplied to you abundantly into the everlasting kingdom of our Lord and Savior Jesus Christ.

—2 Peter 1:5–11

- Obedience brings happiness.

I assure you, most solemnly I tell you, a servant is not greater than his master, and no one who is sent is superior to the one who sent him. If you know these things, blessed and happy and to be envied are you if you practice them—if you act accordingly and really do them.

—John 13:16–17 AMPL

So reading the Bible for "doctrine, reproof, correction and instruction" may have more perks in it than we may have thought! And all of these benefits are part of the blessedness of spiritual growth and drawing closer to God. Yet there is one we have not mentioned: obeying the Bible is wisdom.

This has been left to be said here to prepare us for the "Take 7 Days" concept below. Some Christians think that "wisdom" is merely an intellectual "head trip." The Bible, however, teaches that "wisdom" is moral obedience to God that begins with "the fear of the Lord" (Prov. 9:10). This is the message of Proverbs in particular.

In Proverbs, one's whole person is involved. One's entire life comes under the commands of a holy and moral God. And in ancient times it was the task of Israel's wise men to articulate this to the people. This was one of the purposes of Proverbs, which was largely produced by King Solomon, who at the height of his fame was thought to be the wisest man on the planet.

And because it is God's wisdom, Proverbs, as a book of obedience and discipline, is perennially relevant. It is able to speak to every department of life, showing God's interest in them. Unlike so many modern notions of wisdom which call their disciples merely to contemplate abstract principles, the wisdom of Proverbs calls its followers to enter more deeply into moral obedience to God in concrete situations. God's wisdom, therefore, speaks to a person's attitude and behavior toward his spouse, his children, his work, his friends, his enemies, and even his table manners!

As you take time to participate in the exercises

from Proverbs below, remember that they are about wisdom for living. Obedience to God is a very large issue because it covers the entirety of one's life. The exercises below narrow this down to seven, in the hope that you will afterward be motivated to further examine other areas of your life's wisdom.

TAKE SEVEN DAYS . . .

DAY 1: *The Call and Value of Wisdom*

▶ *Scripture*

Wisdom calls aloud outside;
She raises her voice in the open squares.
She cries out in the chief concourses,
At the openings of the gates in the city
She speaks her words:
"How long, you simple ones, will you love simplicity?
For scorners delight in their scorning,
And fools hate knowledge.
Turn at my rebuke;
Surely I will pour out my spirit on you;
I will make my words known to you.
Because I have called and you refused,
I have stretched out my hand and no one regarded,
Because you disdained all my counsel,
And would have none of my rebuke,
I also will laugh at your calamity;
I will mock when your terror comes,
When your terror comes like a storm,

And your destruction comes like a whirlwind,
When distress and anguish come upon you.
"Then they will call on me, but I will not answer;
They will seek me diligently, but they will not find
    me.
Because they hated knowledge
And did not choose the fear of the LORD,
They would have none of my counsel
And despised my every rebuke.
Therefore they shall eat the fruit of their own way,
And be filled to the full with their own fancies.
For the turning away of the simple will slay them,
And the complacency of fools will destroy them;
But whoever listens to me will dwell safely,
And will be secure, without fear of evil."

My son, if you receive my words,
And treasure my commands within you,
So that you incline your ear to wisdom,
And apply your heart to understanding;
Yes, if you cry out for discernment,
And lift up your voice for understanding,
If you seek her as silver,
And search for her as for hidden treasures;
Then you will understand the fear of the LORD,
And find the knowledge of God.
For the LORD gives wisdom;
From His mouth come knowledge and
    understanding;
He stores up sound wisdom for the upright;
He is a shield to those who walk uprightly;
He guards the paths of justice,
And preserves the way of His saints.
Then you will understand righteousness and justice,
Equity and every good path.

                               —Proverbs 1:20—2:9

▶ *Wisdom Meditation and Application*

This reading introduces one to the wisdom's appeal and the reward for following her, as she stands personified in the midst of the great masses of humanity that refuse to listen to her.

As you thoughtfully read this passage, note that there are three classes of people who won't listen to wisdom: the simple ones, the scorners, and the fools (v. 22). What follows is a description of wisdom being shunned and the dire results of such disobedience.

But then there are those who are the "sons" of wisdom. They are rewarded. Yet even for them wisdom requires diligent search. Such effort, however, is more than worth it because God himself will watch over them and keep them in his will.

After considering the passage, ask yourself if there is anything of the simple one, or the scorner, or the fool in you. Their dominant sin seems to be that they had no fear of the Lord. But it is "the fear of the Lord" that brings wisdom, as Proverbs 1:29 reveals. If you are unable to admit that there is anything of the simple one, the scorner, or the fool in you, maybe you could answer how much "fear of the Lord" determines what you do each day. If someone makes you angry, do you get angry in return? Do you pilfer items from work for your own use? Are you honest about doing your income taxes? Answers to questions like these will help you evaluate how much fear of the Lord influences what you do.

▶ *Prayer*

Lord Jesus Christ, help me to receive your words and treasure your commands within me. By your grace may I notice everyday that the fear of the Lord becomes more real to me. By my obedience may my light shine so as to lead others in the way of wisdom.

DAY 2: *Choosing Friends Carefully*

▶ *Scripture*

> My son, if sinners entice you,
> Do not consent.
> If they say, "Come with us,
> Let us lie in wait to shed blood;
> Let us lurk secretly for the innocent without cause;
> Let us swallow them alive like Sheol,
> And whole, like those who go down to the Pit;
> We shall find all kinds of precious possessions,
> We shall fill our houses with spoil;
> Cast in your lot among us,
> Let us all have one purse"—
> My son, do not walk in the way with them,
> Keep your foot from their path;
> For their feet run to evil,
> And they make haste to shed blood.
> Surely, in vain the net is spread
> In the sight of any bird;
> But they lie in wait for their own blood,
> They lurk secretly for their own lives.
> So are the ways of everyone who is greedy for gain;
> It takes away the life of its owners.
>   —Proverbs 1:10–19

▶ *Wisdom Meditation and Application*

The lawless state described in Proverbs 1:10–19 seems similar to society today. Yet its emphasis on murder, theft, and plunder is probably far from the minds of most Christians, and the passage, therefore, may seem like an extreme example of being led astray by friends. What relevance, we may think, is here for us?

Yet it is the principle we are after, and the principle holds true for all of us. It is possible to be swept away by the enticement of others, to be lured to share in their ill-gotten gain. Even if this is only on a small scale, it is to be consistently refused. Jesus says to us, "Follow me," and the quality of obedience which that demands will become impossible if we let others entice us into even small degrees of ungodly compromise.

After you have read the passage, examine your life to see if any "friends" are awakening desires in you to act against God's will. They may be appealing to something in your sin nature that has lain dormant for years. Are you about to be swept into the world's way of doing things? Perhaps you've seen an employee pilfering small items from work, and now you're justifying the same behavior. Perhaps the influence of a "friend" is making you feel more comfortable around pornographic magazines. Maybe some business partners are slowly beguiling you to cut ethical corners with the promise of quick profit. Maybe you've seen how other secretaries in the office flirt with the boss to get what they want, and now you're starting to "attract" your boss the same way.

How will you answer the appeal, "Come with us, cast in your lot among us?" When you identify an area, what practical steps can you take to disengage yourself from the enticement and turn to walk in God's wisdom?

Take a piece of paper and list the people you work with and socialize with, as well as any others who may influence you. Your list may include a disapproving parent, a demanding boss, a college professor, an annoying neighbor, someone on your bowling team, an office secretary, or an unethical client.

Leave space after each name where you will describe how each person may dominate your mind like a second conscience; e.g., what is the "pull" each person exerts on you, what do you feel you should or should not be doing in his or her presence? Then evaluate which "pulls" are godly or healthy and which are not. Give thanks for the good and take time to seek wisdom for how to respond to the others.

▶ *Prayer*

Father, forgive me for being enticed into _____. I consented to ungodliness for gain, and I am sorry. Help me to no longer walk in that way. Grant the grace to apply your perfect wisdom to my life. Lead me more thoroughly in the fear of the Lord, that by my obedience, my light may shine so as to lead people around me in the way of true wisdom.

▶ *Hymn*

WHAT A FRIEND

What a Friend we have in Jesus,
All our sins and griefs to bear;
What a privilege to carry
Everything to God in prayer.
O, what peace we often forfeit,
O, what needless pain we bear,
All because we do not carry
Everything to God in prayer.

Have we trials and temptations?
Is there trouble anywhere?
We should never be discouraged,
Take it to the Lord in prayer.
Can we find a friend so faithful,
Who will all our sorrows share?
Jesus knows our every weakness:
Take it to the Lord in prayer.

Are we weak and heavy-laden,
Cumbered with a load of care?
Precious Saviour, still our refuge,

> Take it to the Lord in prayer.
> Do thy friends despise, forsake thee?
> Take it to the Lord in prayer;
> In His arms he'll take and shield thee,
> Thou wilt find a solace there.
> —George Scriven

DAY 3: *The Influence of Sexuality*

▶ *Scripture*

> My son, pay attention to my wisdom;
> Lend your ear to my understanding,
> That you may preserve discretion,
> And your lips may keep knowledge.
> For the lips of an immoral woman drip honey,
> And her mouth is smoother than oil;
> But in the end she is bitter as wormwood,
> Sharp as a two-edged sword.
> Her feet go down to death,
> Her steps lay hold of hell.
> Lest you ponder her path of life—
> Her ways are unstable;
> You do not know them.
> Therefore hear me now, my children,
> And do not depart from the words of my mouth.
> Remove your way far from her,
> And do not go near the door of her house,
> Lest you give your honor to others,
> And your years to the cruel one;
> Lest aliens be filled with your wealth,
> And your labors go to the house of a foreigner;
> And you mourn at last,
> When your flesh and your body are consumed,
> And say:

*"How I have hated instruction,
And my heart despised correction!
I have not obeyed the voice of my teachers,
Nor inclined my ear to those who instructed me!
I was on the verge of total ruin,
In the midst of the assembly and congregation."*
*Drink water from your own cistern,
And running water from your own well.
Should your fountains be dispersed abroad,
Streams of water in the streets?
Let them be only your own,
And not for strangers with you.
Let your fountain be blessed,
And rejoice with the wife of your youth.
As a loving deer and a graceful doe,
Let her breasts satisfy you at all times;
And always be enraptured with her love.
For why should you, my son, be enraptured by an
     immoral woman,
And be embraced in the arms of a seductress?
For the ways of man are before the eyes of the
     LORD,
And He ponders all his paths.
His own iniquities entrap the wicked man,
And he is caught in the cords of his sin.
He shall die for lack of instruction,
And in the greatness of his folly he shall go astray.*
                              —Proverbs 5:1–23

▶ Wisdom Meditation and Application

The theme of Proverbs 5:1–23 is God's wisdom in relations between the sexes. For our meditation here, we want to apply the principles in the often ignored area of how we may let the advertising industry mold us into its images of sexuality.

Begin this meditation by thinking of the amount of television, magazine, and other "pictorial" advertisements you take in each week. A large percentage of this will be images of sexuality, which are in back of the product being advertised. Appearing before our eyes with calculated regularity are lean, trim, and muscular males with handsomely chiseled features and svelte women without a hair out of place, at times nearly undressed.

After a time, these images have a kind of "power relationship" over the viewer, who begins to look at his wife with disdain for her figure or wrinkles; or the wife becomes repulsed because of her husband's sagging midsection or creeping baldness. The point is that we can subtly allow our relationships to be influenced by worldly sexuality, which is loaded with idolatries. When this occurs, we are letting a kind of spiritual prostitution or adultery slip into the covenant relationship we have with our spouses.

This is what is meant by the immoral (lit. "strange") woman in verse three. Her lips drip honey, and her mouth is smoother than oil. But notice that "in the end she is bitter as wormwood," (v. 4). Ask those who have associated with her to the end (immorality, adultery, divorce) if this is not so. Then ask yourself how much of an influence the sexuality of the world's wisdom influences your decisions and thoughts.

Maybe it "only" coaxes a bit too much money out of you to spend on how you look. Maybe it "only" encourages you to spend a little too much time with aerobics or playing sports or exercising. But what will the "end" be? Verses nine to eleven teach that the end will be the *loss* of worldly goods and bodily strength—the complete opposite of the promises made by worldly images of sexuality.

"I was on the verge of total ruin, in the midst of the assembly of the congregation," (v. 14). Here are the pangs of remorse. But they came too late. "In the greatness of his folly he shall go astray," (v. 23).

Be wise. It is the "little foxes that spoil the vines [of martial relationships that] have tender grapes," (Song of Sol. 2:15). In fact, it is the Song of Solomon that speaks of the intense longings, fervent desires, and intimacy one is to have only for a spouse:

> *Let him kiss me with the kisses of his mouth—*
> *For your love is better than wine.*
> *Because of the fragrance of your good ointments,*
> *Your name is ointment poured forth. . . .*
> *Draw me away*
> *The king has brought me into his chambers.*
> —Song of Solomon 1:2–4

To nourish such love, the spouse shows interest in the mate's work, seeks to please, and gives compliments:

> *Tell me, O you whom I love,*
> *Where you feed your flock,*
> *Where you make it rest at noon.*
> *While the king is at his table,*
> *My spikenard sends forth its fragrance.*
> *Behold, you are handsome, my beloved!*
> *Yes, pleasant!*
> *Also our bed is green.*
> —Song of Solomon 2:7, 12, 16

And when there is marital trouble or love falters, the spouse does not look for comfort in another lover but in the covenant mate:

> *I sought him, but I did not find him.*
> *"I will rise now," I said,*
> *"And go about the city;*
> *In the streets and in the squares*
> *I will seek the one I love."*
> —Song of Solomon 3:1–2

Here is a godly vision of marital love. We seek deep intimacy arising from faithfulness and a love that appreciates and serves the other for who he or she is—an image bearer of the Divine. What a contrast this rich, full vision is over against the thin, demanding lifestyles anchored in immoral sexuality.

▶ *Prayer*

God of my covenant relationship, help me to ponder where I get my images of sexuality. Help me to stay far away from the influential door of advertised sexuality. Keep me from despising any instruction I may need here. Grant me the grace to draw the images of what my spouse should be like from your wisdom. And may my rejoicing with my wife (husband) be a light shining to lead other couples in the way of true wisdom.

▶ *Hymn*

PURER IN HEART, O GOD

Purer in heart, O God,
Help me to be;
May I devote my life Wholly to Thee.
Watch Thou my wayward feet,
Guide me with counsel sweet;
Purer in heart, Help me to be.

Purer in heart, O God,
Help me to be;
Teach me to do Thy will Most lovingly.
Be Thou my Friend and Guide,
Let me with Thee abide;
Purer in heart, Help me to be.

Purer in heart, O God,
Help me to be;
That I Thy holy face One day may see.

Keep me from secret sin,
Reign Thou my soul within;
Purer in heart, Help me to be.
　　　　　—Mrs. A. L. Davison

DAY 4: *Wisdom Among Men*

▶ *Scripture*

Does not wisdom cry out,
And understanding lift up her voice?
She takes her stand on the top of the high hill,
Beside the way, where the paths meet.
She cries out by the gates, at the entry of the city,
At the entrance of the doors:
"To you, O men, I call,
And my voice is to the sons of men.
O you simple ones, understand prudence,
And you fools, be of an understanding heart.
Listen, for I will speak of excellent things,
And from the opening of my lips will come right
　　things;
For my mouth will speak truth;
Wickedness is an abomination to my lips.
All the words of my mouth are with
　　righteousness;
Nothing crooked or perverse is in them.
They are all plain to him who understands,
And right to those who find knowledge.
Receive my instruction, and not silver,
And knowledge rather than choice gold;
For wisdom is better than rubies,
And all the things one may desire cannot be
　　compared with her.
"I, wisdom, dwell with prudence,

And find out knowledge and discretion.
The fear of the LORD is to hate evil;
Pride and arrogance and the evil way
And the perverse mouth I hate.
Counsel is mine, and sound wisdom;
I am understanding, I have strength.
By me kings reign,
And rulers decree justice.
By me princes rule, and nobles,
All the judges of the earth.
I love those who love me,
And those who seek me diligently will find me.
Riches and honor are with me,
Enduring riches and righteousness.
My fruit is better than gold, yes, than fine gold,
And my revenue than choice silver.
I traverse the way of righteousness,
In the midst of the paths of justice,
That I may cause those who love me to inherit
   wealth,
That I may fill their treasuries.
"The LORD possessed me at the beginning of His
   way,
Before His works of old.
I have been established from everlasting,
From the beginning, before there was ever an
   earth.
When there were no depths I was brought forth,
When there were no fountains abounding with
   water.
Before the mountains were settled,
Before the hills, I was brought forth;
When as yet He had not made the earth or the
   fields,
Or the primal dust of the world.

When He prepared the heavens, I was there,
When He drew a circle on the face of the deep,
When He established the clouds above,
When He strengthened the fountains of the deep,
When He assigned to the sea its limit,
So that the waters would not transgress His
     command,
When He marked out the foundations of the earth,
Then I was beside Him as a master craftsman;
And I was daily His delight,
Rejoicing always before Him,
Rejoicing in His inhabited world,
And my delight was with the sons of men.
"Now therefore, listen to me, my children,
For blessed are those who keep my ways.
Hear instruction and be wise,
And do not disdain it.
Blessed is the man who listens to me,
Watching daily at my gates,
Waiting at the posts of my doors.
For whoever finds me finds life,
And obtains favor from the LORD;
But he who sins against me wrongs his own soul;
All those who hate me love death."

—Proverbs 8:1–36

▶ Wisdom Meditation and Application

As you read through Proverbs 8:1–36 try to get a feel for
wisdom's impassioned plea. Everywhere she cries out to be
heard by men, on the hills, in the pathways, at the entrances
to cities.

To you, O men, I call,
And my voice is to the sons of men.

—v. 4

Wisdom seeks the ear of men in the most conspicuous places, and her words are excellent, right, and true. She offers a rich reward, better than silver, gold, and rubies. She promises counsel and understanding, and thus makes men into princes, nobles, and judges who rule. And for those men who are still doubtful of what is on offer, wisdom "plays the fool" and justifies herself from the beginning of all things (vv. 22–31). Therefore, "Blessed is the man who listens to me," (v. 34).

For many years now, the call has gone out from our Christian thinkers that we must have a biblical "worldview." Our minds must be renewed and our thinking must be more and more Christlike with each passing year. But this is not just about memorizing Scripture or knowing key points of doctrine. It's not just about listening to sermons or leading people to Christ. It's also about identifying and renewing the "conspicuous places" of my life and activities where I'm less biblical in my thinking than I ought to be.

After you have read the above passage, take as much time as necessary to be honest with yourself and God about the mundane areas of your life, where you may need to have your mind renewed and so take on board God's wisdom for those areas. Sometimes these things cannot be sorted out alone, and you may want to talk to your minister or a mature Christian friend.

Look at verses two and three symbolically for clues. The "high hill" could represent *vision*. The "way" and "paths" could represent the *daily grind*. The "gates of the city" could represent *business*. The "entrance of the doors" could represent *family*. These are all very conspicuous places, indeed. And wisdom is waiting to find hearers who will listen to her therein. How may any of these, or others you may think of, relate to you? Where could you use a change of wisdom?

For example, take the area of "vision." Let's talk about "pro-life" for a minute. Many Christians have a vision to see the end of the abortion holocaust, and rightly so. Those who do usually call themselves "pro-life." But what does it really mean to be pro-*life*? Is this not a label that should apply to our attitude towards *all* of life? In other words, would we be willing to adopt a homeless child? Is our attitude towards the very elderly that of seeking to enhance their quality of life? Would we be willing to write a letter voicing our support of a sound environmental package to clean up polluted water? One evangelical now no longers calls himself "pro-life" in public because he realized he was not willing to do some of these things.

In the realm of "business," technical efficiency is often seen only in terms of economic production. Such a single focus can easily demean or crush people and relationships. Human labor, however, is the chief aspect of "business." An employee's human-ness can easily be belittled if he or she has little or no freedom or responsibility on the job. A Christian businessman may never have considered that his employees' work ought to express their humanity. Such a company, run as it may be within a rigid scientific and technical framework, may cause employees to suffer emotionally and perhaps physically. God, however, holds relationships and wholeness in people very high in the scheme of things. A biblical Christian worldview, therefore, would make some godly adjustments in the above scenario. It would, for instance, give employees more access to management and more freedom to create better ways in which to do their tasks.

As far as "the daily grind" goes, let's look at "looking beautiful." Life certainly has an aesthetic dimension, and whenever we can we like to look as best we can. But the pursuit of personal beauty to impress people tends to reduce us to a package that we need to sell. This would be bad enough even if it controlled only our human relationships, but what if it influences how we present ourselves to God?

We are then coming to him in a righteousness of our own and not in Christ's. We hope the outer show of good works will make us attractive to God. A biblical worldview, however, will help us shake off that worldly wisdom by showing us that God is interested in the heart and that outer things, as beautiful as they may be, are perishing:

> But the Lord said to Samuel, "Do not look at his appearance or at his physical stature, because I have refused him. For the Lord does not see as man sees; for man looks at the outward appearance, but the Lord looks at the heart."
>
> —1 Samuel 16:7

> Let the lowly brother glory in his exaltation, but the rich in his humiliation, because as a flower of the field he will pass away. For no sooner has the sun risen with a burning heat than it withers the grass, and its beautiful appearance perishes.
>
> —James 1:9–11

▶ *Prayer*

Jesus Christ, you became for me the wisdom of God. But sometimes I find myself far from living out of that wisdom. Help me now to hear the voice of wisdom crying to me in the mundane areas of my life. Keep me from sinning against my own soul. In the commonplaces of life may I be to other men a light shining true wisdom.

DAY **5**: *Wisdom Among Women (and Men!)*

▶ *Scripture*

> Who can find a virtuous wife?
> For her worth is far above rubies.
> The heart of her husband safely trusts her;

So he will have no lack of gain.
She does him good and not evil
All the days of her life.
She seeks wool and flax,
And willingly works with her hands.
She is like the merchant ships,
She brings her food from afar.
She also rises while it is yet night,
And provides food for her household,
And a portion for her maidservants.
She considers a field and buys it;
From her profits she plants a vineyard.
She girds herself with strength,
And strengthens her arms.
She perceives that her merchandise is good,
And her lamp does not go out by night.
She stretches out her hands to the distaff,
And her hand holds the spindle.
She extends her hand to the poor,
Yes, she reaches out her hands to the needy.
She is not afraid of snow for her household,
For all her household is clothed with scarlet.
She makes tapestry for herself;
Her clothing is fine linen and purple.
Her husband is known in the gates,
When he sits among the elders of the land.
She makes linen garments and sells them,
And supplies sashes for the merchants.
Strength and honor are her clothing;
She shall rejoice in time to come.
She opens her mouth with wisdom,
And on her tongue is the law of kindness.
She watches over the ways of her household,
And does not eat the bread of idleness.
Her children rise up and call her blessed;

Her husband also, *and he praises her:*
"Many daughters have done well,
But you excel them all."
Charm is *deceitful and beauty* is *passing,*
But a woman who *fears the* LORD, *she shall be*
  praised.
Give her of the fruit of her hands,
And let her own works praise her in the gates.
                                              —Proverbs 31:10–31

▶ *Wisdom Meditation and Application*

As Proverbs does elsewhere, this passage exalts the honor and dignity of womanhood as it follows after wisdom. In the Hebrew, the passage is a beautiful acrostic poem, each verse beginning with a successive letter of the Hebrew alphabet. Someone took a lot of time and effort to accomplish that! Perhaps it was done as a symbolic gesture to the graciousness of the woman of wisdom.

As you read through the passage, note the qualities of the woman. You do not need to be a wife or mother to model yourself after her. Here is a hard-working, bright, and resourceful person. She is respected in and outside of the home. She works not only for profit but also among the poor and needy. She is known for her wisdom and kindness, and for the good reputation she has gained for her family. She does not trust in charm or beauty, but, like all those who know true wisdom, she fears the Lord.

Here is a wide range of activities in which the woman of wisdom works, for her God, her husband, her family, and others. There is barely a hint in the passage that she works to get things for herself. Thus she is a humble woman, and perhaps virtuous as a result. The humble person is more concerned for the needs of others than for the needs of self, and so the virtuous woman emulates her Lord, who gave himself up for others.

This is biblical wisdom. It contrasts strikingly with worldly wisdom, and not only for women but for men too. Worldly wisdom coaxes all of us to cast off restraint and to look out for Number One because we owe it to ourselves. Perhaps this has influenced you more than you thought. Whether you are a man or a woman, perhaps you've made a career change for chiefly selfish reasons and now you regret that. Perhaps worldly wisdom seduced you into a divorce. Too much time away from home may be having a harmful affect on your children. Christian men and women both ought to be living more consistently out of a biblical wisdom. What areas of your life do you think ought to be more biblical?

If any of you lacks wisdom, let him ask of God, who gives to all liberally and without reproach, and it will be given to him.

—James 1:5

Who is wise and understanding among you? Let him show by good conduct that his works are done in the meekness of wisdom. But if you have bitter envy and self-seeking in your hearts, do not boast and lie against the truth. This wisdom does not descend from above, but is earthly, sensual, demonic. For where envy and self-seeking exist, confusion and every evil thing are there. But the wisdom that is from above is first pure, then peaceable, gentle, willing to yield, full of mercy and good fruits, without partiality and without hypocrisy.

—James 3:13–18

These things also we speak, not in words which man's wisdom teaches but which the Holy Spirit teaches.

—1 Corinthians 2:13

▶ *Prayer*

Jesus, you have saved me not only from sin but from the wisdom of the world. Expose areas of worldly wisdom in my life. Help me by your grace to shake yourself free and become virtuous. May I be to others a light shining true wisdom in the fear of the Lord.

DAY 6: *Wisdom and Society*

▶ *Scripture*

The preparations of the heart belong to man,
But the answer of the tongue is from the LORD.
All the ways of a man are pure in his own eyes,
But the LORD weighs the spirits.
Commit your works to the LORD,
And your thoughts will be established.
The LORD has made all for Himself,
Yes, even the wicked for the day of doom.
Everyone proud in heart is an abomination to the
LORD;
Though they join forces, none will go unpunished.
In mercy and truth
Atonement is provided for iniquity;
And by the fear of the LORD one departs from evil.
When a man's ways please the LORD,
He makes even his enemies to be at peace with him.
Better is a little with righteousness,
Than vast revenues without justice.
A man's heart plans his way,
But the LORD directs his steps.
Divination is on the lips of the king;
His mouth must not transgress in judgment.
Honest weights and scales are the LORD's;

All the weights in the bag are His work.
It is an abomination for kings to commit wickedness,
For a throne is established by righteousness.
Righteous lips are the delight of kings,
And they love him who speaks what is right.
As messengers of death is the king's wrath,
But a wise man will appease it.
In the light of the king's face is life,
And his favor is like a cloud of the latter rain.
How much better to get wisdom than gold!
And to get understanding is to be chosen rather than
     silver.
The highway of the upright is to depart from evil;
He who keeps his way preserves his soul.
Pride goes before destruction,
And a haughty spirit before a fall.
Better to be of a humble spirit with the lowly,
Than to divide the spoil with the proud.
He who heeds the word wisely will find good,
And whoever trusts in the LORD, happy is he.
The wise in heart will be called prudent,
And sweetness of the lips increases learning.
Understanding is a wellspring of life to him who
     has it.
But the correction of fools is folly.
The heart of the wise teaches his mouth,
And adds learning to his lips.
Pleasant words are like a honeycomb,
Sweetness to the soul and health to the bones.
There is a way that seems right to a man,
But its end is the way of death.
The person who labors, labors for himself,
For his hungry mouth drives him on.
An ungodly man digs up evil,
And it is on his lips like a burning fire.

A perverse man sows strife,
And a whisperer separates the best of friends.
A violent man entices his neighbor,
And leads him in a way that is not good.
He winks his eye to devise perverse things;
He purses his lips and brings about evil.
The silver-haired head is a crown of glory,
If it is found in the way of righteousness.
He who is slow to anger is better than the mighty,
And he who rules his spirit than he who takes a city.
The lot is cast into the lap,
But its every decision is from the LORD.

He who is often rebuked and hardens his neck,
Will suddenly be destroyed, and that without remedy.
When the righteous are in authority, the people
    rejoice;
But when a wicked man rules, the people groan.
Whoever loves wisdom makes his father rejoice,
But a companion of harlots wastes his wealth.
The king establishes the land by justice,
But he who receives bribes overthrows it.
A man who flatters his neighbor
Spreads a net for his feet.
By transgression an evil man is snared,
But the righteous sings and rejoices.
The righteous considers the cause of the poor,
But the wicked does not understand such knowledge.
Scoffers set a city aflame,
But wise men turn away wrath.
If a wise man contends with a foolish man,
Whether the fool rages or laughs, there is no peace.
The bloodthirsty hate the blameless,
But the upright seek his well-being.
A fool vents all his feelings,
But a wise man holds them back.

If a ruler pays attention to lies,
All his servants become wicked.
The poor man and the oppressor have this in
    common:
The LORD gives light to the eyes of both.
The king who judges the poor with truth,
His throne will be established forever.
The rod and rebuke give wisdom,
But a child left to himself brings shame to his mother.
When the wicked are multiplied, transgression
    increases;
But the righteous will see their fall.
Correct your son, and he will give you rest;
Yes, he will give delight to your soul.
Where there is no revelation, the people cast off
    restraint;
But happy is he who keeps the law.
A servant will not be corrected by mere words;
For though he understands, he will not respond.
Do you see a man hasty in his words?
There is more hope for a fool than for him.
He who pampers his servant from childhood
Will have him as a son in the end.
An angry man stirs up strife,
And a furious man abounds in transgression.
A man's pride will bring him low,
But the humble in spirit will retain honor.
Whoever is a partner with a thief hates his own life;
He swears to tell the truth, but reveals nothing.
The fear of man brings a snare,
But whoever trusts in the LORD shall be safe.
Many seek the ruler's favor,
But justice for man comes from the LORD.
An unjust man is an abomination to the righteous,

And he who is *upright in the way* is *an abomination
   to the wicked.*
                                —Proverbs 16:1–33; 29:1–27

▶ *Wisdom Meditation and Application*

We have this saying, and rightly so, "If Jesus is not Lord
of all, then he's not Lord at all." In the two passages above,
we get a glimpse of God's wisdom in the big picture of
society, where he has the final say.

This prayer activity will close with your praying about
God's wisdom entering into society. But first, as you read
through the passages, watch for some areas to be high-
lighted to you for prayer. Here are some suggestions.

- What areas of society clearly have not committed
  their works to the Lord (16:3)?

- In what work(s) have the proud in heart joined forces
  (16:5)?

- Where is society coming apart at the seams because
  of "in-house" fighting (16:7)?

- Where is local or national government particularly
  corrupt and self-serving (16:10–12)?

- How could the newspapers be redemptive in the way
  they use the information they dig up (16:27–30)?

- Are you aware of any *clearly identifiable* unrighteous
  politicians or legislation (29:2)?

- Is there sufficient help for the poor in your neighborhood (29:7)?

- Where is wickedness increasing internationally
  (29:12, 16)?

- Which subcultures have cast off all restraint (29:18)?

- Do you know people of influence who seek to curry
  favor with those in authority only out of self-interest
  (29:26)?

One Christian journalist has earned the trust of her publisher, who now gives her freedom to write an occasional editorial to express overtly biblical views. Other Christians are getting involved in political hustings and also become precinct workers to help elect righteous men and women to replace the unrighteous. A Christian youth group planned part of their Summer vacation to work among the poor in an inner-city area. A Christian attorney has donated part of his time to minister through Christian mediation, working for reconciliation in broken homes and ruptured businesses.

▶ *Prayer*

Pray for the end of the influence of worldly wisdom in any areas you have identified. You may want to make this a matter of ongoing prayer, perhaps with friends. If there is any way your involvement (letter writing, contacts, personal activity?) could release God's wisdom into the situation, why not pray about getting involved to some degree? You could be a part of changing a curse into a blessing.

▶ *Hymn*

DARE TO BE BRAVE, DARE TO BE TRUE

Dare to be brave, dare to be true,
Strive for the right, for the Lord is with you;
Fight with sin bravely, fight and be strong,
Christ is your captain, fear only what's wrong.

Fight then, good soldiers, fight and be brave,
Christ is your captain, mighty to save.

Dare to be brave, dare to be true,
God is your Father, He watches over you;
He knows your trials; when your heart quails,
Call Him to rescue, His grace never fails.
Dare to be brave, dare to be true,

> *God grant you courage to carry you through;*
> *Try to help others, ever be kind,*
> *Let the oppressed a strong friend in you find.*
> —W. J. Rooper

DAY 7: *Cleaving to That Which Is Good*

▶ *Scripture*

> *My son, give attention to my words;*
> *Incline your ear to my sayings.*
> *Do not let them depart from your eyes;*
> *Keep them in the midst of your heart;*
> *For they are life to those who find them,*
> *And health to all their flesh.*
> *Keep your heart with all diligence,*
> *For out of it spring the issues of life.*
> *Put away from you a deceitful mouth,*
> *And put perverse lips far from you.*
> *Let your eyes look straight ahead,*
> *And your eyelids look right before you.*
> *Ponder the path of your feet,*
> *And let all your ways be established.*
> *Do not turn to the right or the left;*
> *Remove your foot from evil.*
> —Proverbs 4:20–27

▶ *Wisdom Meditation and Application*

When all is said and done, here is the appeal of wisdom, as the teacher to the learner, to submit the whole of one's life in the direction that leads to life. Ears, eyes, heart, mouth, and feet are all included in the submission.

As you ponder the passage, notice that for wisdom it is not enough merely to listen to instruction; it must be assimilated and walked out. That is to say it must be at the heart, and if so, "out of it spring the issues of life," (v. 23). This is why "wisdom," according to the Bible, is never divorced from one's actions. It brings together both theory and practice. And all of our senses as well as our hands, feet, and mind are involved in the picture. But at the center is the heart, which is a biblical metonym for "motivation" or "direction." What backslidden Israel needed was "a heart to know . . . the Lord," and to return to him "with their whole heart" (Jeremiah 24:7). When Jesus took this up and taught that it is "not what goes into the mouth that defiles a man; but what comes out of the mouth," he offended many religious people (Matthew 15:10–2).

Therefore it is good to weigh up ("ponder," v. 26) our paths, that we might discover where we are turning (in our hearts) to the right or the left (v. 27). Take some time for pondering. Wherever you detect you have gone amiss, discover the good and cleave to it. That is God's wisdom.

▶ *Prayer*

Merciful God, give attention to my confession. Incline your ear to me. I have fallen short of your wisdom in the area of _____. Forgive my sin. By your grace may my eyes and ears, may my hands, feet, and mind, be thoroughly motivated by your obedience.

▶ *Hymn*

JESUS, KEEP ME NEAR THE CROSS

Jesus, keep me near the cross,
There a precious fountain,
Free to all, a healing stream,
Flows from Calvary's mountain.

In the cross, in the cross
Be my glory ever,

Till my raptured soul shall find
Rest beyond the river.

Near the cross, a trembling soul,
Love and mercy found me;
There the Bright and Morning Star
Shed His beams around me.

Near the cross! O Lamb of God,
Bring its scenes before me;
Help me walk from day to day
With its shadow over me.

Near the cross! I'll watch and wait,
Hoping, trusting ever,
Till I reach the golden strand,
Just beyond the river.
—Fanny J. Crosby

— 10 —

Spirituality and Politics

Politics is a dirty word to many Christians. How many times have we heard people say, "The Church should stay out of politics?" And we have come to believe this. Politics should happen in Washington, D.C. "They" should be left to get on with it. It is a matter for the experts. There have always been exceptions, however. Christian men and women have been part of the political process, and some of them have been very influential. And the Church has admired them (at least in retrospect!) and kept them in its prayers. Christians have rightly struggled with trying to be a holy people, and for many the obvious way to achieve or preserve holiness is to stay clear of anything that might tarnish it. Like politics, which has become a fabled land full of the ogres of compromise, deceit, and—the biggest enemy of all—worldliness. For some, holiness is threatened when they have to move too far outside the Church to become involved in a

world where a strand of theology tells them they
do not belong.

Christians have also favored banishing political discussion from the pulpit or study group
for fear that different opinions would clash and
unity would be destroyed. This is a real fear. But
it needs to be healed rather than avoided. The
problem is that we have narrowed politics down
in such a way that we now feel justified in not
being involved. Perhaps, then, some of the dirt
needs scraping off the word "politics." This may
help liberate politics from too narrow definitions, which may then help us to see that our
involvement is not unspiritual. We could say
that politics, therefore, is simply about how human beings live and organize themselves together in society to meet some needs that cannot
be met by the individual. And this would include how they deal with resources and power
and behave towards one another. This broader
understanding of politics ought to give us room
to see that we are included after all.

Worlds Apart?

Sometimes we think that religion, or spirituality, and politics are worlds apart. Yet Psalm 24:1
states that, "The earth is the LORD'S, and all its
fullness." Now to this we may well agree, but
we generally associate this claim with the beauty
of nature. Yet the psalmist wrote that *everything*
is the Lord's, not only the things of nature. We,
however, tend to separate out of "everything" the

things we think are proper concerns for God and ignore the rest.

The whole world is the object of God's love. His commitment to it is passionate and total and not only for the Church. The God who made the world does not discriminate about which parts he will love.

Human life is generally more comfortable when it is divided up into compartments. Divisions are made between private and public life, between mind, body, and spirit, between the world and the Church. A sense of what is appropriate to each is developed, and this frees, we think, us from the more difficult questions and tensions. There is a pressing need to recover a sense of wholeness.

Because people feel more competent in some areas than in others, the temptation is to downplay or deny the spheres that don't concern us. Yet even the quietest and most retiring member of the human race lives in three main areas of life. The first is the obvious one of personal development. The second is that of the local community, which will include family, friends, work, and social contacts. The third area is more complicated. It is made up of larger structures and systems. For example, when we shop in a supermarket we usually think no further than the meals to be provided. We do not generally consider the means by which the products arrived on the shelves, the destination or amount of the profits, the possible exploitation of people at the root of those profits, or the working conditions of the employees. We feel we have little control or say over these matters, but at the same time *we* are happy to profit by them.

This third area, then, which I am calling "political" in a broad sense, is just as inescapable as the first two. I am not free to say that in the first two I am a Christian but in the third I am merely a citizen. Because being a Christian affects the whole of my life in society, it becomes difficult to say that one area, politics, has nothing to do with my spirituality.

I Am with You

When that scrap of a baby, Jesus, was born in Bethlehem, in an outrageous kind of way God was saying, "I am with you." We had lived as though we saw God through a telescope, believing him to be far away, removed from earthly concerns. He might send instructions or even messengers, but to take on human flesh was surely taking commitment to extremes. Nevertheless, God has met us in Jesus as man and God. He is now part of our human history not just our philosophy.

The implications of the Incarnation challenge us at every turn. Our spirituality becomes moulded by that of Jesus himself, our mind shaped by his:

> Let this mind be in you which was also in Christ Jesus . . . [who] made Himself of no reputation, taking the form of a bondservant.
> —Philippians 2:5–7

Here is a reminder of the total self-giving of Jesus for the world. Faith does not remove us from the world; it plunges us right in, to take risks, to become vulnerable. The challenge to us is the challenge of "God with us" in everything, including politics.

Jesus is our model. He takes us out of the business of theory alone. It is a costly adventure; the cross stands as a stark reminder of that. Often we will get it wrong, patronize, lose courage, or prefer our own interests. Then we too need to know the Jesus who is with us, so we can begin again. A price has to be paid. Jesus did not only comfort those who were pushed out of society. He served and gave his life to see people transformed in society as well. That is to say his life was given to see God's kingdom come.

Your Kingdom Come

Where do we look for the kingdom of God? The answer to this is an important point on the compass of our spiritual journey.

Some will answer that the kingdom is inside us. In this popular view the kingdom (or rule) of God is largely a personal, interior matter. Others will say that the kingdom is in the Church. This usually results in erecting a high barrier between the Church and the world, and retreat becomes the best course of action. Other Christians, however, will say that the kingdom is coming in the future. Yet this implies that it has little, if anything, to do with society now on earth. So we do not need to be greatly concerned with society because what counts is the coming kingdom, and then all this earthly muddle will be behind us.

All these points of view have substantial elements of truth, but even together they miss the force of what Jesus meant when he proclaimed that the kingdom of God was at hand. God's kingdom is about a just and righteous way of living in all areas of life in the here-and-now. When Jesus talked about the kingdom, he was talking about what we might call the "true shape" for human society. It was about the expression of the character and concerns of God in the world at large (as well as privately). This, then, was a kingdom that would transform the face of the earth.

This kingdom is good news precisely because it is God's kingdom and not another human enterprise. It is a challenge to all those who hear, "Today the kingdom has come near you." It is a call to faith, to change, to repentance, and to commitment to God's way revealed in and by Jesus. One of the consequences will be the transformation of our values, which will radically alter the way we see the world and act in it. This means that the values of God's kingdom will often make the Christian community uncomfortable to the rest of society. The presence of kingdom values will question much of the motivation and goals of the world. They may, for example, expose inadequate understandings of justice, abuses of authority, or wrongful oppression.

We cannot simply identify Christianity with a particular political party or even a culture. God's design is far greater. There are many attractions and false securities in settling for a Christianity which fits in with the mainstream. It is all too easy to believe that the issues we hold dear are also God's prime concerns. It calls for clear-sightedness and a courageous faith to be part of what God is doing throughout the world and to accept the responsibility he has given to us even in the larger areas and structures.

Response and Responsibility

One of the uncomfortable gifts God has given to human beings is responsibility. It is intrinsic to our humanity. At the beginning, God gave his good creation into the hands of men and women to care for it. He has not changed his mind. We have a responsibility, then, before God, not only for ourselves but also to the world at large.

Our responsibility to God necessitates a response. And our response, in part, must be to become communities of faith led by the Holy Spirit to challenge and disturb, when necessary, the social order. This is our prophetic role: to proclaim and articulate in word and deed the values of God's kingdom.

Not surprisingly, Christians often find this kind of God disquieting and his demands too much like hard work.

But there is hope. At its heart, spirituality is the expression of our response to God. Because his character, values, concerns, and activities steadily influence our own, as we encounter him more fully, so will our response to him increase.

Finally, just before we move on to the "Take 7 Days" material, it remains to be said that the kind of obedience God requires of us in this wide political sense (care for our "neighbor" and influencing the larger structures) is much more entailed than merely "throwing money" at a need. Compassion and care may fall far short of justice and righteousness when they do not tackle the *causes* of distress. Unless we deal with such causes, we may unconsciously be playing a part in *maintaining* an unjust social order.

Another part of our response, then, is to examine the social structures in the light of God's values, to assess how people are being treated, and to bring justice where needed. The Bible reminds us of this, and part of our obedience is to cooperate with God in it.

Tall order or high ceiling? In a way, it is both, because it is *God* with whom we have to do. And so we both pray and work to see his kingdom come.

TAKE SEVEN DAYS . . .

DAY 1: *Small Beginnings, Big Results*

▶ *Scripture*

Another parable He spoke to them, saying, "The kingdom of heaven is like a mustard seed, which a man took and sowed in his field, which indeed is the least of all the seeds; but when it is grown it is greater than the herbs and becomes a tree, so that the birds of the air can come and nest in its branches." Another parable He spoke to them: "The kingdom of heaven is like leaven, which a woman took and hid in three measures of meal till it was all leavened."

—Matthew 13:31–33

▶ *Exercise*

The modern world is so busy, and it may keep us rushing around so much that it's hard to just stop and take time to really observe what is going on around us. This may prevent us from seeing what God is doing, from observing how he is at work in the things around us.

You'll need to arrange some "stopping time" to participate in this particular exercise. The idea is to take your Bible and go and sit in a public place, perhaps a library, city-county building, or shopping mall. After you have found a place to sit and rest, take fifteen or twenty minutes to really look at what is happening around you. What are people doing? What sorts of transactions are taking place? Are people arguing or laughing? Is everything going smoothly or are there problems occurring for some persons?

After a while, open your Bible and read Matthew 13:31–33 carefully. Its point is that enormous results can stem from small beginnings, in the context of how God's kingdom influences the world.

Now look around again. Can you identify any kingdom values at work in this public place? What are they?

If not, why not?

Is there anything you or your Christian community could do to influence this place with God's kingdom values? Don't worry about how insignificant an influence you think you would be. Zechariah 4:10, asks, "Who has despised the day of small things?" The thought, here, is that we ought not to let ourselves get discouraged by small contributions but understand that God does not place as much importance on the size of things as we do.

▶ Kingdom Witness: England

Josephine Butler was born in England in 1828, the daughter of John and Hannah Grey. The family held a firm Christian faith, believing that God is actively involved in human affairs. From an early age Josephine had a strong sense of what she called "the inequalities, injustices, and cruelties in the world." As an adult, Josephine began to spend time with women who were the outcasts of society. This led her to investigate the causes of poverty. She and her husband, George Butler, then opened their home to destitute women. They also tried to provide alternative work to oakum picking, the occupation of the workhouse, and to prostitution.

Josephine Butler's concern for the injustice of a society that drove women to prostitution led her to mount a campaign against the Contagious Diseases Acts. These Acts in effect violated the civil rights of any woman suspected of being a prostitute, who could then be forcibly examined for venereal disease. If she refused, a woman was liable to imprisonment. Josephine campaigned tirelessly until the Act was repealed in 1883. She also worked to raise the age of consent to 16 and to abolish the practice of selling women into prostitution. Josephine's writing and the testimony of her friends reveal that throughout her life she was sustained by her discipline of prayer and her vision of God. She believed that she was living in the days that would see God usher in the kingdom.

▶ *Prayer*

Either now or later, take time to ask the Lord if there is a way you or your Christian community can make a small beginning with the values of God's kingdom in this place.

DAY 2: *Basic Kingdom Attitudes*

▶ *Scripture*

Then He opened His mouth and taught them, saying,

> *"Blessed are the poor in spirit,*
> *For theirs is the kingdom of heaven.*
> *Blessed are those who mourn,*
> *For they shall be comforted.*
> *Blessed are the meek,*
> *For they shall inherit the earth.*
> *Blessed are those who hunger and thirst*
>   *for righteousness,*
> *For they shall be filled.*
> *Blessed are the merciful,*
> *For they shall obtain mercy.*
> *Blessed are the pure in heart,*
> *For they shall see God.*
> *Blessed are the peacemakers,*
> *For they shall be called sons of God.*
> *Blessed are those who are persecuted for*
>   *righteousness' sake,*
> *For theirs is the kingdom of heaven.*

*Blessed are you when they revile and persecute you,
and say all kinds of evil against you falsely for My sake.
Rejoice and be exceedingly glad, for great is your
reward in heaven, for so they persecuted the prophets
who were before you."*

—Matthew 5:2–12

▶ *Exercise*

When you are out in public (working, shopping, socializing), how consistent is your attitude with the values Jesus presents in Matthew 5:2–12? For example, sometimes we find ourselves around people who are mocking a government leader. It's as if they could do better. Would you be willing to exhibit the opposite attitude, that is, of one who is poor in spirit? Or perhaps fellow employees are saying how Mary or John deserved to be fired. It may be tempting to agree, but it may be more Christian to offer some mercy in this situation.

What other ways could you see yourself applying the values of the Beatitudes in your "public" life?

▶ *Prayer*

Include in your daily prayers a time to ask the Lord to help you identify areas in which you could be more influential with kingdom values.

▶ *Hymn*

O TO BE LIKE THEE!

*O to be like Thee! blessed Redeemer,
This is my constant longing and prayer;
Gladly I'll forfeit all of earth's treasures,
Jesus, Thy perfect likeness to wear.*

O to be like Thee!
O to be like Thee,
Blessed Redeemer, pure as Thou art!
Come in Thy sweetness, come in Thy fullness
Stamp Thine own image deep on my heart.

O to be like Thee! full of compassion,
Loving, forgiving, tender and kind;
Helping the helpless, cheering the fainting,
Seeking the wandering sinner to find.

O to be like Thee! while I am pleading,
Pour out Thy Spirit, fill with Thy love;
Make me a temple meet for Thy dwelling,
Fit me for life and heaven above.
                              —Thomas O. Chisholm

DAY **3**: *Public Reformation*

▶ *Scripture*

For thus says the LORD to the house of Israel:

"Seek Me and live.
Seek the LORD and live,
Lest He break out in fire in the house of Joseph,
And devour it,
With no one to quench it in Bethel—
You who turn justice to wormwood,
And lay righteousness to rest in the earth!"
He made the Pleiades and Orion;
He turns the shadow of death into morning
And makes the day as dark as night;
He calls for the waters of the sea
And pours them out on the face of the earth;
The LORD is His name.

He rains ruin upon the strong,
So that fury comes upon the fortress.
They hate the one who rebukes in the gate,
And they abhor the one who speaks uprightly.
Therefore, because you tread down the poor
And take grain taxes from him,
Though you have built houses of hewn stone,
Yet you shall not dwell in them;
You have planted pleasant vineyards,
But you shall not drink from them.
For I know your manifold transgressions
And your mighty sins:
Afflicting the just and taking bribes;
Diverting the poor from justice at the gate.
Therefore the prudent keep silent at that time,
For it is an evil time.
Seek good and not evil,
That you may live;
So the LORD God of hosts will be with you,
As you have spoken.
Hate evil, love good;
Establish justice in the gate.
It may be that the LORD God of hosts
Will be gracious to the remnant of Joseph.
                                   —Amos 5:4, 6–15

▶ *Exercise*

Here's an easy one, perhaps! Make yourself a cup of tea
or coffee and relax. Go ahead. I'll wait for you here.

Many of us enjoy sitting back comfortably with a cup of
tea or coffee. But don't get too comfortable. When you drink
your cup, reflect on the fact that you are probably the last
link in a chain of exploitation. Though the tea and coffee
industries are some of the biggest in the world, financially,
workers in the field at the start of the process are usually

paid very low wages and may live in overcrowded and un-healthy conditions.

The book of Amos cries out for justice and righteousness to be brought into public spheres. Notice the many areas that are on Amos' heart: public moral error, Godward defiance, lawless and oppressive practices, unjust property management, social evils, a loss of freedom of speech—to name several. Society is ready to be judged by God.

But Amos said that there was hope of transformation instead, as God himself transforms society. In verse eight there are three striking transformational pictures: seasonal changes, day and night, and flood waters. In other words, no injustice is so established that it is inviolable. God himself offers the people in the structures an opportunity to change them for the good.

Think about delivering an "Amos Article" or lesson to your Bible study group or Sunday School class. You will probably need to use a library for this, where you will research a particular "chain of exploitation," like coffee workers. There is also a loud hue and cry these days about overpopulation and the plundering of the earth through deforestation of the world's rainforests. A librarian will help you find both pro and con information regarding these. Let your research be in both areas to discover what points of view are to be trusted. At a local Christian bookstore you will also be able to pick up one or two books on these topics.

Present your "Amos Article" by citing the facts on both sides of a subject and then share a biblical conclusion. Maybe the secular positions are too biased in support of special interest groups. If the biblical conclusion is different from prevailing secular positions, what practical steps can you and/or your class take in an "Amos" direction? One simple thing could be to write an op-ed piece for your newspaper, or write the authors of the books and articles that present weak positions.

▶ *Prayer*

Identify injustice in one or two public spheres and make this a matter for ongoing prayer.

▶ *Hymn*

WHERE CROSS THE CROWDED WAYS OF LIFE

Where cross the crowded ways of life,
Where sound the cries of race and clan,
Above the noise of selfish strife,
We hear Thy voice, O Son of man!

In haunts of wretchedness and need,
On shadowed thresholds dark with fears,
From paths where hide the lures of the greed,
We catch the vision of Thy tears.

From tender childhood's helplessness,
From woman's grief, man's burdened toil,
From famished souls, from sorrow's stress,
Thy heart has never known recoil.

O Master, from the mountain side,
Make haste to heal the hearts of pain;
Among these restless throngs abide;
O tread the city's streets again,

Till sons of men shall learn Thy love
And follow where Thy feet have trod;
Till glorious from Thy heaven above
Shall come the city of our God.
                                        —Frank Mason North

DAY 4: *Rulers with Kingdom Values*

▶ *Scripture*

Give the king your judgments, O God,
And your righteousness to the king's Son.
He will judge Your people with righteousness,
And Your poor with justice.
The mountains will bring peace to the people,
And the little hills, by righteousness.
He will bring justice to the poor of the people;
He will save the children of the needy,
And will break in pieces the oppressor.
They shall fear You
As long as the sun and moon endure,
Throughout all generations.
He shall come down like rain upon the grass before
   mowing,
Like the showers that water the earth.
In His days the righteous shall flourish,
And abundance of peace,
Until the moon is no more.
He shall have dominion also from sea to sea,
And from the River to the ends of the earth.
Those who dwell in the wilderness will bow before
   Him,
And His enemies will lick the dust.
The kings of Tarshish and of the isles
Will bring presents;
The kings of Sheba and Seba
Will offer gifts.
Yes, all the kings shall fall down before Him;
All nations shall serve Him.
For He will deliver the needy when he cries,
The poor also, and him who has no helper.

He will spare the poor and needy,
And will save the souls of the needy.
He will redeem their life from oppression and
   violence;
And precious shall be their blood in His sight.
And He shall live:
And the gold of Sheba will be given to Him;
Prayer also will be made for Him continually,
And daily He shall be praised.
There will be an abundance of grain in the earth,
On the top of the mountains;
Its fruit shall wave like Lebanon;
And those of the city shall flourish like grass on earth.

                                          —Psalm 72:1–16

▶ *Exercise*

Psalm 72 presents a high, godly ideal for those who rule, whether they are presidents, prime ministers, governors, mayors, or city administrators. As you read through the Psalm, notice that it speaks of a ruler's administration of his own nation or jurisdiction as well as how his character is known outside of that. Notice, too, that as a ruler he is subject to God's requirements for him, and out of this will flow a dealing with his people that is consistent with God's character. And a righteous ruler will be acknowledged as such outside his sphere of jurisdiction. Finally, his people pray for him, and they all prosper.

Many of us have watched the news or read a newspaper article about something that rankles us about the actions of one of our elected rulers. And then we get with friends who are like-minded and complain. But that's often as far as we go.

Why not actually *do* something? Take a piece of paper and jot down a few thoughts about what really bothers you regarding a decision your congressman has made, or a wrong way of thinking that exists in your city government. Now write that letter which you have always wanted to write, or phone one of those governmental 800 numbers to voice your righteous opinion. Be respectful; show your concern for the well-being of all; but explain why this particular action seems wrong to you. Request an explanation or a specific corrective action. No threats, just a firm, but winsome appeal for that which is truly good.

► *Prayer*

It is easy to pray only for those rulers whom we elected. But as Christians, we are to pray for all of our rulers, even those for whom we did not vote. Pray for these men and women. Pray that God will give us righteous rulers and transform existing rulers.

► *Hymn*

BE THOU MY VISION

Be Thou my Vision, O Lord of my heart;
Naught be all else to me, save that Thou art
Thou my best thought, by day or by night,
Waking or sleeping, Thy presence my light.
Be Thou my Wisdom, and Thou my true Word;
I ever with Thee and Thou with me, Lord;
Thou my great Father, I Thy true son;
Thou in me dwelling, and I with Thee one.

Riches I heed not, nor man's empty praise,
Thou mine inheritance, now and always:
Thou and Thou only, first in my heart,
High King of heaven, my treasure Thou art.

High King of heaven, my victory won,
May I reach heaven's joys, O bright heaven's Sun!

Heart of my own heart, whatever befall,
Still be my Vision, O Ruler of all.
      —Mary Byrne and Eleanor Hull

DAY 5: *Being Global Christians*

▶ *Scripture*

Now it shall come to pass in the latter days
That the mountain of the LORD's house
Shall be established on the top of the mountains,
And shall be exalted above the hills;
And peoples shall flow into it.
Many nations shall come and say,
"Come, and let us go to the mountain of the LORD,
To the house of the God of Jacob;
He will teach us His ways,
And we shall walk in His paths."
For out of Zion the law shall go forth,
And the word of the LORD from Jerusalem.
He shall judge between many peoples,
And rebuke strong nations afar off;
They shall beat their swords into plowshares,
And their spears into pruning hooks;
Nation shall not lift up sword against nation,
Neither shall they learn war anymore.
      —Micah 4:1–3

▶ *Exercise*

Can you say what was happening around the world in the news last week? When you hear a news story, take time to imagine what it is like to be one of the central figures. Pay attention to news items from one particular country outside of your own. See if you can discover the roots of the problem, and follow the issue during the weeks that it is in the news.

The above passage from Micah is one of the great promises of Scripture: global peace. It shows beyond a doubt that God is interested in international relations. His desire is for peace. For several years now, there have been more than forty global "hot spots." Think what it would be like if there were none! Impossible? With God all things are possible.

In the meantime, wherever the kingdom is being incarnated, we have representations of the wider peace in part, on a smaller scale. We can have a hand in creating that peace through our diligent prayers.

▶ *Kingdom Witness: South Africa*

Many Christians in South Africa are working and praying to see justice in their land. Often it all seems such a large scale that it is difficult to know how ordinary Christians can be directly involved. In mid-1986 a substantial part of the black township of Crossroads, just outside Cape Town, erupted in violence, and many people who had lived in the area were made homeless. Faced with this crisis, the people of Wynberg parish knew they must respond. They opened the church halls and buildings and welcomed in the refugees in the name of Jesus. Church members found many ways to be involved, offering time, money, clothes, food, and other necessities.

This was not the first time the parish had been involved in such activity. It began in 1977 when they opened their doors to those left without shelter when the shanties in Modderdam were demolished. This was more than an act of compassion. Their action meant a deliberate decision to break the law of the Group Areas Act, which designated which race might live in what area. This experience brought much heart searching to the parish and faced the Christian community with the implications of being God's people in

South Africa. The churches which became involved faced the hostility of the police, and there were fines and detention for some of the church leaders.

▶ *Prayer*

In the context of a new heavens and a new earth, a very interesting passage in 2 Peter 3:11–13 suggests that we can "hasten" its coming:

> *Therefore . . . what manner of persons ought you to be in holy conduct and godliness, looking for and hastening the coming of the day of God? . . . We, according to His promise, look for a new heaven and a new earth in which righteousness dwells.*

Pray regularly for God to enter as Arbiter into the moral and ethical questions and dilemmas that surround the jurisprudence of international relations. Here is one way that you can "hasten" the coming of a new heavens and earth, in which there is righteousness and peace.

DAY 6: *Being Conscientious in "Gray" Areas*

▶ *Scripture*

> *When they had come to Capernaum, those who received the temple tax came to Peter and said, "Does your Teacher not pay the temple tax?" He said, "Yes."*
> *And when he had come into the house, Jesus anticipated him, saying, "What do you think, Simon? From whom do the kings of the earth take customs or taxes, from their sons or from strangers?"*
> *Peter said to Him, "From strangers."*
> *Jesus said to him, "Then the sons are free. Nevertheless, lest we offend them, go to the sea, cast in a hook,*

*and take the fish that comes up first. And when you
have opened its mouth, you will find a piece of money;
take that and give it to them for Me and you."*
—Matthew 17:24–27

► *Exercise*

This is such an unusual event that we generally focus on
how the money arrived! But that is of minor importance in
light of how our Lord goes to an extreme so as not to give
offense concerning taxes. This was a very minor religious
tax that some Jews found a way around. But Jesus is willing
to pay it to keep the peace. And when it came to the heavy
political taxes, we already have his word that we are to ren-
der to Caesar the things that are Caesar's.

Here, then, is a matter of personal ethics about paying
taxes. It is tempting to find ways around certain taxes, especially at the end of the year when we are doing income taxes.

► *Prayer*

Ask God to show you how to deal with your tax situation.

► *Hymn*

BEFORE THY THRONE, O GOD

*Before thy throne, O God, we kneel;
Give us a conscience quick to feel,
A ready mind to understand
The meaning of thy chastening hand;
Whatever the pain and shame may be,
Bring us, O Father, nearer thee.*

*Search out our hearts and make us true,
Wishful to give to all their due;
From love of pleasure, lust of gold,
From sins which make the heart grow cold,*

Wean us and train us with thy rod;
Teach us to know our faults, O God.

For sins of heedless word and deed,
For pride ambitious to succeed,
For crafty trade and subtle snare
To catch the simple unaware,
For lives bereft of purpose high,
Forgive, forgive, O Lord, we cry.

Let the fierce fires which burn and try,
Our inmost spirits purify:
Consume the ill; purge out the shame;
O God, be with us in the flame;
A newborn people may we rise,
More pure, more true, more nobly wise.
—William Boyd Carpenter

DAY 7: *Responsibility to the Government*

▶ *Scripture*

Let every soul be subject to the governing authorities.
For there is no authority except from God, and the au-
thorities that exist are appointed by God.
—Romans 13:1

▶ *Exercise*

Think about the subjects of your prayers and those of
your church. What are the topics of most of those prayers?
What percentage would be "personal" in nature and what
percentage would fall into the category that we have called
"political" in this chapter? In many cases, the largest percentage by far falls into the "personal" category.

In what ways could you help both yourself and your

church or prayer group to pray more frequently for the "political" area? Could you put together a teaching to share during Sunday School that might alert people to pray more for local government? Do you have a testimony you could share that would enlighten people to how God answers political prayers?

▶ *Kingdom Witness: United States*

On April 3rd, 1968, Dr. Martin Luther King, Jr. delivered a speech in Memphis, Tennessee, in support of striking sanitation workers: "We have been forced," he said, "to a point where we're going to have to grapple with the problems that men have been trying to grapple with through history, but the demands didn't force them to do it. Survival demands that we grapple with them. Men, for years now, have been talking about war and peace. But now no longer can they just talk about it. It is no longer a choice between violence and nonviolence in this world. It is [between] non-violence and nonexistence. . . . And also in the human rights revolution, if something isn't done, and in a hurry, to bring the colored peoples of the world out of their long years of poverty, their long years of neglect, the whole world is doomed. . . . I don't know what will happen now. We've got some difficult days ahead. But it doesn't matter with me now, because I've been to the mountain top. And I don't mind. Like anybody, I would like to live a long life; longevity has its place. But I'm not concerned about that now. I just want to do God's will."

The next day, he was assassinated.

▶ *Hymn*

GOD OF OUR FATHERS

God of our fathers, whose almighty hand
Leads forth in beauty all the starry band

Of shining worlds in splendor thru the skies,
Our grateful songs before Thy throne arise.

Thy love divine hath led us in the past,
In this free land by Thee our lot is cast;
Be Thou our Ruler, Guardian, Guide, and Stay,
Thy Word our law, Thy paths our chosen way.

From war's alarms, from deadly pestilence,
Be Thy strong arm our eversure defense;
Thy true religion in our hearts increase,
Thy bounteous goodness nourish us in peace.

Refresh Thy people on their toilsome way,
Lead us from night to neverending day;
Fill all our lives with love and grace divine,
And glory, laud, and praise be ever Thine!
—Daniel C. Roberts

▶ *Prayer*

Open our eyes, Lord, that we may see how to pray for our local, state, and national government, that they may pursue justice and treat all people as image-bearers of the Divine.

Practical Spirituality

—————◆—————

At a particular point in time God himself in the person of Jesus Christ suffered and died for you and me. That incredible love must call forth a response. If we have experienced that very great love, we shall want to give God tokens of our love for him. Two ways we can do this are by fasting and giving. Fasting is usually a private gift to God, something between us and him. It is offered to him secretly. Giving is a thank-offering to God, expressed in the form of practical love for our fellow men and women. Let us consider these two disciplines of the normal Christian life.

Fasting

Why Fast?

The modern world is obsessed with diet. It bombards us with books, courses, and the latest schemes. It's big business too. A lot of people, for example, will pay hundreds of dollars to visit a health farm for a supervised fast in an effort to obtain a healthier body. Christians, too, may need to diet for purely physical reasons, but we should also be fasting for spiritual reasons. Fasting is a spiritual discipline that will move us on in our discipleship.

The Bible teaches that the children of God are expected to fast. In the Sermon on the Mount, Jesus spoke of fasting:

> *When you fast, do not be like the hypocrites, with a sad countenance. For they disfigure their faces that they may appear to men to be fasting. Assuredly, I say to you, they have their reward. But you, when you fast, anoint your head and wash your face, so that you do not appear to men to be fasting, but to your Father who is in the secret place; and your Father who sees in secret will reward you openly.*
> —Matthew 6:16–18

While Jesus' words are not an explicit commandment, it is obvious that he took it for granted that his followers would fast, and that we needed instruction about how to do it. The New Testament references to fasting, however, are only the tip of the iceberg. Many more are found in the Old Testament. In the context of a national disaster that had come on Israel, we read:

> *Gird yourselves and lament, you priests;*
> *Wail, you who minister before the altar;*
> *Come, lie all night in sackcloth,*
> *You who minister to my God;*
> *For the grain offering and the drink offering*
> *Are withheld from the house of your God.*
> *Consecrate a fast,*
> *Call a sacred assembly;*
> *Gather the elders*

And all the inhabitants of the land
Into the house of the LORD your God,
And cry out to the LORD.
—Joel 1:13–14

Here is a way to express a corporate response to disaster and national repentance. It is a way to show not only sorrow for sin but also our determination to turn back to God as a nation and take him seriously. Joel calls God's priests to give up both food and sleep in order to give more time to prayer. The whole people, not just a selected few, are called to a solemn fast. In other words fasting is not an exercise for the odd or the very holy; it is for all God's people.

Fasting, like any other spiritual discipline, however, can be abused and degenerate into a religious show or pretense:

In fact, in the day of your fast you find pleasure,
And exploit all your laborers.
Indeed you fast for strife and debate,
And to strike with the fist of wickedness.
You will not fast as you do this day,
To make your voice heard on high.
Would you call this a fast,
And an acceptable day to the Lord?
—Isaiah 58:3–5

The entire passage of Isaiah 58 warns that fasting must not be done for a religious show or pretense, or as a way to manipulate God. It is a discipline we offer in God's service, without forgetting the responsibilities we have toward others.

How Does Fasting Help?

Those who have fasted regularly have discovered that there are four main reasons for fasting. First, it is a straightforward way of making an offering to God which is, in at least a small way, costly. Second, it sets free more time for prayer. If we skip lunch, an extra hour is available when we can give attention to God in worship or intercession. Third, for many people it sharpens and clears the mind for a more concentrated and effective period of prayer. This may not come at once, as it is usually associated with longer fasts or with short, regular fasts when practiced for a long time. Fourth, fasting loosens that which ties us too firmly to a fallen, self-centered world. We live in a consumer culture which conditions us to believe that "more" is "better" and will make us happy. Fasting helps us shake off those claims and demonstrate that it is obedience to God which brings true joy.

Practical Guidelines

What works perfectly well for others may not be right for us. Therefore there will be different ways to fast. It is important that we do only what the Lord requires of us.

The most common pattern is to give up a meal once a week, perhaps on Friday, as a day to remember the Lord's sacrifice. The time saved from eating is spent in some form of prayer. Others are able to fast an entire day. Although some people discover that if they have a demanding day they may need to eat a small breakfast. A lunchtime-to-lunchtime fast, missing only two meals, may be a helpful pattern for such people. If you want to try a twenty-four hour fast, the best way is to begin it by skipping dinner and then the next day's breakfast and lunch. The fast will end as you partake of the next dinner (but make it a small one).

Many people fast three or four days in a row, perhaps making a retreat of it. Some find it necessary to eat very small amounts, like an apple or an orange, and they always drink plenty of water. Other people choose the route of giving up favorite foods for a period of time. Such restriction of diet is a legitimate partial fast. We have an example of it in Daniel 10:2–3, where the prophet Daniel ate no "pleasant food, meat, or wine" for three weeks. And God answered this fast.

Some people are called to more extended fasts, perhaps for a week or two. But no one should fast for more than forty days. In most cases the long period of fasting is offered to God as a prayer for a particular need, perhaps the conversion of a friend or the removal of a "log jam" in the life of a church, business, or the affairs of a nation. No one should go on an extended fast without having had the experience of shorter fasts. And since the digestive system will have had little to do, it is essential to break a long fast slowly and gently, perhaps with a little fruit juice. Some people will need to consult a doctor before thinking about doing an extended period of fasting, and there are certainly people who ought not fast at all.

Giving

Why Do We Give?

Jesus expects us to give:

> Take heed that you do not do your charitable deeds before men, to be seen by them. Otherwise you have no reward from your Father in heaven. Therefore, when you do a charitable deed, do not sound a trumpet before you as the hypocrites do in the synagogues and in the streets, that they may have glory from men. Assuredly I say to you, they have their reward. But when you do a charitable deed, do not let your left hand know what your right hand is doing, that your charitable deed may be in secret; and your Father who sees in secret will Himself reward you openly.
> —Matthew 6:1–4

But we do not give simply because God has told us to. We know that our giving makes a difference to those in need. It will meet the needs of the hungry and deprived, but it will, also, set us free from being too tied to our own possessions. For some of us, money and possessions can be idols. If so, that problem needs sorting out before we can really give wholeheartedly. If we live for money (or for our wife, husband, ambition, or whatever) that will in practice be our "god." If we give our money and possessions to the Lord, however, we shall be making a plain statement about what is important to us, which may be a very practical step toward dethroning false gods and serving the living God. For example, if the setting aside of a tithe (or whatever gift seems right) comes first when we are paid, it may be a visible sign that God comes first in our lives.

Practical Guidelines

Clearly, what matters is that we are serious about giving and not allow it to be dependent upon how much "extra" we have or how emotional we are feeling. In fact, according to Jesus, it is not the amount given but the commitment that is important:

> Now Jesus sat opposite the treasury and saw how the people put money into the treasury. And many who were rich put in much. Then one poor widow came and threw in two mites, which make a quadrans. So He called His disciples to Himself and said to them, "Assuredly, I say to you that this poor widow has put in more than all those who have given to the treasury; for they all put in out of their abundance, but she out of her proverty put in all that she had, her whole livelihood."
>
> —Mark 12:41–44

Besides commitment, this passage also seems to imply that our level of giving does depend on how much we have to start with. Ten percent of $100 a week is in fact much more costly to give than ten percent of a $1000 a week, if only because in the first case so much less is left to live on. It is probably true that poorer people should give no more than one tenth (and, in some cases, less) and richer people ought to be giving much more. Although one's percentages are dependent on many circumstances, such as a person's dependents. The tithe, ultimately, should be seen not as a law but as a guideline.

Giving More Than Money

The principles that the Bible makes clear about giving money can be applied, indeed should be applied, to the use of everything which is at our disposal. Our time, resources, and talents, for example, are to be used not only to make us money but also to forward the work of our church and to help those in need outside the church. Again, the principle of "a tenth" is worth practicing. If you have, say, forty hours a week "free time," why not set aside four hours a week to give your time, resources, or talents in Christian service? There is no space here to work these things out in detail. You will need to do that for yourself. Take time to think about how you could give in this way.

We've homed in on two parts of the Christian life: giving and fasting. It is enlightening that Jesus has linked these matter-of-factly with a third area. In Matthew 6 he mentions giving and fasting with prayer, almost in the same breath. At the least, this suggests that giving and fasting are no less spiritual or required than prayer.

Most of the spiritual exercises in this book encourage the development of the inner life through various forms of prayer. Yet if the emphasis is only on this, the temptation will be to think that prayer is the only means of developing inwardly or being spiritual. This is why we turned a corner with chapter ten and continue to do so with this chapter, emphasizing not so much inner but "outer" activities that are, according to Jesus, seemingly, to be just as regular with us as prayer disciplines. These are no less spiritual than prayer, and they contribute greatly to our spiritual development as well. Without them, we will be as someone has said, "So heavenly minded that we're no earthly good." Fasting and giving may seem too mundane. But as we obey God in these disciplines, who knows how we will grow?

TAKE SEVEN DAYS . . .

DAY 1: *Fast and Pray for Insight*

▶ *Activity*

Make a checklist of your food intake for a week. What items do you really enjoy eating or drinking?

Sometimes we need special insight from God. There's a decision to be made, a new direction to discover, or perhaps we need fresh vision or hope. A one or two week fast in which you give up your favorite foods or drinks may be just the thing to help receive that insight. During such a fast you would set aside a certain amount of time each day to pray for your need.

This is a good way to fast and pray because it should not interfere with normal workday activities. It is suitable for those who cannot sustain a regular fast of entire meals. And another advantage is that you can return to your usual eating habits immediately afterwards without a cautious transition period.

So what would you like to give up? Coffee, tea, cokes, ice cream, cake, cookies, potato chips, french fries, hamburgers, cereal, toast, butter, sugar, salt, ethnic foods? And as with any extended time of fasting and prayer, keep a notebook or your journal handy to write down what the Lord reveals along the way.

> Strict exercise of self-control is an essential feature of the Christian's life. Such customs have only one purpose—to make the disciples more ready and cheerful to accomplish those things which God would have done . . . . When flesh is satisfied it is hard to pray with cheerfulness or to devote oneself to a life of service which calls for much self-renunciation.
> —Dietrich Bonhoeffer

▶ *Hymn*

BREAD OF HEAVEN, ON THEE WE FEED

Bread of heaven, on Thee we feed,
For Thy flesh is meat indeed:
Ever let our souls be fed
With this true and living bread.

Vine of heaven, Thy blood supplies
This blest cup of sacrifice:
Lord, Thy wounds our healing give,
To Thy cross we look and live.

Day by day with strength supplied
Through the life of Him who died,
Lord of life, O let us be
Rooted, grafted, built in Thee!
　　　　　　　—Josiah Conder

DAY 2: *Giving to the Needy*

▶ *Activity*

This is not about writing a check and sending it to a charity organization.

During the several years a Christian worked in an inner-city job, he often went out of the office for lunch. This took him through some rather seedy neighborhoods in which tramps and street people begged for food and money. Whenever he was approached by one of these persons, he usually gave them some money. One day, after encountering many such persons, he gave one man, who begged and pleaded with tears, both money and his lunch. The man grabbed both and promptly walked away mumbling. When he had got half a block away, the beggar threw the entire lunch in the street, pocketed the money, and slipped off to buy some wine.

That's a true story, and it calls into question whether or not it is right to get so personally involved with tramps and street people. Is it right to give to them? Certainly there are many of them. How far do we go to make contact with them? Are we prevented from giving and getting involved because someone abuses our gifts? Besides problems like the one above, what prevents you from getting involved with such people?

Fear is often the problem. One Christian man knew the

Lord was asking him to take a frozen turkey to an inner-city rescue mission, but he was nearly paralyzed with fear of getting robbed or mugged if he went into that part of town. Obeying God, for him, meant working through that fear and become willing to trust God in the act of giving.

Take a time of prayer, alone, with God to ask him how you can make a contribution, a personal contribution, to tramps or street people. Perhaps it will be to take food or clothing to a rescue mission. Perhaps it will be to drive your car through a derelict neighborhood to look for someone to give to. If you would like to do this but want a safer situation, discover an inner-city church that has a ministry to tramps and street people. You may be able to work with it for a few hours on a Saturday. And while you are brainstorming what you can do, remember what Jesus said about giving in secret so that only your heavenly Father knows, which, as Jesus also said, will be very rewarding.

> When a friend of Alexander the Great had asked of him ten talents, he tendered to him fifty, and when the reply was made that ten were sufficient, "True," he said, "ten are sufficient for you to take, but not for me to give."
>
> —Phillip Brooks

▶ *Hymn*

MORE ABOUT JESUS

More about Jesus would I know,
More of His grace to others show;
More of His saving fulness see,
More of His love who died for me.

More, more about Jesus,
More, more about Jesus;

More of His saving fulness see,
More of His love who died for me.

More about Jesus let me learn,
More of His holy will discern;
Spirit of God, my teacher be,
Showing the things of Christ to me.

More about Jesus, in His Word,
Holding communion with my Lord;
Hearing His voice in every line,
Making each faithful saying mine.

More about Jesus on His throne,
Riches in glory all His own;
More of His kingdom's sure increase;
More of His coming, Prince of peace.
—Eliza E. Hewitt

DAY 3: *Fast and Pray for Salvation*

▶ *Activity*

You will give up one meal a week for several weeks to fast and pray for someone's conversion to Christ.

Have you been saying the occasional prayer for a friend or loved one to see him or her become a Christian? A season of fasting as well as praying for the person may be just the thing that is needed. In Luke 11:5–8 Jesus spoke of the man who went with great persistence to a friend to ask for bread. And it was because of that persistence that the man got what he came for. Jesus set the story in the context of prayer, with the point that at times our focused persistence with God is what is needed. Fasting as well as praying for someone's salvation can be that focused persistence.

What meal could you fast each week that would symbolize your deeper commitment to pray for the person's salvation? If you don't eat much of a breakfast, it would not be much of a fast to skip one of those. But perhaps an evening or Sunday meal would be appropriate. Once you have decided that, you will also need to make a decision about how many weeks you will want to fast this meal. You may want to leave it open-ended, which may make it easier for you to know when you have fasted long enough.

Many non-Christians are bound spiritually by habitual, long-term, sin patterns that play a big role in keeping them from turning to God in repentance and humility for salvation. Some are even caught and deceived in forms of occultism. A season of fasting and prayer for your friend or loved one, or even a stranger, like a celebrity or public figure, can give you insight about how to pray with greater clarity for salvation. It can help free the person from deep sinful patterns to respond to God's offer of forgiveness and love. Another advantage is that if you are in contact with the person, you can be talking to him or her to discern how things are going at the time of your fasting, which should give you further clues for prayer and identify how God is at work in the situation. You will want to become sensitive to the person's softening to the Gospel so that you will know when it is appropriate to speak to him or her about it.

Fasting and praying, therefore, for a person's salvation will give you both insight into the person's life as well as authority from God to speak with power about the Gospel.

> *Is not this the fast that I have chosen:*
> *To loose the bonds of wickedness,*
> *To undo the heavy burdens,*
> *To let the oppressed go free,*
> *And that you break every yoke?*
> —Isaiah 58:6

DAY 4: *Giving through Giving Up*

▶ *Activity*

This is a fairly challenging activity because it involves incorporating it into your life for a long period, if not for the rest of your life.

Many western Christians are waking up to the fact that even the poorest of us are rich when compared to the per capita income of people in non-western nations. And these Christians are discovering that in being "rich," they have unconsciously used their money, time, and resources to accumulate many things that they don't really need. Let's call these "extras." Author Tom Sine in his book *Why Settle For More And Miss The Best* has written about such Christians. He tells many superb stories about Christians who have cut back on "extras" in an effort to give their money, time, and resources more creatively for the kingdom of God. It seems to be a long-awaited act of obedience that many Christians are learning to live with less so they can give more to the poor and needy.

Some Christians have taken to purchasing less expensive clothes, cars, or houses. Others are cutting back on unnecessary social activities to use that time to serve in the community. Some people have stopped spending so much money in restaurants to eat more frequently at home.

Of course, setting out on such a course is going to take planning and agreements within families as structures are rearranged. Take some time to sit down with your spouse or family to have an initial discussion about this. It will probably take several prayerful conversations to arrive at an agreed upon course of action. But if you are unmarried, or without children, such a decision may be easier to arrive at.

One of the advantages of this is that it will help us trust more deeply in God. In Matthew 6:25–34 Jesus told us not to worry about what we should eat, drink, or wear because our heavenly Father knows that we need these things and will provide them. We must be careful that in our "rich" Christian lifestyles we do not slowly slip from trusting God for our needs into being dependent on our "richness."

In using riches where they have no real use, nor we any real [need], we only use them to our great hurt, in creating unreasonable desires, in nourishing ill tempers, in indulging foolish passions, and supporting a vain turn of mind. Money thus spent is not merely wasted or lost, but it is spent to bad purposes and miserable effects; to the corruption and disorder of our hearts; to the making us unable to follow the sublime doctrines of the gospel. It is like keeping money for the poor, to buy poison for ourselves.

—John Wesley

▶ *Hymn*

I GAVE MY LIFE FOR THEE

I gave my life for thee,
My precious blood I shed,
That thou mightest ransomed be,
And quickened from the dead;
I gave, I gave My life for thee,
What hast thou given for Me?
I gave, I gave My life for thee,
What hast thou given for Me?

My Father's house of light,

My glory-circled throne,
I left for earthly night,
For wanderings sad and lone;
I left, I left it all for thee,
Hast thou left aught for Me?
I left, I left it all for thee,
Hast thou left aught for Me?

I suffered much for thee,
More than thy tongue can tell,
Of bitterest agony,
To rescue thee from hell;
I've borne, I've borne it all for thee,
What hast thou borne for Me?
I've borne, I've borne it all for thee,
What hast thou borne for Me?

And I have brought to thee,
Down from My home above,
Salvation full and free,
My pardon and My love;
I bring, I bring rich gifts to thee,
What hast thou brought to me?
I bring, I bring rich gifts to thee,
What hast thou brought to me?
—Frances R. Havergal

DAY 5: *Fast and Pray for Personal Problems*

▶ *Activity*

You will fast one meal a day for two or three days and spend the time you would be eating in prayer.

Humility is the soil in which grace flourishes, and it takes God's grace to deliver us from besetting sins and failures.

Because fasting is a mark of humility, we can expect grace from God to help us in especially difficult problems.

Can you identify areas in your life that are not pleasing to God but you find it hard to change? Perhaps it is anger toward a spouse or gossiping with neighbors. Perhaps there is lingering bitterness toward a parent or too much yelling at the children. You've tried to stop it, but still it goes on. Or perhaps you are in deep financial difficulties. A two- or three-day fast of a meal each day may help you appropriate grace to see a release from a besetting problem. It is a way to "come boldly to the throne of grace," as Hebrews 4:16 puts it, "that we may obtain mercy and grace to help in time of need."

Fasting and praying like this helps to further our sanctification. It is a self-humbling process that can lead us into mourning and repentance for our sin. There may be times when we are not enjoying the true freedom we want because we're not really too upset or sorry for particular sins or failures. Our nonchalance can be a hindrance to receiving grace to change. Fasting can help produce the necessary mourning and repentance that will show our earnest desire to be free. Into this context God will bring great grace.

Take time alone to decide what area you would like to fast and pray about. And remember to find a quiet spot to pray and read the Bible during the times when you would normally be eating the meals.

If you have been brought low through personal defeat; if there is a call in your soul to a deeper purifying, to a renewed consecration; if there is the challenge of some new task for which you feel ill-equipped—then it is time to enquire of God whether He would not have you separate yourself unto Him in fasting.

—Arthur Wallis

▶ *Hymn*

TAKE TIME TO BE HOLY

Take time to be holy,
Speak oft with thy Lord;
Abide in Him always,
And feed on His Word:
Make friends of God's children,
Help those who are weak;
Forgetting in nothing
His blessing to seek.

Take time to be holy,
The world rushes on;
Spend much time in secret
With Jesus alone:
By looking to Jesus
Like Him thou shalt be:
Thy friends in thy conduct
His likeness shall see.

Take time to be holy,
Let Him be thy guide,
And run not before Him
Whatever betide;
In joy or in sorrow
Still follow thy Lord,
And looking to Jesus,
Still trust in His Word.

Take time to be holy,
Be calm in thy soul;
Each thought and each motive
Beneath His control;
Thus led by His Spirit

To fountains of love,
Thou soon shalt be fitted
For service above.
—William D. Longstaff

DAY 6: *Giving Sacrificially to God*

▶ *Activity*

You will apply one of the biblical injunctions for New Testament types of sacrifices.

In the Old Testament times, people generally used sacrifices to appease the wrath of some god or to seal covenants. But with the sacrifice of Christ on the Cross, the nature of sacrifices in New Testament times changes. The justice of God has been satisfied at Calvary, the New Covenant sealed. Yet the New Testament mentions sacrifices that we can make to God. These usually come under the general heading of "spiritual sacrifices." Below are several of these, and as you discover what they are, make a note of the ways you can offer them to God.

> *I beseech you therefore, brethren, by the mercies of God, that you present your bodies a living sacrifice, holy, acceptable to God, which is your reasonable service.*
>
> —Romans 12:1

We are to present our bodies as a living sacrifice because, as 1 Corinthians 6:19 says, our bodies are the temple of the *Holy* Spirit. Is there a part of your body that you are withholding from God because of a pattern of unholy behavior? It would be a sacrifice for you to stop that behavior and give it to God. Yet this, after all, is the "reasonable" thing to do. Think about it. Then give it up to God.

Walk in love, as Christ also has loved us and given Himself for us, an offering and a sacrifice to God for a sweet-smelling aroma.

—Ephesians 5:2

True love may be a sacrifice simply because we may not "feel" like loving someone the way we ought to. Take time to think about your realm of relationships. Are there a few persons whom you have difficulty in loving? Take time to pray to ask God to help you to walk in love toward them, and know that when you do it is a sweet-smelling aroma to God.

If I am being poured out as a drink offering on the sacrifice and service of your faith, I am glad and rejoice with you all.

—Philippians 2:17

The sacrifice of faith is that we will continue to serve God and others even despite all odds and doubts. We pour out ourselves regardless, because we trust God. If you can identify areas of your life where you lack faith, but you know God is calling, be bold to step out in obedience, and you will find gladness and joy.

Even in Thessalonica you sent aid once and again for my necessities. Not that I seek the gift, but I seek the fruit that abounds to your account. Indeed, I have all and abound. I am full, having received from Epaphroditus the things sent from you, a sweet-smelling aroma, an acceptable sacrifice, well pleasing to God.

—Philippians 4:16–18

Do you know any full-time workers for the Gospel who serve without being paid by a mission board and so have to drum up their own finances? Many large-scale, reputable mission organizations are set up like that. Ask around in your church or friends for the name of a proven missionary who serves voluntarily like this. Then write a letter to the person to discover any pressing needs, or you may be able to discover that from your friends or church. Afterward, take time for prayerful consideration as to how you can give into the situation. And when you give, imagine this, that you will be well-pleasing to God.

> *Therefore by Him let us continue to offer the sacrifice of praise to God, that is, the fruit of our lips, giving thanks to Him*
>
> —Hebrews 13:15

It's not difficult to praise God when all is well. But when things are difficult or depressing, then it is a sacrifice. The old saying "count your blessings" in adversity is a good one. You may not as yet see anything to thank God for in times of suffering, but as a sacrifice to God you can praise him with the fruit of your lips for past blessings. If you are struggling, try to do this, and in so doing you will be giving thanks to his name even in the tough places.

> *But do not forget to do good and to share, for with such sacrifices God is well pleased.*
>
> —Hebrews 13:16

It's really that simple to please God: do good and share. Well done. Keep up the good work.

DAY 7: *Fast and Pray to Remove a Log Jam*

► *Activity*

This will be a full fast, except for water and/or juices, for one to three days.

A full fast like this is often done by one or more persons when praying for a particular need in a church or community. Has your church been struggling for a long time with a particular problem? This may be an indication of the need for a full fast by members of the church. Take some time to gather with your pastor and elders to suggest this. Not everyone has to participate in the fast.

Keep good notes among those who are fasting and praying, to refer to during and after the time.

Of course, you will get hungry doing this kind of a fast. Because of this it is advisable to set your mind firmly to finish the fast before it begins, otherwise a longing for food may be too much of a temptation.

Breaking a one or two day fast usually presents no problems, but for three or more days caution is necessary. A glass or two of tomato juice is a good way to start breaking a fast. But the longing to eat a lot, which will follow that, must be resisted with a slow, steady build up of food intake until normal eating patterns return. Work with your own body and desires to discover the length of adjustment back to normal. Take care as to how much you eat, what you eat, and how you eat it. In other words, watch your quantities, stay away from spicy or hard-to-digest food, and chew your food well.

One disadvantage of such a fast is that it may hinder your usual workday activities. If so, you will need to decide how to deal with this, perhaps by taking some vacation days from work.

So we fasted and entreated our God for this, and He answered our prayer.

—Ezra 8:23

▶ *Hymn*

IN THE HOUR OF TRIAL

*In the hour of trial,
Jesus, plead for me,
Lest by base denial
I depart from Thee:*

When Thou see'st me waver,
With a look recall,
Nor for fear or favor
Suffer me to fall.

With forbidden pleasures
Would this vain world charm,
And its sordid treasures
Spread to work me harm:
Bring to my remembrance
Sad Gethsemane,
Or, in darker semblance,
Cross-crowned Calvary.

When my last hour cometh,
Fraught with strife and pain,
When my dust returneth
To the dust again,
On Thy truth relying,
Through that mortal strife,
Jesus, take me, dying,
To eternal life.
—James Montgomery

— 12 —

Corporate Spirituality

———— ◆ ————

Praying with the Church

When Jesus was asked by his disciples how they should pray, he replied by teaching them a prayer that has been on the lips of Christians ever since:

> *Our Father in heaven,*
> *Hallowed be Your name.*
> *Your kingdom come.*
> *Your will be done*
> *On earth as it is in heaven.*
> *Give us this day our daily bread,*
> *And forgive us our debts.*
> *As we forgive our debtors.*
> *And do not lead us into temptation,*
> *But deliver us from the evil one.*
> *For Yours is the kingdom and the power and*
>   *the glory forever. Amen.*
>   —Matthew 6:9–13

Children learn it, and it is said frequently in church services. It is also prayed during times of distress or confusion and even on one's death-bed. Its words are simple, yet profound; and they have helped bring men and women of many cultures into the knowledge of God.

A wide range of human concerns are found in the prayer, and its short petitions have helped Christians to place their hope in a God who changes things. The prayer's name for God—Father—brings comfort, and yet at the same time stretches the greatest minds as they try to fathom how the invisible God becomes our Father through Jesus' relationship to him. It is, of course, The Lord's Prayer (more accurately, The Disciples' Prayer).

We have already spent some time with this prayer in the Take 7 Days exercises in Chapters 3 and 7, but something else remains to be said. Embedded in The Lord's Prayer is a corporate perspective on spirituality. It shows us that in prayer we enter the vast sea of the Church's prayers. The plural pronouns used by Jesus throughout the prayer reveal that we are not merely individual units within Christianity but that we are joined through him into one people. We have a *corporate* identity. This becomes clear in such phrases as "*Our* Father," "give *us*," "forgive *us*," "*we* also forgive," and "do not lead *us* into temptation." Jesus showed us this identity, and it means that Christians are never alone when they pray.

It may seem to be stating the obvious to say that we are never really alone when we pray in private. Of course, we think, God is present and we are thinking about those for whom we are in prayer. So we're not really "alone." And yet, because of traditional western ways of viewing ourselves and our societies (especially so in the U.S.), it is difficult for Christians to resist getting caught in a kind of private religion that robs them of any concern for their corporate identity with the Church. In fact, it is not uncommon that western, and especially American, Christians need to appreciate that their identity is understood, characterized, recognized and *established* properly only within Christ's Church. Simply, one's individual spiritual identity as a believer becomes grossly deformed when it is not grounded in the Church. The Lord's Prayer, in particular, prevents us from thinking that Christian existence itself or prayer can ever escape life with others. Let's take a moment, here, to dig a bit deeper into this important issue.

One or Many?

Each individual is uniquely precious to Jesus, who, as The Good Shepherd, will leave ninety-nine sheep in the wilderness to "go after the one which is lost until he finds it," (Luke 15:4). The Bible, therefore, places great value on the individual. But this is something quite different from the way the individual is regarded in western culture, which stresses independence, isolation, and rugged individualism. This view is reflected, for example, in our economic arrangements in which the "normal" individual is seen as a single "unit of labor." Deeper still in our intellectual tradition lies the famous statement of Descartes: "I think, therefore I am," which emphasizes *individual* perception and judgment and devalues the same *corporate* activities. A needed adjustment to this would be the saying of African theologian John Mbiti, who said, "I am, because we are." Mbiti is emphasizing that we exist as *human* beings because communities form us in ways more profound than we often acknowledge. What is generally true of us as individuals within geographic communities is equally true of who we are spiritually.

For example, a newborn child needs help from within a community to grow into adulthood. It is not merely enough that the child is provided with food and clothing. In order to mature, the child needs to become immersed in the language, culture, and social projects of the community. It is through and with this that his individuality finds expression. Now what is true of human development in general—individual growth is made possible as one is part of a community—is true of spiritual development too.

Because of this, the Bible shows us individual lives lived within a corporate life. Yes, the Bible has its share of loners, persons like Jeremiah, Elijah, John the Baptist and others. But such "aloneness" is never a kind of spiritual aloofness. It is never a statement endorsing independence, isolationism, or individualism. Quite the opposite. Even their aloneness is part of a calling in which they serve the *community* by crying to it (from the wilderness, as it were) with a message of correction or repentance. Any "apartness" that may be their lot still keeps them related to the community which, in fact, gives them a large part of their identity as individuals.

This way of thinking about our corporate identity does not come naturally to us, but it is part of the fabric of a biblical worldview. So much so that entire communities are occasionally personified as individuals:

> *Woe to you, Chorazin! Woe to you Bethsaida! For if the mighty works which were done in you had been done in Tyre and Sidon, they would have repented long ago, sitting in sackcloth and ashes. But it will be more tolerable for Tyre and Sidon at the judgment than for you. And you, Capernaum, who are exalted to heaven, will be brought down to Hades.*
>
> —Luke 10:13–15

When we talk about our corporate identity as Christians, therefore, we are not Christianizing humanist or Marxist sociology. We are discussing that which is utterly biblical.

Abraham and Jesus

Another reason why we have trouble appreciating our corporate Christian identity derives from how we think about "salvation." Most western Christians think in terms of getting the *individual* saved. A person is lost in his or her sin, and Jesus is the way of salvation for the person.

Fair enough. But the early Christians often started rather differently. They saw Abraham, a Mesopotamian city-dweller who was called to leave his country, family, and way of life, as the founder and father of a pilgrim people. The early Christians saw that God's plan of salvation was to call out of the world *a people* who would live in relationship to him, expressing his character and fulfilling his purposes together:

> *You are a chosen generation, a royal priest-hood, a holy nation, His own special people, that you may proclaim the praises of Him who called you out of darkness into His marvelous light; who once were not a people but are now the people of God, who had not obtained mercy but now have obtained mercy. Beloved, I beg you as sojourners and pilgrims, abstain from fleshly lusts which war against the soul, having your conduct honorable among the Gentiles, that when they speak against you as evildoers, they may, by your good works which they observe, glorify God in the day of visitation.*
> —1 Peter 2:9–12

In our time we are generally unfamiliar with this view of salvation because the language of the modern West orients us to think wrongly about what it means to be an "individual." God's promise to Abraham, however, was that in him all *nations* would be blessed (Gen. 12:3). This promise was fulfilled in Jesus Christ. As the "second," or "last," Adam (1 Cor. 15:45–49), Jesus Christ identified with us in a fully human but sinless life as well as in his lonely sin-bearing death in order to become in his resurrection "the firstborn among many brethren," (Rom. 8:29). Jesus' coming, therefore, does not mean the abandonment of God's plan to create a people in favor of a host of isolated persons. Rather, it was to fulfill God's promise to Abraham to create "a single new humanity," (Eph. 2:15 NEB).

We see just how real and ever-present this corporate identity was to Jesus when he prayed in John 17:

> *I have manifested Your name to the men whom You have given Me out of the world. . . I do not pray for these alone, but also for those who will believe in Me through their word; that they all may be one, as You, Father, are in Me, and I in You; that they also may be one in Us, that the world may believe that You sent Me. And the glory which You gave Me I have given them; that they may be one just as We are one. I in them, and You in Me; that they may be perfect in one.*
> —John 17:6, 20–23

Jesus is not praying for the "oneness" of eastern mysticism, in which everyone's personalities become subsumed and lost in some sort of cosmic energy. There is neither individual nor corporate identity at the end of the day in that. Jesus is praying that his people will be more fully individuals while being more closely at one (with one another and with God). *That* is the miracle of saving grace. It gives us both an individual and a corporate identity as God's people living in peace and harmony with one another.

This process appears at Pentecost, which, with the coming of the Holy Spirit, may be seen as the reversal of the chaos and division begun at the Tower of Babel (see Genesis 11 and Acts 2). The Holy Spirit began to draw people out of every language into the people of God. For the early disciples this was a bewildering and costly experience. As we know, the apostle Peter had great difficulty in accepting God's inclusion of Cornelius and his household into the Church (Acts 10). And there was much division between the Hebrew and Hellenist Christians as to how their widows were to be taken care of (Acts 6). There was also an ongoing rift between those of the circumcision party and the Gentile believers (Acts 15). Life in the early Spirit-filled Church was neither perfect nor comfortable whenever God stressed its corporate identity.

Two thousand years later we experience a similar stretching by the Spirit, but in different forms. These may be cultural, technological, or economic. Many structures may blind us to the reality of the corporate. We may think that our particular church or denomination is "the way" and so put down the others. We may make a dichotomy between charismatics and noncharismatics or Third World and First World Christians. We may have become cynical about the excesses of the hyper-faith/prosperity theology or alienated ourselves from Christians who don't care about "prosperity." And then there are the divisions that arise between the mega-churches and the small churches or between those who speak in tongues and those who do not. These are only several of many differences with which we are uncomfortable, and thus we resist fully identifying with the larger corporate identity of the Church today.

Rediscovering the Church

The way back to rediscovering the Church, and by implication our corporate identity, begins with repentance. We must identify any bad attitudes, confess them to God, and forsake them. Then we will feel free to get to know the Church for who and what she is: the individuals, communities, adventures, triumphs and sorrows, acts of worship and service, prayers, songs, and writings that are our corporate identity, our true glory.

An important step in any Christian's growth is the first time she looks out from her primary Christian group, where her initial identity has been formed, and recognizes the work of the Holy Spirit in other Christian communities, churches, and denominations, past or present.

Two Cities

Christians often see the Church as God's alternative society, simply a place of refuge from the world. And yet, God's concern clearly is for the world as well as for the Church. The Church, therefore, is not so much an alternative society as it is a resistance movement. We are a company of people living in hostile territory, and here, then, is a part of our corporate identity. From the Church we will draw the resources to be courageous and willing to live dangerously and to spend even our lives to establish the values and love of our true allegiance. We draw grace from the Church to name the true King's name and to encourage others to do the same. We know there will be setbacks but that one day the reign of Love will come. In the meantime, the Church must teach us both how to live as individuals in our private worlds as well as how to influence the public spheres of life individually and corporately.

In his great work *The City of God*, St. Augustine develops this theme, seeing the history of the world as the interwoven history of two cities which exist alongside each other until the end of time. His starting points are the biblical cities of Babylon and Jerusalem, which symbolize two ways of life, two different projects; the former human, the latter Divine. The splendor of the heavenly city will not be revealed until Jesus Christ comes in glory; thus its present existence often passes unnoticed even though it is full of beauty, holiness, and love. This present age is the age of the earthly city, Babylon, which is built on the love of self and of human pride. At the end of time the bankruptcy of the earthly city will become obvious. In the meantime, Augustine does not suggest that we can or should withdraw from the earthly city even though our citizenship is now in heaven (Philippians 3:20). Rather, as citizens of heaven we influence the earthly city accordingly. Christian spirituality means living within this tension.

This stance toward private and public life has very practical, down-to-earth ramifications. For instance, "love of neighbor" means that, in part, we will work for the well-being of the earthly city. And so Jeremiah wrote to the exiled Jews in Babylon:

> Seek the peace of the city where I [God] have caused you to be carried away captive, and pray to the Lord for it; for in its peace you will have peace.
>
> —Jeremiah 29:7

We cannot fulfill such a calling without appreciating and consciously indwelling our identity as the Church. It is too much of a burden for lone individuals to bear.

The Family

Many Christians today find the picture of the "family of God" as the one that makes the Church most real to them and from which they derive a corporate identity. This is because the family is for many people a place of refuge and belonging where people are valued and human contributions are given and received freely rather than exchanged for money.

But for the early Church, the idea of "family"

was quite different than our modern one. The Greek word in the New Testament that corresponds with "family" in English is the word "household." And the household in those times was seen as a portion of society, not as a refuge from it. Besides parents and their children, the household included relatives, servants, friends and possibly other dependents. Thus the household formed a microcosm of the city, not an alternative to it. Further back in the tribal society of Abraham's time, family (household) and city were nearly one. And as societies developed throughout biblical times, household and city were complementary modes of common life, not alternatives.

These forms of family, of course, are different than our modern ideal of the nuclear family, in which the small unit of "parent and child" alone, or "parents and children" alone, are elevated as the norm for humanity and belonging. We should not be afraid to question this ideal, if only because it lends itself to unwise choices. For example, it gives us a notion that birth control is not so much about planning a family as it is about preserving the comfortable lifestyle of the four-member nuclear family. The Church, then, serves us four, no more. Consequently, our actual corporate identity will stop with our home's front door. And Jesus' words about family in the "new humanity" of God's kingdom will seem odd:

While He was still talking to the multitudes, behold, His mother and brothers stood outside, seeking to speak with Him. Then one said to Him, "Look, Your mother and Your brothers are standing outside, seeking to speak with you."

But He answered and said to the one who told Him, "Who is My mother and who are My brothers?"

And He stretched out His hand toward His disciples and said, "Here are My mother and My brothers! For whoever does the will of My Father in heaven is My brother and sister and mother."

—Matthew 12:46–50

Jesus . . . said, "Assuredly, I say to you, there is no one who has left house or brothers or sisters or father or mother or wife or children or lands, for My sake and the gospel's, who shall not receive a hundredfold now in this time—houses and brothers and sisters and mothers and children and lands, with persecutions—and in the age to come, eternal life."

—Mark 10:29–30

We must be wise. The symbol of the nuclear family can pit self-love against the wider human community. It can isolate us from redemptive interaction with those who are not represented in "standard" families, including singles (whether never married, separated or divorced, or widowed) living alone or with others and single parents with their children. It can limit expectations and restrict friendships and relationships that older societies valued and regarded as normal. In short, it can detour us from participating in the wider purposes of God.

The symbol of "family" today is two-edged and must be used with care. It affirms values we do not want to lose, yet it can blind us to the diversity of human life. It is not that we want to lose our passion for our immediate families, but we may need to redirect it through our families into the larger context of the Church household, which encompasses all believers in Christ.

Christian Worship

In the world we serve an unseen King, and to belong to him is to belong to our fellow Christians worldwide. It is in gathering for worship that we see a small expression of our corporate identity as God's people.

This book, with some intentional exceptions, is chiefly about one's private devotions to God. Yet this would give us a distorted picture of spirituality if we did not focus finally on the corporate Church. For this reason, Christian private prayer must never be seen as unrelated to or more important than the public worship and prayer of one's church. In fact, private prayer grows out of corporate worship and corporate worship feeds private prayer.

The way that private prayer is influenced by public worship can be seen by the way that hymns and songs, for instance, are used by many Christians. Martin Luther told Christians to recite The Lord's Prayer and The Apostles'

Creed in the morning. He also suggested that they say other prayers, "and then shouldst thou go with joy to thy work." The Apostles' Creed is also used in the baptismal rite of some churches. (The Creed comes from the baptismal rite of the ancient Western Church.). The person being baptized learns the creed by heart and recites it to the gathered church during the baptismal service.

Of course, there is a tremendous variety to Christian worship. It gets its color from the cultures, musical styles, social patterns and so forth that particular individuals bring to it. Yet fixed patterns can be discerned within all the variety.

Four elements provide a God-given, grace-motivated shape to Christian worship the world over. First, almost all Christians gather on Sundays to celebrate the death and resurrection of Christ. Another element is baptism, in which a repentant individual becomes identified with the life of the Church. A third element is the partaking of The Lord's Table (known in various traditions also as Holy Communion or The Eucharist), which requires Christians to think about and examine their relationships with one another. A fourth element is the public reading of Scripture, which proclaims the Gospel and summons the Church to listen to Christ. A common denominator of all these elements is their corporate dimension. None of the four elements can be done solo. All call for a group, a body of believers, for their observance.

The pattern of worship can be compared to language. Both belong to the community and not to the individual alone, although individuals may express themselves through the resources the community has provided. Forms of worship can also be seen as a kind of corporate art form, rather like community music or dance in some cultures. The range of this corporate pattern is very wide, from simple songs and prayers to larger or seasonal celebrations or the solemn ceremonial.

Sometimes groups of Christians become alienated from parts of the most basic, common pattern. They may find it hard to "get inside" less familiar parts of the pattern when it is needed. Examples could be funerals or civic services. And then there is the tendency for groups of Christians to seize upon certain parts of the common pattern to make them into rallying points at the expense of the other parts. Neither practice truly helps the Church or individuals.

If these elements disclose the skeleton of Christian worship, it is then fleshed out and clothed by the individuals who make up a particular church, and this generally depends on the larger structure of the denomination in which the church exists. Many things determine the practical shape and form. Some are theological, and these would influence a church's prayers, praise, and preaching. Some reflect the particular biases of human nature, and these would affect how music is played and the posture and movement used to express ourselves. Other determining factors are technological. The invention of mass printing, for example, has placed Bibles, congregational prayer books, and song books in the hands of every congregant. A great blessing, yes. It has changed and enriched Christian worship dramatically. But not without a price. For it has tended to "fix" worship; it costs a lot of money for a church to change a hymn book!

The private prayer of Christians can be shaped by similar influences. Before the invention of watches, which helped to privatize time, Christians tended to pray at common times that were determined by a household's routine, the church bell, or even the sound of a city. Our awareness of our vulnerability in the early morning or at night often dictates prayer at those times. And it may be that the invention of the electric light has shifted evening prayer to a later night time. Economic and work structures, too, have changed radically this century, and these too have helped to alter the way we go about our private prayers.

But the resources for personal prayer provided through the Church are many. Collections of Christian prayer from the days of the early church are available, as well as collections valued by the ancient churches, Roman Catholic and Eastern Orthodox. Traditions rising from the

Reformation have also produced collections of prayers, Psalms, and other scripture readings. These would include Lutheran, Methodist, and Presbyterian books, as well as the well-known Episcopalian *Book of Common Prayer*. Even free-church traditions, which have typically emphasized the use of printed prayers less than others, have produced similar collections. Along with these are the many books of devotions, increasingly popular and targeted to quite specific audiences. A visit to your local bookstore and to a church leader will probably introduce you to several sources of prayers, readings, and meditations that offer some of the devotional riches of the Church for your private or small-group use. An excellent resource that should not be overlooked is the church hymnal. While some do not include many prayers, many do, and with them Scripture and other readings and meditations. Good hymnals are actually handbooks for worship, and they are equally useful for public and private worship.

And so there is much to be said in favor of the Christian's corporate spirituality and identity. As we recognize the variety, the richness, and the breadth of public worship that is our Christian heritage, we discover an environment in which our private prayer life and devotions to God can be enriched and grow. Even in our most private prayers we are one with the Church. We may consciously cultivate this oneness through participating regularly in the Church's life. As we do, our personal devotion to God becomes more fully biblical, more fully Christian. And our private practice of spiritual disciplines transports us more deeply into His presence.

TAKE SEVEN DAYS . . .

DAY **1**: *With the Church*

▶ *Scripture*

> *To the church of God which is at Corinth, to those who are sanctified in Christ Jesus, called to be saints, with all who in every place call on the name of Jesus Christ our Lord, both theirs and ours: Grace to you and peace from God our Father and the Lord Jesus Christ.*
> —1 Corinthians 1:2–3

Note how Paul begins his letter with a reminder of the geographical and universal dimensions of the church and with the call and promise of the gospel.

▶ *Exercise*

Picture the Christian communities of your town or city, and relate them to this passage. Then picture Christian congregations in other parts of the world. Now let God help you to pray for some of these Christians.

▶ *Scripture*

> *18 For you have not come to the mountain that may be touched and that burned with fire, and to blackness and darkness and tempest, 19 and the sound of a*

trumpet and the voice of words, so that those who heard it begged that the word should not be spoken to them anymore. 20 (For they could not endure what was commanded: "And if so much as a beast touches the mountain, it shall be stoned or shot with an arrow." 21 And so terrifying was the sight that Moses said, "I am exceedingly afraid and trembling.")

22 But you have come to Mount Zion and to the city of the living God, the heavenly Jerusalem, to an innumerable company of angels, 23 to the general assembly and church of the firstborn who are registered in heaven, to God the Judge of all, to the spirits of just men made perfect, 24 to Jesus the Mediator of the new covenant, and to the blood of sprinkling that speaks better things than that of Abel.

25 See that you do not refuse Him who speaks. For if they did not escape who refused Him who spoke on earth, much more shall we not escape if we turn away from Him who speaks from heaven, 26 whose voice then shook the earth; but now He has promised, saying, "Yet once more I shake not only the earth, but also heaven."

27 Now this, "Yet once more," indicates the removal of those things that are being shaken, as of things that are made, that the things which cannot be shaken may remain. 28 Therefore, since we are receiving a kingdom which cannot be shaken, let us have grace, by which we may serve God acceptably with reverence and godly fear. 29 For our God is a consuming fire.

—Hebrews 12:18–29

These words are written to some discouraged Jewish Christians who are feeling that their new life in Christ offered them less than their previous home in Judaism. It seemed to them less impressive (Hebrews 12:18–21) and less per-

manent or secure (Hebrews 12:25–29). Allow the images of
verses 22–24 to grip you.

▶ *Prayer*

Almighty God, you have knit together your elect into one
communion and fellowship in the mystical body of your Son.
Give us grace so to follow your blessed saints in all virtuous
and godly living, that we may come to those unspeakable
joys which you have preferred for those who truly love you:
through Jesus Christ our Lord. Amen.

▶ *Hymn*

THE PILGRIM MARCH

*Through the night of doubt and sorrow
Onward goes the pilgrim band,
Singing songs of expectation,
Marching to the promised land.
Clear before us through the darkness
Gleams and burns the guiding light:
Brother clasps the hand of brother,
Stepping fearless through the night.*

*One the light of God's own presence,
Over his ransomed people shed,
Chasing far the gloom and terror,
Brightening all the path we tread:
One the object of our journey,
One the faith which never tires,
One the earnest looking forward,
One the hope of God inspires.*

*One the strain the lips of thousands
Lift as from the heart of one;
One the conflict, one the peril,
One the march in God begun:*

> *One the gladness of rejoicing*
> *On the far eternal shore,*
> *Where the one Almighty Father*
> *Reigns in love for evermore.*
>   —Bernard Severin Ingemann

DAY 2: *Baptism*

The twentieth century has seen the various parts of the church struggling to rediscover the reality of baptism. Conversion disrupts life, and it is therefore not surprising that the rediscovery of baptism is not a tidy process. Baptism means change for both the individual and the church. The body has to adjust to the arrival of a new member.

▶ Meditation

The water of baptism is a picture of the call and promise of God. Allow some of the images to take hold of you. Note how often there is a corporate dimension to the picture.

- Passing through judgment to life:

     Then he said to the multitudes that came out to be baptized by him, "Brood of vipers! Who warned you to flee from the wrath to come?

           —Luke 3:7

     Moreover, brethren, I do not want you to be unaware that all our fathers were under the cloud, all passed through the sea, all were baptized into Moses in the cloud and in the sea. . . .

           —1 Corinthians 10:1–2

     For Christ also suffered once for sins, the just for the unjust, that He might bring us to God, being put to death in the flesh but made alive by the Spirit, by whom also He went and preached to the spirits in prison, who formerly were disobedient, when once the Divine longsuffering waited in the days of Noah, while the ark was being prepared, in which a few, that is, eight souls, were saved through water.

There is also an antitype which now saves us— baptism (not the removal of the filth of the flesh, but the answer of a good conscience toward God), through the resurrection of Jesus Christ.

—1 Peter 3:18–21

• Cleansing and forgiveness:

And such were some of you. But you were washed, but you were sanctified, but you were justified in the name of the Lord Jesus and by the Spirit of our God.

—1 Corinthians 6:11

• Renewal in the Spirit:

. . . not by works of righteousness which we have done, but according to His mercy He saved us, through the washing of regeneration and renewing of the Holy Spirit, whom He poured out on us abundantly through Jesus Christ our Savior, that having been justified by His grace we should become heirs according to the hope of eternal life.

—Titus 3:5–7

"Therefore being exalted to the right hand of God, and having received from the Father the promise of the Holy Spirit, He poured out this which you now see and hear."

. . .

Then Peter said to them, "Repent, and let every one of you be baptized in the name of Jesus Christ for the remission of sins; and you shall receive the gift of the Holy Spirit.

"For the promise is to you and to your children, and to all who are afar off, as many as the Lord our God will call."

—Acts 2:33, 38–39

- New birth into the body of Christ:

Jesus answered, "Most assuredly, I say to you, unless one is born of water and the Spirit, he cannot enter the kingdom of God.

—John 3:5

For as the body is one and has many members, but all the members of that one body, being many, are one body, so also is Christ. For by one Spirit we were all baptized into one body—whether Jews or Greeks, whether slaves or free—and have all been made to drink into one Spirit.

—1 Corinthians 12:12–13

- Moving from death to life:

For You cast me into the deep,
Into the heart of the seas,
And the floods surrounded me;
All Your billows and Your waves passed
    over me.
Then I said, 'I have been cast out of Your
    sight;
Yet I will look again toward Your holy
    temple.'
The waters surrounded me, even to my
    soul;
The deep closed around me;
Weeds were wrapped around my head.
I went down to the moorings of the
    mountains;
The earth with its bars closed behind me
    forever;

*Yet You have brought up my life from the pit,
O LORD, my God.*

—Jonah 2:3–6

*Or do you not know that as many of us as were
baptized into Christ Jesus were baptized into His
death? Therefore we were buried with Him through
baptism into death, that just as Christ was raised from
the dead by the glory of the Father, even so we also
should walk in newness of life.*

—Romans 6:3–4

- The unity of the church:

*There is one body and one Spirit, just as you were
called in one hope of your calling; one Lord, one faith,
one baptism.*

—Ephesians 4:4–5

▶ *Prayer*

Think first of those who sponsored you at your baptism
and who have supported your life in the church. (If baptism
in your church tradition does not involve sponsors, think of
those who have been your spiritual 'parents.') Ask what God
is saying to you through the baptism that other Christians
have received.

*Baptism is the sign of new life through Jesus Christ.
It unites the one baptised with Christ and his people.
The New Testament scriptures and the liturgy of the
Church unfold the meaning of baptism in various images which express the riches of Christ and the gifts of
his salvation . . . Baptism is both God's gift and our
human response to that gift. It looks towards a growth
into the measure of the stature of the fullness of Christ.*

This comes from a statement on baptism agreed on by
major Christian traditions in 1982 in Lima, Peru. It is pub-

lished in *Baptism, Eucharist and Ministry* and provides a good starting point for thinking about baptism.

DAY 3: *Your Kingdom Come*

Imagine the meeting for worship you normally attend on a Sunday. Picture who is there and who feels most at home or left out. What people or topics will be prayed for?

▶ *Scripture*

Therefore I exhort first of all that supplications, prayers, intercessions, and giving of thanks be made for all men, for kings and all who are in authority, that we may lead a quiet and peaceable life in all godliness and reverence.

For this is good and acceptable in the sight of God our Savior, who desires all men to be saved and to come to the knowledge of the truth.

For there is one God and one Mediator between God and men, the Man Christ Jesus, who gave Himself a ransom for all, to be testified in due time, for which I was appointed a preacher and an apostle—I am speaking the truth in Christ and not lying—a teacher of the Gentiles in faith and truth.

I desire therefore that the men pray everywhere, lifting up holy hands, without wrath and doubting; in like manner also, that the women adorn themselves in modest apparel, with propriety and moderation, not with braided hair or gold or pearls or costly clothing, but, which is proper for women professing godliness, with good works.

—1 Timothy 2:1–10

What topics did these Christians pray for? How did they see their place and calling in God's purpose?

▶ *Prayer*

Allow the passage to guide you in prayer.

▶ *Reflection*

Is there anything you can do to deepen or direct the prayer life of your church? Do you know what projects, Christian workers or organizations your church supports? Do you know much about them? Should they be part of your regular private prayer?

> Christ look upon us in this city and keep our sympathy and pity Fresh, and our faces heavenward Lest we grow hard.
>
> —Thomas Ashe

▶ *Hymn*

BRETHREN, WE HAVE MET TO WORSHIP

Brethren, we have met to worship
And adore the Lord our God;
Will you pray with all your power,
While we try to preach the Word?
All is vain unless the Spirit
Of the Holy One comes down;
Brethren, pray, and holy manna
Will be showered all around.

Brethren, see poor sinners round you
Slumbering on the brink of woe;
Death is coming, hell is moving,
Can you bear to let them go?
See our fathers and our mothers,
And our children sinking down;
Brethren, pray, and holy manna
Will be showered all around.

Sisters, will you join and help us?
Moses' sister aided him;
Will you help the trembling mourners
Who are struggling hard with sin?
Tell them all about the Saviour,
Tell them that He will be found;
Sisters, pray, and holy manna
Will be showered all around.

Let us love our God supremely,
Let us love each other too;
Let us love and pray for sinners,
Till our God makes all things new.
Then He'll call us home to heaven,
At His table we'll sit down,
Christ will gird Himself, and serve us
With sweet manna all around.
—George Atkins

DAY 4: *Sing Us One of the Songs of Zion*

▶ *Scripture*

By the rivers of Babylon,
There we sat down, yea, we wept
When we remembered Zion.
We hung our harps
Upon the willows in the midst of it.
For there those who carried us away captive asked of
us a song,
And those who plundered us requested mirth,
Saying, "Sing us one of the songs of Zion!"
How shall we sing the LORD's song
In a foreign land?
—Psalm 137:1–4

▶ *Exercise*

Find one or two hymns or songs that are important to a different generation or group of Christians than yourself. You may find such hymns throughout this book. Read or sing through them. If possible get someone for whom they are important to talk to you about them.

▶ *Meditation and Prayer*

Read through them quietly, imagining the people and situations they represent. Reflect on the diversity of the Church shown by the hymns that appeal to different people, sometimes different generations. Pray that God will help you appreciate and take joy in such diversity, rather than wishing that all were just like you. Pray that God will help you appreciate different doctrinal emphases of hymns that do not much appeal to you.

▶ *Hymn*

WE'RE MARCHING TO ZION

Come, we that love the Lord,
And let our joys be known;
Join in a song with sweet accord,
Join in a song with sweet accord,
And thus surround the throne,
And thus surround the throne.

We're marching to Zion,
Beautiful, beautiful Zion;
We're marching upward to Zion,
The beautiful city of God.

Let those refuse to sing
Who never knew our God;
But children of the heavenly King,
But children of the heavenly King,

May speak their joys abroad,
May speak their joys abroad.

The hill of Zion yields
A thousand sacred sweets,
Before we reach the heavenly fields,
Before we reach the heavenly fields,
Or walk the golden streets,
Or walk the golden streets,

Then let our songs abound,
And every tear be dry;
We're marching through Immanuel's ground,
We're marching through Immanuel's ground,
To fairer worlds on high,
To fairer worlds on high.

—Isaac Watts

DAY 5: *Until He Comes*

▶ *Scripture*

For I received from the Lord that which I also delivered to you: that the Lord Jesus on the same night in which He was betrayed took bread; and when He had given thanks, He broke it and said, "Take, eat; this is My body which is broken for you; do this in remembrance of Me."

In the same manner He also took the cup after supper, saying, "This cup is the new covenant in My blood. This do, as often as you drink it, in remembrance of Me."

For as often as you eat this bread and drink this cup, you proclaim the Lord's death till He comes.

—1 Corinthians 11:23–26

▶ *Meditation on Scripture*

The scene is familiar. Jesus is accepting his lonely call to the cross. He gathers his apostles and bequeathes them this sign. He gives to them shared bread, which begins a Jewish meal, and the shared cup, which lends the meal a new significance. The action which Jesus gives the Church, and which Christians have enacted and interpreted in many different ways, has a very simple shape: saying grace and partaking—thanksgiving and communion.

Jesus words, 'Do this in remembrance of me,' were addressed to the twelve apostles to the Church in miniature, and not simply to individual Christians. Only corporate obedience is possible. To receive and obey Jesus' command the Church has to be together.

> *Now in giving these instructions I do not praise you, since you come together not for the better but for the worse. For first of all, when you come together as a church, I hear that there are divisions among you, and in part I believe it. For there must also be factions among you, that those who are approved may be recognized among you. Therefore when you come together in one place, it is not to eat the Lord's Supper. For in eating, each one takes his own supper ahead of others; and one is hungry and another is drunk.*
>
> *What! Do you not have houses to eat and drink in? Or do you despise the church of God and shame those who have nothing? What shall I say to you? Shall I praise you in this? I do not praise you.*
>
> • • •
>
> *Therefore, my brethren, when you come together to eat, wait for one another. But if anyone is hungry, let him eat at home, lest you come together for judgment. And the rest I will set in order when I come.*
>
> —1 Corinthians 11:17–22, 33–34

This passage shows part of what this meant in one city. The Christians in Corinth may have met in different homes and groupings (1:11–12; 16:15, 19) as well as together (Romans 16:23; it seems this letter was written from Corinth). The Eucharist brought them together in a way that made them face the differences, such as wealth and class, that divided them.

▶ *Exercise*

Look at the order of service and prayers that your church uses to celebrate the Lord's Supper. Can you see the shape of thanksgiving and communion? How has the church performed these actions? What do they mean for you and your fellow worshippers?

> *For whenever you eat this bread and drink this cup, you proclaim the Lord's death until he comes.*
> —1 Corinthians 11:26

> *Is not the cup of thanksgiving for which we give thanks a participation in the blood of Christ? And is not the bread that we break a participation in the body of Christ? Because there is one loaf, we, who are many, are one body, for we all partake of the one loaf.*
> —1 Corinthians 10:16, 17 RSV

> *Love each other as I have loved you.*
> —John 15:12

DAY 6: *Honor and Remember*

▶ *Scripture*

> *Yet I considered it necessary to send to you Epaphroditus, my brother, fellow worker, and fellow soldier, but*

your messenger and the one who ministered to my need; since he was longing for you all, and was distressed because you had heard that he was sick. For indeed he was sick almost unto death; but God had mercy on him, and not only on him but on me also, lest I should have sorrow upon sorrow. Therefore I sent him the more eagerly, that when you see him again you may rejoice, and I may be less sorrowful.

Receive him therefore in the Lord with all gladness, and hold such men in esteem; because for the work of Christ he came close to death, not regarding his life, to supply what was lacking in your service toward me.

—Philippians 2:25–30

At Joppa there was a certain disciple named Tabitha, which is translated Dorcas. This woman was full of good works and charitable deeds which she did. But it happened in those days that she became sick and died. When they had washed her, they laid her in an upper room. And since Lydda was near Joppa, and the disciples had heard that Peter was there, they sent two men to him, imploring him not to delay in coming to them.

Then Peter arose and went with them. When he had come, they brought him to the upper room. And all the widows stood by him weeping, showing the tunics and garments which Dorcas had made while she was with them.

But Peter put them all out, and knelt down and prayed. And turning to the body he said. "Tabitha, arise." And she opened her eyes, and when she saw Peter she sat up. Then he gave her his hand and lifted her up; and when he had called the saints and widows, he presented her alive.

—Acts 9:36–41

> *Remember those who rule over you, who have spoken the word of God to you, whose faith follow, considering the outcome of their conduct.*
> —Hebrews 13:7

Who do Epaphroditus or Dorcas remind you of? Who were the Christians who brought you the word of God or have given you an example of faith? What do you know about the history of your church and of other churches in your town or city? Who first brought the message of Christ to your town and country?

Remembering is a very important aspect of biblical faith and remembering God's work through individuals is part of this. Example is an important part of Christian growth. Enjoyment of people and thanksgiving to God are part of how we honor and remember.

▶ *Prayer*

Remember and give thanks for those whom God brings to mind.

▶ *Exercise*

Find out who the heroes are of Christians round you. Are there Christians of the past you ought to be learning about?

There are two traps it is easy to fall into. One is using past figures as rallying points without understanding the real meaning of their lives, as the following words of Jesus show:

> *"Woe to you, scribes and Pharisees, hypocrites! Because you build the tombs of the prophets and adorn the monuments of the righteous, and say, 'If we had*

lived in the days of our fathers, we would not have been partakers with them in the blood of the prophets.'"
—Matthew 23:29–30

Another is not noticing how wonderfully varied, eccentric and imperfect God's servants are.

▶ *Hymn*

THE CHURCH'S ONE FOUNDATION

*The Church's one foundation
Is Jesus Christ her Lord;
She is his new creation
By water and the word:
From heaven he came and sought her
To be his holy bride;
With his own blood he bought her,
And for her life he died.*

*Elect from every nation,
Yet one over all the earth,
Her charter of salvation,
One Lord, one faith, one birth;
One holy Name she blesses,
Partakes one holy food,
And to one hope she presses,
With every grace endued.*

*Though with a scornful wonder
Men see her sore opprest,
By schisms rent asunder,
By heresies distrest;
Yet saints their watch are keeping,
Their cry goes up, "How long?"
And soon the night of weeping
Shall be the morn of song.*

> 'Mid toil and tribulation,
> And tumult of her war,
> She waits the consummation
> Of peace for evermore;
> Till with the vision glorious
> Her longing eyes are blest,
> And the great Church victorious
> Shall be the Church at rest.
>
> Yet she on earth hath union
> With God, the Three in One,
> And mystic sweet communion
> With those whose rest is won.
> O happy ones and holy!
> Lord, give us grace that we
> Like them, the meek and lowly,
> On high may dwell with thee.
> —Samuel John Stone

DAY 7: *The New Jerusalem*

▶ *Scripture*

Now I saw a new heaven and a new earth, for the first heaven and the first earth had passed away. Also there was no more sea.

Then I, John, saw the holy city, New Jerusalem, coming down out of heaven from God, prepared as a bride adorned for her husband. And I heard a loud voice from heaven saying, "Behold, the tabernacle of God is with men, and He will dwell with them, and they shall be His people. God Himself will be with them and be their God. And God will wipe away every tear from their eyes; there *shall be no more death, nor sorrow, nor crying. There shall be no more pain, for the former things have passed away."*

Then He who sat on the throne said, "Behold, I make all things new." And He said to me, "Write, for these words are true and faithful."

And He said to me, "It is done! I am the Alpha and the Omega, the Beginning and the End. I will give of the fountain of the water of life freely to him who thirsts. He who overcomes shall inherit all things, and I will be his God and he shall be My son. But the cowardly, unbelieving, abominable, murderers, sexually immoral, sorcerers, idolaters, and all liars shall have their part in the lake which burns with fire and brimstone, which is the second death."

Then one of the seven angels who had the seven bowls filled with the seven last plagues came to me and talked with me, saying, "Come, I will show you the bride, the Lamb's wife."

And he carried me away in the Spirit to a great and high mountain, and showed me the great city, the holy Jerusalem, descending out of heaven from God, having the glory of God. Her light was like a most precious stone, like a jasper stone, clear as crystal.

Also she had a great and high wall with twelve gates, and twelve angels at the gates, and names written on them, which are the names of the twelve tribes of the children of Israel: three gates on the east, three gates on the north, three gates on the south, and three gates on the west.

Now the wall of the city had twelve foundations, and on them were the names of the twelve apostles of the Lamb.

—Revelation 21:1–14

▶ *Exercise*

Imagine what this vision might say to different people—for example:

- St. John in exile on a small island in the Aegean.
- a poor widow in the slums of Brazil
- a Christian artist or poet or gardener
- a politician struggling to improve society
- a ten-year-old child
- Christians in prison for their faith in Turkey or Nepal
- someone planning to retire after a successful business career
- a Christian pastor
- a Christian dying of hunger in Ethiopia
- a young worker
- a single-parent family not quite making it on a small income
- members of a Christian co-operative in a Mexican slum
- a Christian black leader detained in South Africa

▶ *Prayer*

Bring the different feelings and people that this has brought to mind to God. Pray these prayers:

Almighty God, you have entrusted this earth to the children of men, and through your Son Jesus Christ have called us to a heavenly citizenship; grant us such shame and repentance for the disorder, injustice, and cruelty which are among us, that, fleeing to you for pardon and grace, we may henceforth set ourselves to establish that city which has justice for its foundation and love for its law, of which you are the architect and builder; through the same Jesus Christ, your Son, our Lord. Amen.

Merciful God, you have prepared for those who love you such good things as pass man's understanding. Pour into our hearts such love towards you that we, loving you above all things, may obtain your promises, which exceed all that we can desire; through Jesus Christ our Lord. Amen.

— 13 —

To Be a Pilgrim

———— ◆ ————

On her way out of the house, a small girl called to her mother that she was going outside "to play with God." Not too sure what that meant, the mother asked for an explanation. "Oh,'" said the little girl, "I throw my ball up in the air and he throws it back!" Prayer brings us into a two-way relationship like this with God.

Who Am I?

As you reach the end of this book, reflection on its contents will indicate your preferences in prayer. Some chapters and exercises will have spoken to you more clearly than others. This is as it should be. People are different. For example, one person may find that being alone in prayer for an extended period is undesirable, while another person finds group prayer overpowering. This is not necessarily a cause for guilt in either person. God understands us perfectly, and he wants us to know him as we are. So there must be a means of communication that is right for each individual. In our search to discover various kinds of prayer relationships with God, we will need to consider who we are and what we are like.

So, who am I? For the Christian, the easiest answer may be that I am a child of God who is becoming increasingly like Jesus. This, of course, immediately brings us to the question of change, growth, and development—the subject of this book. And this implies that what was considered maturity and growth when we were young in the faith may no longer be appropriate measures five, ten, or fifty years later.

It has been said of Moses that he spent forty years learning to be somebody, forty years learning to be nobody, and forty years learning what God can do with a somebody who has learnt to be a nobody! Clearly God is in the business of transformation:

> But we all, with unveiled face, beholding as in a mirror the glory of the Lord, are being transformed into the same image from glory to glory, just as by the Spirit of the Lord.
> —2 Corinthians 3:18

Where Am I?

The Bible gives us a number of images that depict the Christian life as a journey. The Old Testament records many journeys. God taught Abraham, Jacob, and Joseph through their travels, and in the wilderness wanderings of the Israelites God taught them the basics of being his people. Jesus spoke of the narrow road that leads to life and described himself as the way.

Even since New Testament times Christians have used the image of a journey to describe God's leading and guidance. For Celtic Christians, such as Patrick in Ireland, the idea of being a perpetual pilgrim was central to their faith. In his *Pilgrim's Progress*, John Bunyan popularized the idea that we might see ourselves as travelers. And Horatius Bonar wrote:

> I heard the voice of Jesus say:
> "I am this dark world's light;
> Look unto Me, thy morn shall rise,
> And all thy day be bright."
> I looked to Jesus, and I found
> In Him my Star, my Sun:
> And in that light of life I'll walk,
> 'Till travelling days are done!

It is not surprising that the picture of a journey has become such a widely used description, for the Christian life includes the uphill slog, the mountain top experience, the drabness of the plain, and the frustration of getting lost. Christians experience these times. Journeys also involve maps, routes, guides, directions, fellow travelers, and former pilgrims. And, yet, there is a reluctance within many Christians to ask for directions, which may help explain why people waste precious time going backwards, around in circles, or standing still. The assumption that we seek direction or help only if we have "a

problem" is a chief cause for countless unnecessary wanderings.

———————◆———————

*If we could see beneath the surface of many a
life, we would see that thousands of people
within the Church are suffering spiritually
from "arrested development"; they never reach
spiritual maturity; they never do all the good
they were intended to do; and this is due to
the fact that at some point in their lives they
refused to go further; some act of self-sacrifice
was required of them, and they felt they could
not and would not make it; some habits had
to be given up, some personal relation altered
and renounced, and they refused to take the
one step which would have opened up for them
a new and vital development. They are
"stunted souls."*

—Olive Wyon

———————◆———————

Journaling

Throughout Scripture God tells his people to
remember their history. The rainbow, circumcision and the Passover were all given that men
and women might remember what God had done
in the past and what he had promised for the
future. It is all too easy, however, to forget how
Jesus has led us or to remember many of the
things we have learned. This may actually hin-

der our growing in the knowledge of God, because if we forget then we may need to re-learn.

Keeping a "spiritual" diary, or journal, however, can be of great value. It can help to prevent us from going backward, around in circles, or standing still. An elderly lady once told me that the secret of her prayer life was her blessings book, in which she recorded God's work in her life over the years. Not only did this provide a wonderful account of God's goodness to her, it prodded her memory, which gave her a continual springboard for praise and thanksgiving. It was also instrumental in helping her to recall where she had been so that she would not have to repeat old "lessons." These are the great benefits of keeping a diary, or journal.

Two main reasons, however, may hinder us from journaling. One is the time factor; it is hard enough to make time for prayer and Bible study, let alone writing in a journal. The other is a more subtle reason. Deep down there may be a feeling that it is self-indulgent to keep a diary. It hints at an over-preoccupation with one's problems and accomplishments.

On the other hand, the benefits of journal keeping are many. The very act of writing something down is often therapeutic and an aid to understanding in the clarity it can produce. It can reveal the hand or presence of God at work in unexpected places and events, or in times of difficulty and darkness. It can be a great asset during periods of decision making, helping you to keep a growing list of the pros and cons of proposed future actions. And as progress in the Christian life is often slow, a written record becomes a permanent reminder of where we have come from. A journal is also the place where we can record our inner life, a collection of our personal "God thoughts and experiences" to have with us on the journey.

A spiritual diary is essentially an intimate piece of writing. It is not intended for public sharing. Therefore you can write exactly what you feel and think in the manner you wish to. Spelling, punctuation, and grammar are not to be worried about. The idea is to be completely honest. You're not going to surprise God! He knows your every thought and fantasy. It's not worth trying to pretend or to impress God. You are writing so that you can understand more of who you are, and what's really going on inside of you, and what you are learning and where you are going. You are keeping the record to know God better and yourself more thoroughly. You can't fool God; don't be dishonest in your journaling, and he's not looking for you to impress him with your writing style.

What Do I Include?

The fundamental rule of keeping a spiritual journal is that anything can be included, the bad as well as the good, the failures as well as the successes. Some people find it hard to get started. If you have completed any of the previous exercises in this book on paper, they can be a start. If you haven't done any of them yet, you have plenty of material to form your embryonic journal!

Include:

- descriptions or thoughts of events, people, situations
- relationships and decisions
- notes of helpful talks, sermons, Bible studies
- significant quotations from books, hymns, poems, prayers
- personal struggles or questions
- photographs, pictures, postcards, drawings, diagrams
- meaningful snippets of conversation
- special newspaper or magazine cuttings
- favorite Bible verses
- prayer requests
- mountain top experiences
- expressions of anger or anguish
- wilderness experiences
- outpourings of praise, psalms, songs
- dreams, "pictures," or words from the Lord,
- book/record/tape/film titles you want to remember
- letters received or copies of those you have sent

It is your book. You may not like some of the above suggestions. You may include others. It is not written for anyone else. Include anything that will help you better understand yourself and increase you relationship with God.

Other tips for journaling:

- Don't wait for a significant date with which to begin. It won't be easier to find time to write then than it is now.

- Choose a notebook that is easy to manage. A commercially produced diary is not recommended because it assumes something will be written every day and the space available is limited. A spiral notebook is perhaps the best.

- Be realistic about your aims. It may not be feasible to write in your journal everyday. Some persons prefer keeping a daily record. Others prefer a weekly, monthly, or yearly record. While still others prefer only recording significant moments or irregular entries.

- Date each entry.

- Entries can be as short as a word or a sentence, or many pages in length.

- Be honest. The temptation is either to paint oneself in a better light, or to put oneself down.

- Re-read regularly, but don't revise.

Spiritual Directors

Fasting, the use of the imagination in prayer and meditation, and discerning God's voice through the Bible all increase their value in our lives if we have someone with whom we can discuss things. Our day by day pilgrimage can be greatly enhanced by having someone with whom we might reflect. However much we learn about ourselves from keeping a journal, it is by talking with a trusted human being that we learn more about ourselves. Paul Tournier, a Swiss psychologist, has written, "It is only by expressing [our] convictions to others that [we] become really conscious of them." The value of turning to a mature Christian who has more experience of prayer and God has become far more widely recognized.

———————◆———————

He who makes himself his own teacher becomes the pupil of a fool.
—*Thomas Aquinas*

———————◆———————

In the past, spiritual direction was seen largely as a Roman Catholic activity. It carried connotations of authoritarianism, which many Protestants felt was not for them. It was also, like journaling, thought to be somewhat self-indulgent, an activity for those with plenty of spare time. As a result, many Evangelicals are ignorant of the benefits of a spiritual director.

The task of a spiritual director is largely to listen. A wise director will act as a second pair of ears. He will also be suggesting ways to recognize God's guiding voice in your life. And he will ask questions to help the directee see what God is doing in his life. Futhermore, a spiritual director may help the individual to hear what God is saying during extremely confusing, depressing, or difficult times, such as during unemployment, bereavement, major decisions, or personal upheaval.

So you ascribe all the knowledge you have to God, and in this respect you are humble. But if you think you have more than you really have, or if you think you are so taught of God as no longer to need man's teaching, pride lieth at the door.

—John Wesley

An individual goes to a counselor because he has an ongoing problem. He goes to a director because he wants to grow spiritually. Visits to a counselor are generally frequent and continue until the problem is resolved or dealt with. Visits to a director are usually infrequent and the relationship may last many years.

Finding a Director

Martin Thornton, who wrote widely on the subject of spiritual direction, advised that people should seek a director as they might a dentist after they have moved to a new area. In other words, ask friends, ministers, or anyone who might be able to help. Local monasteries and convents may be a source. The value of the right spiritual director is incalculable, and seeking the person should be a matter of serious prayer. If you make a few false starts, don't give up. You are not looking for a best friend, although your director may one day become such. You are looking for a wise listener whose Christian experience of life and God you respect and value. "Competence is the only essential," wrote Martin Thornton, so don't be too fussy!

What you don't want to settle for is a spiritual director who is over-riding your will or being legalistic. That can be dangerous, leading at times as it does to a heavy-handed "shepherding" role or even a cult situation. You want someone who, like the Holy Spirit, is going to respect your free will, someone who appreciates denominational structures, and someone who is not going to "direct" you away from your family.

Types of Direction

- Traditional one-to-one:
    An individual chooses someone to talk to about his prayer life and spiritual direction. After an initial period of regular sessions (weekly or semi-weekly) the relationship will usually settle into a pattern of two or three meetings per year.

- Congregational:

A growing number of churches are recognizing the value of having spiritual directors in their congregations. This is not to usurp pastoral counseling but to stick within the above guidelines for directors.

- Group:

This is usually direction of limited duration. It's aim is to bring together individuals who are following a particular pattern of prayer, such as the exercises of St. Ignatius. Prayer is undertaken individually, but participants meet together with a director regularly to share their experiences.

- Two-way:

This involves mutual direction in which two individuals encourage one another. However, in order for this to operate successfully, the "sessions" need to be arranged so that both persons have the opportunity to speak and listen. And perhaps at some stage a third-party director could be involved.

TAKE SEVEN DAYS . . .

DAY 1: *Describe Your Conversion Experience*

▶ *Journal Entry*

Some persons have had rather dramatic conversions to Christ, while others have kind of "seeped" into the kingdom of God. Whatever kind you had, take twenty or thirty minutes alone with your journal to write about how you became a Christian.

Write about how you felt. Were you surprised or did you have an idea about what would occur?

Write about the event itself. What specific things led up to it? Did one particular thing trigger it?

Write about what changed. How did your views about God, the Bible, Christianity, and people in general change? Had you been going to a church, or did you have to start looking for one? What was that like?

Write about how it affected your family and friends. Did they accept or reject you? Did any become Christians as a result of what happened?

What was the hardest thing to do immediately or shortly afterward? Did you need to make some restitution? Did you have to apologize to anyone for previous offenses? Did it mean changing jobs, or being reconciled with your family?

The idea is not to force your thoughts to come, neither is it to worry about grammar or spelling, nor is it to fuss over saying it perfectly. The thing is to just start writing down your thoughts as they come. It's really that simple.

You may not even like the above topical suggestions and so think of others that are more relevant to you. Or you may, in all liklihood, find that writing about the topics triggers precious forgotten moments of your conversion process. Jot a brief record of these down on another sheet of paper; you may want to enter them in your journal at another time.

▶ *Hymn*

THE HAVEN OF REST

My soul in sad exile was out on life's sea,
So burdened with sin and distrest,

Till I heard a sweet voice saying
"Make Me your choice,"
And I entered the haven of rest.

I've anchored my soul in the haven of rest,
I'll sail the wide seas no more;
The tempest may sweep over the wild stormy deep,
In Jesus I'm safe evermore.

I yielded myself to His tender embrace,
And faith taking hold of the word,
My fetters fell off, and I anchored my soul:
The haven of rest is my Lord.

The song of my soul, since the Lord made me whole,
Has been the old story so blest,
Of Jesus who'll save whosoever will have
A home in the haven of rest.

Oh, come to the Saviour, He patiently waits
To save by His power divine;
Come, anchor your soul in the haven of rest,
And say, "My Beloved is mine."
    —Henry L. Gilmour

DAY 2: *List Favorite Verses*

▶ *Journal Entry*

Take twenty or thirty minutes alone with your journal to write in several of your favorite verses from Scripture. You can write them out in your own words or look them up and write them down verbatim.

Recall where you were or what you were doing when you received these promises or exhortations. Include the contexts also in the journal entry. Describe why the contexts and the verses were (are) meaningful. Do they still carry weight with you today? A brother in the Lord once complained to a spiritual confidant that he hadn't received a "word from the Lord" for a long time, and he then told about one he had received years earlier. To this his confidant aptly replied, "Brother, if God gave that to you, it's just as good today as back then. His word is eternal." This changed the brother's perspective, and he went away with renewed joy. Having your meaningful verses in the journal can be an immediate source to turn to for comfort and hope.

You may also want to include how these promises or exhortations altered your mood, behavior, or perhaps even your lifestyle. How did you take strength from them? Were you able to share insights with others who also found strength, comfort, or hope?

If you are like many people who keep a journal, you may find that so much information starts flooding in that you will want to use further entries to "catch" it all.

▶ *Hymn*

I WILL NOT FORGET THEE

Sweet is the promise, "I will not forget thee,"
Nothing can molest or turn my soul away;
Even though the night be dark within the valley,
Just beyond is shining one eternal day.

"I will not forget thee or leave thee;
In My hands I'll hold thee, in My arms I'll fold thee;
I will not forget thee or leave thee;
I am thy Redeemer, I will care for thee."

Trusting the promise, "I will not forget thee,"
Onward will I go with songs of joy and love;
Though earth despise me, though
my friends forsake me,
I shall be remembered in my home above.

When at the golden portals I am standing,
All my tribulations, all my sorrows past,
How sweet to hear the blessed proclamation,
"Enter, faithful servant, welcome home at last!"
                                    —Charles H. Gabriel

DAY 3: *Recall a Mountain Top Experience with God*

▶ *Journal Entry*

You may have been at a church service, a Christian conference, a retreat, or alone on your knees with God and had a mountain top experience. In your journal, describe what made this so special.

Where were you? What were you doing? Were you alone or with people? How long did it last, several minutes, days, weeks?

This was a period of special grace. Whenever we receive grace, there is a responsibility implied. We need to be good stewards of it. Record how this has worked out in your life. How are you being a good steward of that grace?

Why do you suppose this occurred? Often, we do not spend much time thinking about why God sent a mountain top experience; we're too busy enjoying it! But in understanding why, we can become better stewards of the grace received. Did it alter the direction of your journey? Did it deliver you from despair? Was it a dramatic answer to persistent prayer? As you answer these questions in your journal and think about how they relate to your life today, you may also get discernment about the stewardship question. But these are merely several of the benefits you will discover from this entry.

▶ *Hymn*

I SAW THE CROSS OF JESUS

I saw the cross of Jesus,
When burdened with my sin;
I sought the cross of Jesus,
To give me peace within;
I brought my soul to Jesus,
He cleansed it in His blood;
And in the cross of Jesus,
I found my peace with God.

I love the cross of Jesus,
It tells me what I am—
A vile and guilty creature,
Saved only through the Lamb;
No righteousness nor merit,
No beauty can I plead;
Yet in the cross I glory,
My title there I read.

I trust the cross of Jesus,
In every trying hour,
My sure and certain refuge,
My neverfailing tower;
In every fear and conflict,
I more than conqueror am;
Living, I'm safe, or dying,
Through Christ, the risen Lamb.
Safe in the cross of Jesus!
There let my weary heart
Still rest in peace unshaken,
Till with Him, never to part;
And then in strains of glory
I'll sing His wondrous power,

Where sin can never enter,
And death is known no more.
                    —Frederick Whitfield

DAY 4: *Describe a Valley Experience*

▶ *Journal Entry*

Sooner or later all Christians enter the wilderness, or the valley. This may be due to our fault or someone else's, or no one's at all. Tragedy, depression, spiritual confusion, a recurring illness, loss of vision, unemployment, and long-term suffering affect us all once in a while.

Writing about your wilderness experience in your journal can be very therapeutic, clarifying, and renewing. Choose an experience that you think you would like to write down.

You may want to write about the general events that led up to it. Did you feel God sustaining you? Sometimes we feel this, other times we don't. Did you increase in your knowledge of God, or did you slide away from him? Did you fear losing something? Did you lose something or someone? How long did this valley experience last?

Such an experience is occasionally quite dry or dark spiritually. Were you able to persevere? Did your trust in God deepen? Did you overcome some evil through it? Did so many doubts arise that you wondered why you ever became a Christian? Did you learn more about Christ's sufferings? If so, describe how. Perhaps you could also describe how you learned humility, or if any Christians helped to get you through.

Often, after we are free of the wilderness, we are so thankful that the tendency is to forget about what we learned, both about ourselves and God. If you record your valley experiences in the journal, you will see how that highlights lessons learned, which may prevent a recurrence, especially if you later take times of meditation and prayer about them.

▶ *Hymn*

> *JESUS IS TENDERLY CALLING*
>
> *Jesus is tenderly calling thee home,*
> *Calling today, calling today;*
> *Why from the sunshine of love wilt thou roam*
> *Farther and farther away?*
>
> *Calling today,*
> *Calling today,*
> *Jesus is calling,*
> *Is tenderly calling today.*
>
> *Jesus is calling the weary to rest,*
> *Calling today, calling today;*
> *Bring Him thy burden and thou shalt be blest;*
> *He will not turn thee away.*
>
> *Jesus is waiting; O come to Him now,*
> *Waiting today, waiting today;*
> *Come with thy sins; at His feet lowly bow;*
> *Come, and no longer delay.*
>
> *Jesus is pleading; O list to His voice,*
> *Hear Him today, hear Him today;*
> *They who believe on His name shall rejoice;*
> *Quickly arise and away.*
> —Fanny J. Crosby

DAY 5: *Describe a Personal Struggle or Dilemma*

▶ *Journal Entry*

In his book *Born Again*, Charles Colson told how he got out a legal pad and made long lists of the pros and cons surrounding the tough decisions he faced. You don't have to use his lawyer's discipline in your journal! Again, it's merely a matter of jotting down ideas and thoughts as they come.

Set aside time to enter in your journal a recent or current struggle you are going through. It could involve decision-making, wrestling with God over an issue, a conflict with a friend or spouse, a touchy situation with a child, a dilemma about changing jobs, or any of a host of other personal struggles.

One way to do this, and it often helps resolve issues, is to have a conversation with yourself about the struggle and write down that conversation. You'll play two roles here. One will be how you really feel, and the other will be objections and insights from the point of view that is contributing to the struggle. It will be as if you were two persons.

For example, let's say you want to change jobs but you've been procrastinating for months. Take two chairs and face them towards each other. Now take your journal and sit in one of the chairs. This is the side of you that wants to change jobs. It may seem silly at first, but make a statement to the other chair, which will be the side of you that's procrastinating, that you want to switch jobs. Record that statement in your journal.

Now go and sit in the other chair. Be that side of you which is not so sure it wants to change jobs, and answer the statement you just made. Then sit in the other chair and answer that statement from the point of view of wanting to switch jobs. And then sit in the other chair and answer that statement for the other viewpoint. (People are often laughing a lot at themselves by this point, which in itself has been known to bring the issue to near resolution because some of the answers we return, to either "self," become pretty ridiculous.) And remember to enter the conversation in the journal.

Here is a short sample:

First Chair: I want to take a job with _____.

Opposite Chair: But you wouldn't be making any more money, and its a longer drive to work.

F.C.: But I've been unhappy with this employer for a long time.

O.C.: You won't really know what kind of situation you're getting into. It could turn out to be worse.

F.C.: It might be worth the risk. After all, they are interested in me.

O.C.: But you'd have to re-learn almost everything, make new contacts, risk being the new person on the block.

Of course, the conversation will continue for a while, but probably not as long as you might think, especially with some issues and situations. And when you include very practical considerations and what you think the Lord may be saying, it becomes even more clarifying.

Of course, you may choose simply to describe your feelings, impressions and insights about a personal struggle without using the above model. Remember, it's *your* journal. The idea is to record the entries however you want to. There's no right or wrong way.

DAY 6: *Describe a Recent Helpful Sermon or Book*

▶ *Journal Entry*

Spend time entering how a significant message affected you.

Why was it special? Did you take notes? If so, you could recopy them in your journal. Who was the preacher or author? What was the name of the message or book? What did it teach you? Have you shared that with another person? Did it alter your life significantly? If so, how?

Was it passages of Scripture used in an unusual way that helped make this happen? If so, you may want to write that down. Perhaps it was certain points in the book's chapters, and you may want to record your interpretation of those. You may find that those insights will become good material for further meditation or consideration.

How will you build upon the insights to help you understand yourself better and know God more deeply? Did you speak to others who were moved by the message? What did they say? Was it similar to your observations or different?

Significant moments can easily get forgotten, but if they are recorded in the journal it usually doesn't take long to see just how much God has been showing to you. This, in turn, may help you discover more clearly what kind of a journey you are on, where you are currently, and where you are headed.

DAY 7: *What Is God Saying to You These Days?*

▶ *Journal Entry*

Have you ever asked a Christian friend, "What's God been saying to you lately?" Some persons almost freeze up; others immediately bubble over with an answer.

Which sort of person are you? Are you able to take time with your journal to record an answer to that question? You may need to begin with what you *think* the Lord is saying. From there you may get something specific. But if it is difficult recording even that, you will probably be able to make a start by answering, "What is God saying to me about _____?" Here you will fill in the blank. Is it school, finances, a spouse, the children, income taxes, Easter, your vacation, an apology, the car? Making it a specific question may help you to put pen to paper. And if you can work it around to what the Lord is saying about your life overall, this can be a good way to discover where you are on the journey.

Is the Lord speaking by way of encouragement or direction, or perhaps reproof or discipline? Did he speak it through a verse? Which one? Were you expecting this? If it was a surprise, why were you unaware of something that was important enough that God spoke? If it is a word concerning direction, reproof, or discipline, how are you following through? Is there a blockage keeping you from taking the next step? Describe the blockage. Can you get past it on your own, or will you need help from a fellow sojourner or more grace from God? What do you think is the best way to pray about it?

You want to record as much of this as you think necessary. And, again, you will discover tangents important enough to write about also.

The entries in the above "Take 7 Days" should get you familiar with journeying through journaling. You will think of almost countless other entries you can make as you get used to the enjoyment that can come through journaling. And remember to consult the list of topics that appeared earlier in this chapter.